Urban Regeneration in Europe

Books are to be returned on or before
the last date below.

Urban Regeneration in Europe

Edited by

Chris Couch

Professor of Urban Planning
Liverpool John Moores University

Charles Fraser

Visiting Research Fellow
Faculty of the Built Environment
South Bank University

and

Susan Percy

Senior Lecturer in Urban & Environmental Planning
South Bank University

Blackwell
Science

© 2003 by Blackwell Science Ltd,
a Blackwell Publishing Company
Editorial Offices:
9600 Garsington Road, Oxford OX4 2DQ,
UK
  Tel: 01865 776868
Blackwell Publishing, Inc., 350 Main
Street, Malden, MA 02148-5018, USA
  Tel: +1 781 388 8250
Iowa State Press, a Blackwell Publishing
Company, 2121 State Avenue, Ames, Iowa
50014-8300, USA
  Tel: +1 515 292 0140
Blackwell Publishing Asia Pty Ltd,
550 Swanston Street, Carlton South,
Victoria 3053, Australia
  Tel: +61 (0)3 9347 0300
Blackwell Verlag, Kurfürstendamm 57,
10707 Berlin, Germany
  Tel: +49 (0)30 32 79 060

The right of the Author to be identified as
the Author of this Work has been asserted
in accordance with the Copyright, Designs
and Patents Act 1988.

First published 2003 by Blackwell Science Ltd

Library of Congress
Cataloging-in-Publication Data
Urban regeneration in Europe/[edited] by
Chris Couch, Charles Fraser, and Susan
Percy.
    p. cm.
Includes bibliographical references and
index.
    ISBN 0-632-05841-2 (pbk. : alk. paper)
    1. Urban renewal – Europe, Western.
2. Deindustrialization – Europe, Western.
3. Land use, Urban – Europe, Western. 4.
Urban policy – Europe, Western. 5. Urban
ecology – Europe, Western. 6. Europe,
Western – Social conditions. 7. Europe,
Western – Economic conditions. 8. Europe,
Western – Environmental conditions. I.
Couch, Chris. II. Fraser, Charles. III. Percy,
Susan, 1965–

HT178.E8U734 2003
307.3′416′094–dc21   2003001127

ISBN 0-632-05841-2

A catalogue record for this title is available
from the British Library

Set in 10/13 pt Trump Mediaeval
by Sparks Computer Solutions Ltd, Oxford
http://www.sparks.co.uk
Printed and bound in Great Britain by
CPI Antony Rowe, Eastbourne

For further information on
Blackwell Publishing, visit our website:
www.blackwellpublishing.com

Real Estate Issues

Series Managing Editors
Stephen Brown RICS Foundation
John Henneberry Department of Town & Regional Planning,
    University of Sheffield
James Shilling Department of Real Estate and Urban Land Economics,
    University of Wisconsin – Madison

Real Estate Issues is a book series presenting the latest thinking into how
real estate markets operate. Based on strong theoretical concepts and a clear
undertanding of market dynamics, it is inclusive in nature, drawing both
upon established techniques for real estate market analysis and on those
from other academic disciplines. It embraces a comparative approach, allowing best practice to be put forward and tested for its applicability and relevance to the understanding of new situations. It does not impose solutions,
but provides a means by which solutions can be found. *Real Estate Issues*
does not make any presumptions as to the significance of real estate markets,
but presents the real significance of the operation of these markets.

Books in this series

Guy & Henneberry *Development and Developers*
Adams & Watkins *Greenfields, Brownfields and Housing Development*
O'Sullivan & Gibb *Housing Economics and Public Policy*
Couch, Fraser & Percy *Urban Regeneration in Europe*
Barlow, Allan, Padovani, Maloutas & Leal *Housing in Southern Europe*
Seabrooke, Kent & How *International Real Estate*
Leece *Economics of the Mortgage Market*
Ball *Markets and Institutions in Real Estate and Construction*
Stephens *Housing Finance and Owner-Occupation*
Brown & Jaffe *Real Estate Investment*

RICS **FOUNDATION**

Contents

Contributors

The editors

Chris Couch

Chris Couch is Professor of Urban Planning and Head of Planning and Housing Studies at Liverpool John Moores University. He is a Member of the Royal Institution of Chartered Surveyors and a Member of the Royal Town Planning Institute. His career has included work on planning and urban design in British new towns as well as involvement with the early development of urban regeneration policies in Liverpool. He has been at John Moores University since the late 1970s. In 1988 he set up the MSc Urban Renewal (Urban Regeneration & Urban Design) at the university, one of the UK's first specialist Masters programmes in the field. His main research interests are in urban regeneration, particularly from a European comparative perspective, as well as the study of urban change and policy development in Liverpool and Merseyside. He has written widely on these subjects. Publications include *Urban Renewal: Theory and Practice* (1990) and *Economic Restructuring, Urban Change and Policy in the Ruhr and Merseyside* (ed., with Boemer, H.) (2000). A book about planning and urban regeneration in Liverpool, *City of Change and Challenge*, is forthcoming.

Charles Fraser

Charles Fraser has been concerned with urban regeneration and particularly the housing aspects of it throughout his career. From early beginnings in the urban renewal team in Middlesex County Council and the urban renewal programme of the Canadian federal agency (Central Mortgage and Housing Corporation), he developed both an interest in the process of renewal and the analysis of various national approaches to it. As Head of the Planning Division at South Bank University he shaped the course programmes to include a central place for urban regeneration. Allied to this was an emphasis on comparing practice from Europe, derived from the knowledge of colleagues on the Netherlands, Germany and Italy, and his own involvement in study and teaching of French practice. As a Visiting Research Fellow at the Faculty of the Built Environment he has been involved in recent EU Interreg projects with a regeneration objective, notably the 'Living in Towns' project for which he was co-ordinator and the 'Working Party on Urban Regeneration in North West Europe', led by the Agence de Lille, on which he was an advisor. He is currently engaged on developing further similar ventures that will spread the knowledge of European practices and enhance the effectiveness of regeneration programmes in an urban Europe. He has contributed articles on housing and renewal to journals in Britain and France and papers to professional and academic conferences and symposia.

Susan Percy

Susan Percy is Head of the Division of Urban and Environmental Studies at London's South Bank University. She has worked as a town planner in the public sector and is a member of the Royal Town Planning Institute. At South Bank there is a strong tradition of urban regeneration in both course provision and research delivered through multidisciplinary working. This is supported by the Local Economy Policy Unit, a nationally recognised resource for local area regeneration and economic development with a unique mix of research, consultancy and training. Susan has edited *Constructing Local Environmental Agendas* (1999) with Susan Buckingham-Hatfield and has published papers on urban and environmental planning and policy. Currently her work is on urban sustainability, local government policymaking and the green economy and is conducted in the context of informing practice and theory through applied research. Susan is deputy editor of the journal *Planning Practice and Research*.

Other contributors

Thierry Baert

Thierry Baert is an architect and urbaniste. He studied architecture at the Ecole St Luc in Tournai, followed by landscape and spatial development at the Ecole d'Architecture de Lille.

His career started in architecture before turning to urban development (aménageur) in the mid-1980s. He joined the Agence de Développement et d'Urbanisme de Lille Métropole in 1993 in order to create monitoring and decision-making systems. Since 1997 he has developed the European studies department and the Cultural studies team, both of which he currently leads. He has participated in several European exchange programmes. From 1998 to 2000 he led the Economic Development and Urban Regeneration Committee of Eurocities and, from 1999 to 2002, the Working Party on Urban Regeneration in NW Europe. He has been a member of the French delegation (on behalf of major cities) to the European 'Urban Development Group'.

Greg Lloyd

Professor Greg Lloyd is Head of the School of Town & Regional Planning at the University of Dundee. He is a land economist and planner with considerable teaching and research experience in both fields. He was recently adviser to the House of Commons Scottish Affairs Committee. He is active in the Regional Studies Association and serves on the editorial boards of the *Town Planning Review* and *Journal of Property Research*. He has published widely in the fields of strategic planning, regional development agencies and economic development and planning policy guidance. He is currently undertaking research funded by the ESRC, Department of the Environment, Transport and the Regions, Scottish Executive, Dundee Partnership and the Carnegie Trust. He serves on the DETR Planning Research Advisory Group.

John McCarthy

John is at the School of Town & Regional Planning at the University of Dundee. His background is in urban planning and regeneration practice, including experience as a senior planner in inner London. His research interests in the fields of urban planning and regeneration have resulted in the publication of numerous journal articles, many with a comparative aspect in relation to international practice. John is currently the Conference Organiser for the Scottish Branch of the Regional Studies Association and a member of the National Executive Committee of the Regional Studies Association.

Stephen McKay

Dr Stephen McKay is a lecturer in the School of Environmental Planning at Queen's University, Belfast. His work is mainly focused upon planning methods and practice, with a specialist interest in planning law and enforcement issues. Since 1998 he has undertaken extensive funded research into the workings of the planning system in Northern Ireland and has written widely on this and other related topics.

Luc Marechal

Luc Marechal served for many years in the Direction Générale de Aménagement du Territoire du Logement et du Patrimoine of the Ministere de la Region Wallone in the capacity of Inspecteur Général. As a consequence he

was at the centre of a period of considerable dynamism in the development
of the new tools for planning and regeneration in the newly created Regional
Government which led to the production of the Regional Plan and its various
implementation instruments. He has recently transferred to work at Cabinet level with the Federal Government in Brussels on wider issues of urban
policy. He has written widely on urban issues and policy in Belgium.

Corinna Morandi

Corinna Morandi is Associate Professor in Town Planning at the Politecnico
di Milano where she teaches on urban planning, specialising in retailing
and related matters. She is also Vice President of the International Relations Committee of the Politecnico. Professor Morandi has been engaged in
research at the Dipartimento di Architectura e Planificazione since 1980.
Her research has been concerned with the evolution of town planning in
metropolitan Milan and its relationship to other regional and urban planning
strategies in the rest of Europe. This work has included a number of major
international research projects. She has published extensively on topics related to Italian planning and the planning of Milan.

Preface

Cities undergo constant change. They are never static, never finished, always adjusting to new circumstances. But over the last 30 years many European cities have experienced a pace of change far more rapid than at any other time in their recent history. The causes of such rapid evolution in the nature and functioning of cities lie in two main areas. The first is the radical restructuring of the economic base of cities that has occurred as they have ceased to be centres of manufacturing production and have become instead the locus for services and centres of consumption. The second is the process of decentralisation, or suburbanisation, that has pulled many functions out from central and inner-city areas towards the periphery of conurbations.

Both trends have resulted in large-scale abandonment and dereliction of land and buildings, degraded environments, unemployment of labour, and acute social deprivation. The public policy response to these problems has become known as *urban regeneration*: that is to say, policies that attempt to return derelict and vacant land and buildings to beneficial use, create new forms of employment where jobs have been lost, improve the urban environment, and tackle an array of urban social problems.

These trends have been particularly severe in older industrial areas: towns, cities or regions that were, until recently, dependent upon mining, traditional manufacturing (such as steel production, chemicals, textiles, heavy engineering and shipbuilding), ports and rail transport. Such areas are to be found throughout western Europe, but are concentrated in the United Kingdom in South Wales, Northern England, the central belt of Scotland and the Belfast area of Northern Ireland. In France the areas of Lorraine and Nord are particularly affected. In the Netherlands the problems are less pronounced, but Rotterdam has suffered from restructuring of the port and related industries. In the Walloon region of Belgium the industrial valleys of the Sambre and Meuse have been badly affected. In Germany, the Saarland, the Ruhr and much of former East Germany have experienced rapid change. In Italy, Milan is one of a number of northern cities adjusting to new, more service-oriented functions.

The United Kingdom, being one of the first of these countries to industrialise, and failing to make the productivity gains of some of its competitors during the post-war period, was among the first of the European countries to face these winds of change. It is no surprise that some of the earliest policies to tackle the decline and restructuring of urban areas can be found here. Indeed the very term 'urban regeneration' appears to have its origins in

British metropolitan planning in the mid-1970s. Dutch city planners were also innovative in their approaches to the renewal of urban areas, especially residential areas, from an early date. By the 1980s a number of French and German cities were experiencing urban problems similar to those of their British counterparts, and were adopting broadly similar policy responses.

Although these urban trends in each country appear similar in general terms, in each country and in each city different circumstances apply. In consequence there is considerable variation in the detail of problems and policies. Through both theoretical discussion and the examination of a series of case studies this book debates the extent to which larger older industrial conurbations in different European countries are indeed facing similar problems, and examines whether the urban regeneration policies they have developed are fundamentally different in approach or are merely locally adapted variations of a common strategy.

The key issues to be examined include the effects and influence on regeneration policies of local geography, built form, land ownership and tenure, local economic circumstances, political agendas and ambitions. Through discussion of these issues insights are provided into the relationship between urban problems and solutions, and the extent to which the issues have a generic aspect.

The contributing authors are all specialists in urban development and planning within particular European countries, and are able to provide a comprehensive view of regeneration within particular localities. Through these lenses the editors consider the similarities and differences between, and influences on, the processes of urban regeneration and policy responses in different European situations.

Chris Couch, Charles Fraser, Sue Percy
February 2003

Acknowledgements

The following figures were drawn by Paul Hodgkinson:

3.1, 4.1, 5.1, 5.2, 5.3, 6.3, 7.1, 8.1, 9.1, 10.1.

The following photographs were taken by Chris Couch:

3.2, 3.3, 3.4, 7.2, 7.3, 7.4, 7.5, 10.2, 10.3, 10.4.

Acronyms

The following is a list of acronyms by country of use, as referred to in the relevant parts of the text.

General and European

DG: Directorate General
EIUA: European Institute for Urban Affairs
ESDP: European Spatial Development Perspective

United Kingdom

BCC: Belfast City Council
BCCMSC: Belfast City Council Management Steering Committee
BCP: Belfast City Partnership
CDP: community development project
DETR: Department of the Environment, Transport and the Regions
DoE: Department of the Environment
          also in Northern Ireland: DoE(NI)
DTI: Department for Trade and Industry
DTLR: Department of Transport, Local Government and the Regions
GEAR: Glasgow Eastern Area Renewal
LEC: local enterprise companies
LIPA: Liverpool Institute for the Performing Arts
MBW: Making Belfast Work
MDC: Merseyside Development Corporation
NDC: New Deal for Communities
NIHE: Northern Ireland Housing Executive
NWDA: North West Development Agency
PPA: priority partnership area
RDA: regional development agency
RDS: Regional Development Strategy (Northern Ireland)
RICS: Royal Institution of Chartered Surveyors
SDA: Scottish Development Agency
SET: Scottish Enterprise Tayside
SIP: Social Inclusion Programme (Scotland)
SRB: Single Regeneration Budget
UDC: urban development corporation
UDP: unitary development plan
UTF: urban task force
VNC: Vauxhall Neighbourhood Council

The Netherlands

VROM: Ministry of Housing, Spatial Planning and the Environment

Belgium

SAED: site d'activité économique désaffecté
SDER: Schéma Directeur de l'Èspace Régional
ZIP: zone d'initiative priviligée

France

CDC: Caisse des Dépôts et Consignations
CFF: Credit Foncier de France
CHR :   Centre Hospitalier Régional
CUDL: Communauté Urbaine de Lille
DIV :   Direction Interministerielle des Villes
HLM :   habitations à loyer modéré
SEM: societe d'économie mixte
SRU :   Loi de Solidarité et Renouvellement Urbain
TGV :   Train á Grande Vitesse
ZAC: Zone d'Amenagement Concerté

Germany

IBA: Internationale Bauaustellung
KVR: Kommunalverband Ruhrgebiet (Ruhr District Association of
             Communities)
NRW: North Rhine Westphalia
ZIM: Zukunftsinitiative Montanregionen

Italy

SFR   regional integrated railway system
STU: società per la trasformazione urbana

1

Introduction: the European Context and Theoretical Framework

Chris Couch and Charles Fraser

The contemporary European context

After the initial post-war rebuilding, the countries of western Europe experienced a long period of economic growth that brought ever greater wealth. Individuals were able to afford more and better housing, and the consumption of consumer goods increased dramatically. Public services and welfare benefits were also improved by tax-rich governments. Countries urbanised apace as workers left the increasingly mechanised agricultural sector to take better-paid jobs in manufacturing and the expanding service industries. However, this era of continuous growth, seemingly without cost, was interrupted by the Arab-Israeli war of 1973 and the oil price rises and recession that followed. Thereafter growth was more erratic, and the social costs of late capitalism became apparent. Unemployment and industrial dereliction rose sharply as firms sought to increase productivity, or where they closed down through a failure to compete. Since then many of Europe's older urban areas have experienced a radical restructuring of their economic base: traditional industries have declined or vanished from the urban scene while the service sector has grown (see Table 1.1).

Declining profits and the rising social costs of unemployment and economic competition put ever greater fiscal strains on national and local governments, leading to cutbacks in public expenditure and services. Growing urban deprivation and the fracturing of traditional communities were causing growing social problems: alienation, racial tension, crime, marital breakdown and mental illness. At the same time the physical infrastructure of many cities, particularly those that had expanded rapidly in the late eighteenth or nineteenth centuries, was becoming obsolete and in need of replacement, often at great cost. Other problems were also becoming apparent: over the last 30 years societies have become ever more aware of the growing environmental

Table 1.1   The changing industrial structure of selected regions in western Europe.

	1981			1997		
	Agriculture %	Industry %	Services %	Agriculture %	Industry %	Services %
Wallonia	3.9	31.2	64.9	2.9	24.5	72.6
Nord-Pas-de-Calais	3.7	44.6	51.7	2.9	31.4	65.6
Northrhein-Westphalia	2.2	46.7	51.1	2.0	35.9	62.2
Lombardy	4.1	52.1	43.8	2.7	40.7	56.6
West Netherlands	8.2	34.7	57.1	2.8	17.2	74.1
North West England	1.3	43.4	55.2	1.2	29.2	69.6
Scotland	4.1	38.3	58.1	2.7	26.8	70.6
Northern Ireland	5.4	36.5	58.1	5.2	27.3	67.5

Source: *Regional Trends*, The Stationery Office, London.

costs of economic competition and urbanisation and the need for more sustainable forms of development.

Thus European cities are facing a complex array of economic, social, physical, environmental and fiscal problems. Cities have to compete for investment and economic growth at the same time as dealing with the dereliction left by previous generations. The social legacy of change also has to be tackled in an era when the dominant aims of political hegemony are concerned with cuts in taxation, privatisation and 'value for money'. The demand for travel in ever more sprawling cities has to be accommodated while trying to reduce energy consumption and environmental pollution.

Urban regeneration is the field of public policy that deals with all these issues. In biology, regeneration means the regrowth of lost or injured tissue, or the restoration of a system to its initial state. And so it is with urban areas. Regeneration is concerned with the regrowth of economic activity where it has been lost; the restoration of social function where there has been dysfunction, or social inclusion where there has been exclusion; and the restoration of environmental quality or ecological balance where it has been lost. Thus urban regeneration is an aspect of the management and planning of existing urban areas rather than the planning and development of new urbanisation. This type of urban policy is unique to the last quarter of a century. Some types of intervention, such as slum clearance and the improvement of transport infrastructure, can be traced back through the whole of the twentieth century and even earlier. Haussmann's restructuring of central Paris in the mid-nineteenth century was a programme of urban regeneration, as was the rebuilding of the metropolis after the Great Fire of London. What is different about recent decades is the size and complexity of the problems, the speed of change, and the concomitant scale and sophistication of policy.

British cities were among the earliest in Europe to experience this wave of economic restructuring and social change, partly as a result of poor industrial competitiveness, outworn infrastructure and social tensions in the inner cities. Modern British urban policy is generally dated from 1968, when a Labour government facing social unrest in the inner cities introduced the Urban Programme to tackle what it identified as areas of severe social deprivation in a number of cities and towns that required special help to meet their social needs and to bring their services to an adequate level (Gibson & Langstaff 1982, p. 147). Thus it was social dysfunction that was amongst the first problem to be identified.

Since the Second World War most western European cities had tackled the problem of obsolete housing through policies of mass slum clearance and replacement. Gradually, from the late 1960s, each country moved to more sensitive programmes of housing renovation and area improvement. The UK was one of the first to change policy after the 1969 Housing Act, followed by the Netherlands after confrontations between communities and city governments in Amsterdam and Rotterdam in the early 1970s (Couch 1990, p. 109). In Germany, as the post-war housing shortage diminished, the passing of the Städtebauforderungsgesetz in 1971 allowed the upgrading of rented property in the inner cities (Power 1993, p. 124). In France, legislation was changed in the 1970s to facilitate small-scale area improvement zones known as *opérations programmée*.

By the mid-1970s in the UK, and by the mid-1980s across western Europe, the traditional industrial structure of many cities was undergoing rapid change. Unemployment and urban deprivation became the major political concerns. In the UK, but not elsewhere, the role of local authorities became increasingly marginalised as central government sought solutions that involved direct action in partnership with private sector investors. Other countries took different approaches: in France solutions were sought in the devolution of power to local communities supported by massive state expenditure; and in Germany wealthy regional and local governments tried to spend their way out of the crisis, at least until reunification changed the priorities for investment.

By the 1990s the long-term environmental benefits of maintaining and improving existing urban areas had been recognised. The *Green Paper on the Urban Environment* (CEC 1990) argued that global environmental protection could be enhanced by urban policies that had as their primary objectives 'the creation, or recreation, of towns and cities which provide an attractive environment for their inhabitants', and that 'strategies which emphasized mixed use and denser development' were to be favoured (CEC 1990, pp. 48, 60).

Thus today there is much interest in urban regeneration as an instrument of urban policy at all political levels, coupled with massive capital investment – both public and private – in the process. At the European level the Commission and its various Directorates are engaged in changing the focus of European policy from issues such as agriculture to an urban one. This is reflected in the introduction of structural fund programmes such as URBAN, and the promotion of several projects under research and structural programmes such as Interreg IIc, III and the 5th and 6th Framework 'City of Tomorrow' research programme.

At the national level most countries have recently re-examined their urban policies and have put new legislation into place to emphasise the need for greater effort to improve the condition of urban areas. The UK government's Urban White Paper, which built on the report of Lord Rogers, *Towards an Urban Renaissance*, is a prime example of this. The French government also has produced a new Planning Act, the SRU of 2000, picking up many of the ideas of the Sueur report of 1998. The Social Cities programme in Germany, the Major Cities programme in the Netherlands and recent initiatives in urban planning in both Brussels and the Walloon region of Belgium and in Italy reinforce the continent-wide nature of this awakening of interest in the future of our towns and cities. This is therefore an auspicious time to examine and review the regeneration process so far, in order to offer a reflection on the capacity of regeneration strategies to meet social, political, economic and environmental goals.

The emergence of a new stream of action in the urban environment, which is dominating the urban policy of several countries, in a way places the spotlight on the more traditional processes of intervention, and raises the question of why the traditional approaches of mainstream urban planning appear to be inadequate for the task of managing the regeneration of our cities and solving, or at least alleviating, the many other social and economic problems that have arisen as the economies of the Western world have evolved.

This book therefore aims to:

- provide a comprehensive and informed presentation of urban regeneration problems and policies in a number of European cities;

- identify and critically discuss the challenges and opportunities to urban regeneration and the extent to which these issues have a generic aspect;

- inform developers, investors, landowners, policy makers and decision takers of key influences in urban change through a framework of urban regeneration issues;

- develop the current knowledge of and understanding about the urban regeneration process in European cities.

It will therefore make a unique European contribution to the debate on urban regeneration by offering a discussion of the relevant theoretical perspectives based on the analysis of case studies of major urban renewal projects and strategies in a number of European cities. These are provided by authors who are specialists in urban development and planning within their own countries and are able to provide comprehensive insights into regeneration in their own national contexts. Drawn from both academic and practical backgrounds the writers are well placed to assess the success or otherwise of their own local urban regeneration projects. Through these studies the editors examine the similarities and differences in the processes of urban regeneration between different situations, drawing out conclusions around key aspects of the process. Thus factors such as location, regional economic conditions, previous land-use patterns and building forms, together with the nature of local land markets, administrative structures, tools and mechanisms of intervention, are all shown to be important in shaping local differences in urban regeneration policy and its outcomes.

Following the next chapter, which considers the nature of change in the European industrial city, there follows a series of chapters, each devoted to a case study of one city or region. These are Liverpool, Dundee, Belfast, Lille, Rotterdam, Wallonie, Milan and the Ruhr. These are followed by three cross-cutting chapters that consider economic and physical conditions; the administrative and financial context; and how new agendas are being accommodated in urban regeneration policies across Europe.

The book concludes that urban regeneration is now a major activity in every country considered and is increasingly a major policy objective of the European Commission itself. In each country the starting point for intervention is in theoretical terms different. For example, in Belgium the country is moving from a social philosophy based upon its traditions of self-help and charity, whereas in France urban regeneration fits into the *dirigiste* philosophy of the French state. In the UK it is market-oriented approaches that have become dominant in recent years. As a result of these differences each country has devised its own formula for state intervention and its own tools and mechanisms for urban regeneration. Nevertheless, all show evidence of concern for environmental improvement, economic development and social inclusion as fundamental goals of urban regeneration, albeit to varying degrees. Success is difficult to measure. In Lille it appears assured, in Liverpool less so. This raises the question of whether regeneration programmes are as effective in cities where there are inherent problems such as peripherality compared with those close to markets. The devolution of power and the 'competence' to tackle problems appears in every case to be having a beneficial effect. In its efforts to devolve power to the countries and regions, the UK government is doing no more than catching up with these other countries. The key actors outside government are landowners and investors, and there is an enormous variety to deal with. Seeking synergies and harmony between the divergent goals of all three is the main public policy challenge, and failure in this area is the main reason for public intervention, whether through direct government action, regulation, taxation or subsidy. Indeed, the most obviously successful examples of urban regeneration have been where the land has been in public ownership from the start. The relation between urban regeneration and 'normal' planning mechanisms varies between countries. For example, in the Netherlands and Belgium urban regeneration is largely an extension of urban planning, whereas in the UK it appears to be a virtually separate arm of public policy, poorly coordinated with the mainstream of land-use planning.

Comparison is at the centre of our approach to writing and editing this book. Comparative theory therefore provides the main framework within which the various case studies are examined. With this in mind we have devoted the following section to a consideration of the merits and problems of the comparative method and the use of case studies from both the theoretical and practical points of view. In writing and editing this work we have been very conscious of the problems and constraints that limit the value of international comparative urban research. We take heed of the conclusions of Ball *et al.* (1988) and Oxley & Smith (1996), who, writing about the field of housing research, note that too many studies fail to get beyond description, and offer little rigorous social scientific analysis of their findings. With this in mind we have taken the opportunity to review the nature and purposes of a selection of previous studies in this field and to consider the alternative research approaches before arriving at our own choice of methodology and places to be compared. This chapter therefore contains both a theoretical discussion of the purposes and problems of international comparative urban research and an outline of the approach adopted in this study.

Issues in international comparative urban research

Most recent writing has suggested that there are two general reasons for undertaking international comparative research in the social sciences: the furtherance of explanatory and predictive theory, and the understanding and transfer of policy from one country to another. Faludi & Hamnett (in Breakell 1975) put forward three aims for comparative planning research: to advance theory; to improve planning practice (urban policy); and to bring about a unification of policy between countries. White (1978), reporting on a seminar discussing the problems of international comparative research in the context of UK/USSR studies, concludes that a further objective might be to understand the processes that prompt the exchange of ideas between nations. He then suggests that the comparative method has a number of potential uses in planning research as an aid to understanding:

- past successes and failures in planning policy;

- contemporary planning processes;

- future developments in planning systems (likely scenarios);

- innovation diffusion processes in the exchange of ideas between nations.

In a discussion of the problems of international comparative research in the social sciences, Jan Berting (Berting *et al.* 1979) provides one of the clearest categorisations of the purposes of international comparative studies:

(1) to develop theory, usually within a particular discipline;

(2) to explain or interpret social phenomena (essentially the converse of the above);

(3) to describe social reality (a prerequisite of 2);

(4) policy development;

(5) policy evaluation.

More specific expressions of research objectives can be found in examples of actual empirical work. There are as many different purposes as there are studies, but an analysis of some recent examples from this and related fields shows that most work fits comfortably within one or other of these categories. For example, Wilmott expressed the aim of his work on poverty and social policy in Europe as being the starting point for a comparative study of social policies (Wilmott & McDowell 1977). The purpose of this was to then suggest how individual countries could learn from each other to improve the effectiveness of their own anti-poverty policies, an approach that he regarded as crucial to the development of a genuinely European strategy to reduce and relieve poverty. George & Lawson (1980), in their study of poverty and inequality in Europe, set out to answer a mixture of theoretical and policy-related questions:

- How is poverty defined in each country, and what government policies are there to deal with the problem?

- How extensive is inequality in income and wealth in each country?

- What trends can be established in the understanding, treatment and prevalence of poverty and inequality?

In contrast to these examples, the study of population movement by Hall & Hay (1980) was clearly designed to test the international validity of a theory of urban change that had been developed in one country, the USA. It sought to describe and categorise urban change and then to proceed to a deeper analysis of economic change and policy responses. Some studies seek only to undertake bi-national comparisons, such as those published by the Anglo-German Foundation. In a study of planning, transport and conservation in British and German cities (Hass-Klau 1988), the central purpose was to explore the scope for policy transfer, particularly towards the UK. By contrast, the rather broader aims of Wild & Jones (1991) in their collection of essays on economic change and policy in the two countries were expressed as understanding:

> the role of industrial policy in both countries, the part played in this by local and regional development policies, identifying differences in policy and implementation, and indicating where lessons may be transferred from one country to the other. (Wild & Jones 1991, p. ix.)

Norton & Novy (1991) sought only to survey British and German housing problems and policies, and to discuss key themes of common interest. Power (1993) seeks to analyse the role of governments in helping to provide housing, especially social housing. Her study traces the evolution of state-sponsored housing in five European countries and evaluates current and emerging policies in this field, identifying a growing international consensus about the future role of social housing. Nijkamp & Perrels are clearly concerned with policy development in their comparative analysis of energy-environmental policies in a number of European cities. Their aim is to 'bring together experiences from various European cities aiming at developing a sustainable development for their urban territory' (Nijkamp & Perrels 1994, preface).

In *Urban Planning in Europe*, Newman & Thornley (1996) see their task as focusing on the 'political and economic forces which create common trends in urban planning and [exploring] the scope for national and urban governments to deviate from these trends and adopt their own approach' (p. 4), thus seeking to develop the theory that explains the nature of urban planning systems and policies and to provide a framework for further policy development.

From these examples it is evident that most of these different purposes and orientations can be accommodated within Berting's fivefold classification or Faludi & Hamnett's more generalised divisions. Certainly there are a great variety of reasons for international comparative research, and each of these studies has, in one way or another, yielded useful findings that could not have been achieved without an international dimension. So where do we see our own study fitting into these categories? The title *Urban Regeneration in Europe* makes clear our concern with urban areas and their regeneration, but we can be more precise than this. Cooke (1989) has explored the ways in which the pervasive experience of economic restructuring has interacted with local characteristics to produce variations in response and outcomes from one locality to another, and posed the question:

> While people's lives continue to be mainly circumscribed by the localities in which they live and work, can they exert an influence on the fate of those places given that so much [of] their destiny is increasingly controlled by global political and economic forces? (Cooke 1989, p. 2.)

This is our area of interest: given the 'pervasive experience of economic restructuring' in a number of different European cities, to what extent and why do local policy responses and the local outcomes vary from place to place and country to country? Thus we are primarily concerned with the development of theory that seeks to explain the interaction between urban change and urban policy within the context of older industrial conurbations that have experienced substantial economic and spatial restructuring.

Research methodology

There are difficult problems to overcome in international comparative urban research. A central issue is the choice between quantitative and qualitative methods. As in any other field of social science research, quantitative approaches give a strong impression of rigour, but in urban research this can be unhelpful and even misleading. If the quantitative analysis is based on secondary data, international researchers are likely to come up against immense problems of lack of comparability of data in terms of availability, definition of terms, periodicity and methods of collection, level of aggregation, and questions of interpretation. A quick glance at, for example, the comparative housing statistics published by Eurostat for the European Commission will quickly reveal how, even at the highest level of European administration, there are major problems with the comparability of data. If these problems are difficult at the level of the nation, then they are intensified at the level of the conurbation, the focus of our research interest.

These problems force many international researchers to consider primary data collection: *surveys*. These are potentially attractive for many purposes, but we did not feel that we had the capacity to carry out extensive and expensive comparative surveys. Furthermore, given the variety of places and circumstances that we were investigating, we did not feel that any quantitative survey could reveal the kind of information that we required for our analysis.

Masser, extensively quoting Yin (1982), argues that situations such as cross-national studies, where context (the history, geography, institutions, economy and culture of the country) and phenomenon (the planning issue being studied) are entwined to such an extent that the boundaries of the study become unclear, are common in the social sciences. In these circumstances he argues in favour of a case study approach:

> Yin sees the case study as a research strategy which can be likened to an experiment, a history, or a simulation. He points out that it does not imply the use of any particular type of evidence or data collection technique. It can draw on both quantitative or on qualitative evidence and make use of fieldwork techniques, verbal reports, and observations, either separately or collectively. The essential strengths of case studies lie in their ability to take account of a large amount of local detail at the same time as generally comparable information, and in their essential flexibility in practice. (Masser 1986, p. 14.)

Power agrees, suggesting that:

> the local approach makes it possible to go beyond the more standard international studies in pursuing a central theme to its roots – why are social housing areas becoming more polarised and more popular across the European Community at the advent of the Single Market? (Power 1993, p. 13.)

To be successful, Masser argues that:

It is necessary to proceed step by step and to develop in the first place an adequate explanation for each case in its own right, before going on to evaluate the findings for several cases and then proceeding to develop a common explanation relating to the phenomenon ... [It is important that] readers are able to follow the argument and draw their own conclusions from the evidence. For this purpose graphical representation and tables of events have been found to be particularly useful. (Masser 1986, p. 15.)

A major limitation on the usefulness of case studies in comparative research is the competence of the researcher to investigate and analyse the country in question. Most researchers would agree that there are no short cuts in this process and that it is necessary to invest considerable time and effort in getting to grips with the country and culture under investigation before serious research can be undertaken. The ability of any one researcher to investigate case studies in more than two or three countries, including their own, is therefore extremely limited. This tends to lead to studies being either comparative between only two or three countries, or employing a number of researchers, or using alternative methods of investigation reliant upon secondary sources of data. Whereas the majority of multinational studies are carried out by research teams drawn from the countries under investigation, Power's study of social housing was unusual for the fact that a single author achieved a rigorous investigation in five different countries:

The approach adopted here was direct and deliberately responsive – an exhaustive and in-depth quest, country by country, for live experiences and examples. The approach was orientated towards 'discovery' rather than 'standardisation'. By following up on important issues as they arose, the author was able to uncover a pattern of urban development that was surprisingly uniform and that gave unexpected prominence to social housing in the current period. (Power 1993, p. 12.)

A contrasting approach was taken by Parkinson *et al.*:

The aim of the study was to assess the contribution that cities have made to the changing Europe during recent decades and identify the broad implications for cities within the European Community during the 1990s. The approach taken in the study was essentially qualitative, rather than quantitative. Its primary database was that created by individual city case-studies which were carefully selected to represent the different types of change that have been occurring in the different regions of Europe. The purpose of the study was not to compile a superficial set of indicators of urban conditions across all the urban areas of Europe. Rather it was to understand in depth the dynamics of the economic, social and environmental

changes at work in European cities which would allow us to evaluate their
consequences for the European urban system, anticipate future changes
and assess their policy implications. (EIUA 1992, p. 11)

It is often argued that one of the main limitations on the value of case studies
is the difficulty of generalising from the results. But case studies can reveal
a depth and richness of detail and expose differences that more rigorously
comparative but less precise quantitative studies cannot show. Case studies
expose similarities and differences of experience and policy, and pose questions for future research. They can also help to provide local explanations for
the findings of more generalised quantitative comparisons. However, to be
successful, multiple case studies must conform to a common design – a common template – in order to facilitate comparisons. Without such a template
the case studies become little more than a collection of parallel descriptions.
Masser draws attention to the high rate of failure in international comparative research based upon case studies, arguing that many lack any serious
attempt at a comprehensive evaluation in cross-national terms. One of the
few studies he regarded as successful at that time was the Leiden–Oxford
Project (Thomas *et al.* 1983), in which the British and Dutch teams shared
a common British experience that permitted a much more sustained and
richer comparison than might otherwise have been the case. Significantly,
many of the most interesting insights related to the workings of the British
planning system.

Taking account of this wealth of previous experience we have chosen to examine the situation in each country through the use of case studies. As well
as being theoretically justified there were a number of practical reasons for
this approach. First, there already exist a number of published studies that
describe and seek to explain urban trends and policy responses on a cross-national or international comparative basis across Europe. Second, within each
country there exist, to varying degrees, detailed analyses of urban trends and
approaches to urban regeneration. We felt that there was little to be gained
by attempting to replicate such studies with our own limited resources.
Instead, as we have stated above, one of our key aims was to explore ways
in which the characteristics of locality in each conurbation (the particular
characteristics of the local urban fabric, the urban economy, society and the
policy-making process) could modify the experience of urban change and
affect the nature or effectiveness of urban policy.

With this aim in mind much of our work is qualitative in nature and depends
for its worth on the detail obtained for each place. The only way to achieve
the depth we required was to undertake a series of case studies within a common template. Our comparative statements therefore rely heavily upon our

understanding and interpretation of these case studies. We are fully aware that there are severe limitations on the extent to which it is possible to generalise from this kind of work. It is for this reason that we have constantly attempted to relate the case studies to the wider context of national and international trends and events so that we 'know where we are' and can assess the typicality of each case. These limitations on our study are, we think, common to many international comparative studies of this type but do mean that our conclusions are restricted to comments on the validity of previous research findings or assumed truths and the development of new hypotheses for future research investigation.

Our study uses a number of researchers, each with appropriate country-specific knowledge. This approach raises some issues. Within the social sciences it is always possible to identify a variety of theoretical approaches and methods. In our project we have eight contributors from six countries, and in these circumstances it becomes very difficult to agree common approaches and interpretations. Therefore, on the one hand, each researcher has had to make compromises and to accept the template for the case study provided by the editors; on the other hand, we have also had to accept that to some degree each researcher would adopt their own approach, priorities and interpretations.

The choice of localities

Although we are interested in international variations in urban change and policy across Europe, it was necessary for us to recognise the limitations of our own capacity to investigate such a vast array of experiences in many different countries: we had to be selective in what we studied. Europe may be subdivided in a number of ways. There are large geographical regions whose boundaries may vary in detail, but most observers will accept that western Europe may be distinguished from eastern Europe, and that northern Europe may be distinguished from southern Europe, in terms of physical geography, history, economy and society, such that the differences between these regions are generally greater than those within them. There are substantial administrative regions: the most important by far is the division between those countries within the European Union and those outside its boundaries, and the EU itself identifies a series of internal regions such as the Atlantic Arc or the Baltic region. There are economic divisions between the more and less prosperous countries of Europe, and socio-political divisions between the countries of the former Soviet bloc and the Western democracies.

We felt that it would be too problematic for our purposes to study case studies from all European countries: we did not have the capacity, and the difference of experience between the richer North and West and the poorer East and South would be such that the exploration of similarities between countries in one region would most likely be overwhelmed by the differences between regions. Besides, we were not interested in producing a European compendium. We were interested in exploring a theoretical question: what was the impact of locality on urban change and policy? This could be achieved by studying cases in just a few countries with what would be, in the European context, a broadly similar experience of economic development, urbanisation and economic restructuring. Thus we chose to study cases from countries within the European Union that met these criteria. The United Kingdom (from which we have case examples from three of its constituent parts, England, Scotland, and Northern Ireland), the Netherlands, Belgium, Germany, France and Italy are all prosperous industrialised countries within the EU and have all, in one form or another, experienced massive urban restructuring in recent years.

The spatial focus of interest is the obsolescent urban area (frequently the inner city, but in some examples, such as the Ruhr and Wallonia, more widely spread). Thus we are not concerned in detail in this work with either the problems of rural areas or the urban periphery, except where they interact with areas of obsolescence in terms of problems or policies. The case studies tend therefore to operate at two levels of detail: the conurbation, and selected obsolescent districts within each conurbation chosen to illustrate particular circumstances.

The choice of case study was also constrained by the need for similarity. We were interested primarily in second-tier urban areas that met certain criteria:

- conurbations large enough to be regional centres but not capital cities (where a whole different range of international economic forces would have come into play);

- conurbations that had experienced the kind of large-scale restructuring we wished to investigate;

- conurbations that had some distinctive characteristics of locality that could be easily identified and whose impacts could be examined.

We have to be honest and say that we were also constrained by the practicalities of research, with localities of which we had some prior knowledge and where we had local academic contacts being favoured over others. In the end the choice came down to the following:

- **Liverpool**, a conurbation with more experience of urban restructuring and change than almost any other British city. It is among the poorest conurbations in western Europe, and has been the subject of an extensive variety of urban policy initiatives over the past 30 years. As a case study it provides an opportunity to study the possibilities for and limitations of regeneration in a situation of extremely limited demand for land, property, goods and services coupled with low levels of both consumer and business confidence.

- **Dundee**, in many ways the forgotten city in the Scottish story of urban regeneration. Much has been written about Glasgow and Edinburgh, but a study of Dundee can offer different insights in an area that has seen the decline of traditional industries coupled with some successes in the regeneration process.

- **Belfast**, the primary city of Northern Ireland, where urban restructuring and urban policy have become intertwined with internal civil and political conflict with important consequences for economic development, social structures and the nature of governance.

- **Lille**, the centre of a former textile and mining region in northern France, has, in recent years, undergone a transformation to become an icon of the new Europe at the heart of the London–Köln–Paris 'golden triangle'.

- **Milan** provides contrasting experiences to those of the northern European cities: a prosperous city in a growing region, the impacts of restructuring are more subtle in Italian society.

- **Rotterdam**, the largest port in Europe and largely rebuilt after the Second World War, provides an interesting contrast to Liverpool and, to a lesser extent, Dundee. A successful port city in a prosperous region; the case study illustrates a process of urban restructuring and decentralisation in a growing conurbation and a strong local government that provided a number of early innovations in community participation in the regeneration process. Nevertheless, deprivation and social exclusion remain serious issues.

- **Wallonia**, especially the valley of the Sambre-Meuse from Mons through Charleroi to Namur and Liège, has seen the collapse of its former prosperity and political influence, which was dependent upon the industrial base of coal, steel, chemicals and textiles. Here regional and local governments are struggling to get to grips with social, economic and environmental problems of immense complexity and scale.

- **The Ruhr**, in North-Rhine Westphalia, has endured more than 20 years of economic restructuring and regeneration activity. The area has become famous for the activities of the recent high-profile Emscher Park IBA. The environmental problems of this region are substantial, but within a strong economy and a stable political framework some novel solutions are emerging.

The structure of the case studies

Contributors worked at two levels of study: the conurbation, and selected examples of obsolescent districts or areas. The definition of each conurbation was left to each contributor, based upon their own informed judgement about the nature of the area, the issues and the constraints imposed by administrative boundaries, and the availability of data. Below this, contributors were free to select and study whatever local districts, areas or projects they felt would illustrate the processes of urban change and regeneration to best advantage. Reflecting our interest in locality, the template for each case study asked contributors to consider: the nature of the economic restructuring and urban change that had occurred over the last 20 years, or whatever other period seemed locally significant; the nature of the public policy responses to the restructuring processes; and the outcomes of these processes up to the time of writing. Beyond this, contributors were asked to discuss the extent and ways in which policy might have been influenced by the characteristics of the locality, such as: geography (topography, climate, etc); environment (physical conditions, nature of the built form, such as flats or houses, buildings and areas of architectural or historic interest); economic circumstances (industrial change, personal and institutional income and wealth); social characteristics (population change and structure, including the presence of ethnic minorities); political circumstances (party control, stability/instability in local governance, leadership); patterns of land ownership, the workings of the local property market); and specific political agendas such as social exclusion and environmentally sustainable development.

2

Change in the European Industrial City

Charles Fraser

The origins of the industrial city

To understand what is happening to Europe's major urban centres today one has to understand why and how they were created, and why and how they have declined. Only then can the efficacy of the remedial measures be judged and improved. To do so, it would be instructive, in the imagination, to take a walk in the Pennines or along the banks of the Clyde in or around 1750. There would be no 'dark satanic mills' or, for the inhabitant, little inkling of the vast changes to the rural and urban scene that were about to unfold. To take the same walk in 1875, at the height of the industrial might of these areas, would reveal a totally different scene. To take the walk today would reveal that that which was created and appeared so permanent has begun to disappear and mutate into something quite different.

In short, the process of urban change is continuous, and that which was created and has enjoyed such permanence in our history for almost 200 years can disappear as easily as it begun. To Machu Pichu, Mohenjo Daro and a thousand other 'lost' cities are we about to add the names of Liverpool, Glasgow, Lille, the Ruhr and many smaller towns? We do not want to do so, and therefore in order to prevent the disappearance of our urban society entirely to the forces of natural economics and shifting capitalism, conscious decisions have been made to arrest this process. However, to do so is not that easy. To begin with, there is a gap between the desire to retain a city and the knowledge of how this can be done. We cannot recreate the immediate industrial past any more than we can recreate the more distant rural past. Therefore we have to create a new future. But how? Decrees and policy decisions do not create anything. They are more often than not shown to be hollow shams. The management and redirection of the process of city creation is in itself a complex exercise, and we have to begin by knowing what factors we have to manage. Some light can be shed on this by identifying the factors that were important in the formation of those first industrial towns and the nature of the dynamics that drove the process forward.

Analysts of the British scene point to the happy coincidence of a multitude of factors in the mid-seventeenth century, which blossomed in the eighteenth century to create the conditions for take-off of the first industrial society (Hoskins 1957). Throughout the United Kingdom, except the southern rural parts of Ireland, a class of capitalist landowners had emerged with rights to encourage the exploitation of their property. To this was added the availability of capital for investment through a sound banking system and an emerging labour force of rural migrants, untrammelled by the ties of a feudal peasant society, set in the context of a society that had achieved internal security and stability, hardly disturbed by the eruptions of the Jacobite rebellions from 1688 to 1745. This process gathered momentum until, by the time that James Watt had uncovered the way to harness the power of the steam engine in 1776, it had developed a dynamism that changed the economic scene radically. Despite the loss of most of the American colonies by 1780 new markets had emerged, and the basis for an industrial society was assured. In Britain, cities – some old, some new – emerged or expanded to prosper in this new economy: Glasgow, Birmingham, Sheffield, Manchester, Leeds and the West Riding towns, and with them new ports such as Liverpool, Hull and Dundee to bring raw materials such as cotton and export the products.

On the continent of Europe such conditions did not exist in the same order, and although the new technologies were available, and there were cities with a rich history of trade and banking such as Antwerp and Amsterdam, much of the land was still held in feudal tenure, making its commercial exploitation difficult. Equally, much of the labour force was still rural and held in feudal bondage of one type or another. It was not really until the French Revolution that the spread of new structures struck at this medieval legacy. It was through the revolutionary armies of France, and later Napoleon, that these barriers were swept away and the conditions for economic innovation appeared. This is best exemplified in the case of the Walloon region of what is now Belgium, the first area of continental Europe to industrialise. Here the markets for industrial products existed, and the technology was available. There was a plentiful supply of investment capital from the rich port and textile cities of Flanders, such as Antwerp, Ghent and Brussels. Land and resources, such as coal and the labour supply, were however still trapped in age-old feudal systems, which were liberated only by the incorporation of the region into the new French Republic. Similar processes were set in motion in the Netherlands, France and the German states, but did not percolate till much later to the Hapsburg Empire or Russia.

A further significant difference between the continent and Britain was the extent to which the new elites related to the old guard in terms of who exercised most political control over the emerging industrial towns and cities. It would be generally true, and perhaps not too much of an oversimplification, to state that in the UK the new cities soon came under the sway of the new industrial capitalist classes, whereas on the continent the control of the developing industrial centres was still shaped by the long-standing institutions, families and processes that they had possessed for centuries. On the one hand the city served the industrialist; on the other the industrialist served the city (Cipolla 1973).

The decline of the industrial city

Thus by the middle of the nineteenth century an entire new urban society had been put in place throughout much of western Europe, exploiting roughly similar combinations of land, labour and capital as well as internal stability in each nation state and systems of urban governance that adapted to the new society and enabled it to flourish. However, much of the growth and success of each national grouping of industry and towns was at the expense of the others, and the competition for resources and growth led inevitably to conflict between the major national states. This took place on the continent itself and in the far-flung corners of the world, where Europeans competed for influence, resources and markets. This conflict resulted in two 'world' wars and did not end until 1945, when the futility of such conflicts became apparent. What became most apparent was the fact that this European industrial society was about to face structural economic changes that would have a destabilising effect on what was apparently a permanent and unchangeable society.

To begin with, the core of industrial countries had grown to encompass the United States, Russia and other states. Secondly, the technological basis of society had shifted from coal (although it still remained an important energy source) to oil and electrical energy. Chemical industries had replaced older mechanical-based processes, and the products of industry had evolved and multiplied, dramatically altering the location criteria for new industries. The raw materials that were once plentiful in western Europe were being exhausted, or abandoned in favour of cheaper sources in colonial countries. Thus several of the factors that had been at the root of nineteenth century industrialisation had changed dramatically. The others, however, appeared stable. Capital resources still remained essentially national in their origin, although American investment had began to increase, especially in Britain. Labour markets were still essentially national, although there was some cross-border migration, such as the movement of Italians to France and Germany, Poles to the French coalfields, and the Irish to Britain. Land markets and land management systems remained as they had been, although possession of capital rather than land resources was the essential requirement for new industrial and commercial growth.

With hindsight it can be seen that even those 'stable' factors were about to change equally dramatically, and that further changes in the entire structure were around the corner. However, in all countries there was a common reaction to the economic problems that emerged in the post-war era. In essence the local political and governance systems that existed in western Europe at that time derived their legitimacy from the dominant urban pattern of industrial towns and cities. Their reaction to the forces of change, to the destruction of the war, and to the drive for better living conditions to eradicate the insalubrious legacy of nineteenth century industrialisation, was to rebuild their cities as if no further changes to their industrial and economic dominance were likely to occur. Liverpool, Rotterdam, Lille, Charleroi, Essen and many other cities would be reconstructed in the anticipation that they would remain the powerhouses of the western European economy and still be managed within *national* labour, capital and political structures.

Thus from the immediate post-war years each country responded with programmes of slum clearance, reconstruction or economic renewal that built on the existing fabric and sought to enhance it. To varying degrees, each nation state succeeded in these ambitions. However, structural economic changes *did* occur. The role of these great cities as powerhouses of production began to decline sharply, and each has subsequently faced the challenge of a new wave of economic and social change that was not foreseen in that optimistic era, and which has in many ways undone much of the effort to reconstruct European cities in the post-war era. It is these external *winds of change*, which were particularly fierce in the 1970s and 1980s, that have brought about the contemporary need for the regeneration of urban economies: to adapt these cities to their new roles hosting service employment and as centres of consumption.

Thus although it is true that there has been fairly continuous economic growth and a general improvement in most aspects of living conditions in western Europe over the last 50 years, these structural economic changes have pushed the economies of many of these industrial cities into relative decline for substantial periods of time, and have caused a deterioration in living conditions. Furthermore, the benefits of growth and the costs of structural change have not been distributed equally between areas or across the population. The result has been that some areas and some groups in the population have gained massively from change, while others have suffered on an equal scale.

The process of suburbanisation, which was most evident in British cities in the inter-war era (Jackson 1973), has become a universal process of *peri-urbanisation* (Dezert *et al.* 1991). This has not only been reflected in residential housing markets, but is equally pervasive in the commercial, retail and industrial areas, and has become a feature of prosperous and declining city regions at the same time. Thus core area decay may run hand in hand with increasing regional affluence. Paralleling this process has been the restructuring of major service industries in almost the whole of western Europe. By adopting new technologies for their operation, industries such as railways, gas and electricity suppliers and port authorities have been able to continue their businesses with fewer employees and on smaller land areas. In consequence much loyal and skilled labour has been cast aside, and huge areas of urban land have been released for other uses. The transport sector was particularly affected as ports switched to the new technologies such as containerisation, as ship sizes became ever larger, and as railways lost business to the road transport industry and their need for huge marshalling yards began to disappear.

The aggregate result of all these processes is that, without exception, the morphology of cities throughout the continent began to display the common characteristics of unplanned and unforeseen change. Spaces, varying from huge sites to empty city centre apartments or shops, have been left abandoned in and around the core of all major urban areas. This leaves a visual legacy of dereliction that imparts an air of decay to these areas, and is a disincentive to investors.

Allied to this is the growth of sectoral unemployment where specific industries have gone and their former employees are left jobless. This is often exacerbated by the fact that many of the labour forces in traditional industries such as textiles are now essentially made up of new migrants who have come in to take up jobs vacated in the process of social mobility of the indigenous population. They in turn have become entrapped in the downward cycle of deprivation caused by the collapse of the industries they came to work in. This adds a social problem to the physical one. This manifests itself in varying forms of social disruption: crime, racism and social exclusion fuelled by poverty, which are often spatially expressed in the areas of the city most affected by the malign effects of this process of change. Paradoxically these areas tend to be either the large social housing estates built in the 20 years after the Second World War, which were intended to eradicate the very problems that they now perpetuate, or the remaining areas of poor-quality older nineteenth century housing, which the bulldozers of the 1950s and 1960s did not eradicate.

To these can be added a range of environmental problems such as polluted sites, unclean rivers and watercourses, air pollution and derelict buildings, many often of historic or architectural value, which add further to the unpleasantness of the declining areas. The whole adds up to a set of social, economic and environmental problems of mind-boggling complexity. It must be tempting for politicians to walk away and turn their backs on the problems of older cities, but there are in fact strong arguments for intervention.

The case for intervention

Thus from the 1960s, when early city redevelopment programmes were at their height, we have not gone on to a more secure, more pleasant, more comfortable future, but have been bequeathed a legacy of intractable problems that are common to all of western Europe's urban complexes. By the mid-1980s, economic decline of traditional industries, related unemployment, dereliction of sites, social exclusion and racism and ubiquitous environmental degradation were the hallmarks of large areas of the industrial cities born out of the Industrial Revolution.

Persistent out-migration of younger and skilled labour to more prosperous regions and new industries was a parallel process. The message was clear. The economic processes that had created these cities had turned against them, and they were faced with stark alternatives: either to decline further or to attempt to counter this process. This required a conscious choice on the part of someone, but whom? If left to the 'market', those investors whose criteria for success related to sound economic returns for shareholders, a secure if not too long-term future, and an absence of need to invest in the social capital (roads, schools, hospitals, etc.), would choose not to invest in the older urban areas. Indeed, some economists would argue that to invest in such areas does not make economic sense, at either a micro or a macro scale, but merely diverts capital from areas where better returns are to be had due to 'natural' processes of spatial change in our capitalistic economy. Furthermore, the contemporary movement of capital away from older industrial cities is no different from that which created those 'dark satanic mills' in the first place.

But such a simplistic economic model is fundamentally flawed, for it fails to discount the many social costs caused by the abandonment of obsolete operations, and it erroneously regards labour as a totally mobile factor of production.

Many of the people left stranded in one location by such economic changes might be able to 'get on their bikes' and move away, but many more – for a variety of reasons – cannot do so. We have in western Europe a society that sees it as civilised to pay social costs to those disrupted by this economic change, and therefore it is not so easy to take this simplistic course of action and write off people as one would a stretch of redundant railway line.

It is possible to view the industrial city as being similar to the mining village that first appeared on our maps in the eighteenth or nineteenth century and has now disappeared from them as the coal has run out and the economic raison d'être of the place has gone. If this were the case then great cities such as Liverpool, Lille, Rotterdam, Essen, Charleroi, even Milan and many others should be vanishing as new centres took their place. However, this is not what is happening, and every city and town that has suffered from the effects of restructuring of the 'post-industrial' economy is attempting to find a new rationale for its existence and re-creation of its former prosperity. It is a matter of conscious choice to do so. This conscious choice is based on the realisation that these cities are not small, simple creations such as a mining village; they are large and complex, and possess many attributes that are worthy of sustaining and enhancing.

First, they possess a rich structure of *social capital* – of schools and universities, hospitals, libraries and cultural facilities that are the consequence of generations of investment and which are irreplaceable at any reasonable cost. In addition, in most, although the basic economic rationale may have gone, the other functions of the city may still thrive, such as its role as a shopping, commercial or cultural centre, as a transport hub, or as a tourist destination. These major centres are not to be compared to the mining village. They are not reliant upon a single firm or even a single industrial sector. While one sector is in decline, there are others that persist and will not be planned or wished away. These other sectors provide a continuing rationale for the existence of the place and a wealth of resources and facilities that can form the basis for future regeneration and development.

To this can be added a *sense of place*, a special character or feeling in and for that place, which attracts loyalty from inhabitants and identifies the city or town in the geography of the continent. Underpinning this is the existence of local administrations, often exemplified by grand or indeed magnificent public buildings, such as Glasgow's City Chambers or the City Hall in Leeds, which add identity and purpose to the activities of inhabitants. Finally, there is the rest of the *built fabric* of the city. Often the accent has been on the problems created by those buildings that were of poor quality and had to be renewed, but there are often many more that are fine and well built, and cannot either physically or economically be written off as obsolete and allowed to decay and vanish.

Thus throughout western Europe there are scores of such towns and cities that could be left to wither, but which we have chosen to renew because of these attributes. This is a conscious choice, taken not only by the local populations who have chosen to remain there and their administrations, but also by governments, and often by capitalists, large and small, local and international, to retain and renew this urban fabric. Despite the shift of much of our economic and social activity to new locations in the geography of each state or the continent and within the urban regions themselves to suburban and peri-urban locations, there is a clear policy choice at all levels (an act of faith?) that means that we have chosen to retain our urban centres and to reincorporate them into our cultural life. Although we possess a preference for more spacious suburban lifestyles, no different from that of the North Americans, we also possess a desire to add in to that lifestyle the strong urban focus that the more recent industrial cities on our continent have inherited from the older medieval and Renaissance cities that we value. Society at large is saying that the retention and enhancement of Duisburg, or Sheffield, Norrkoping or Lens is as important to our shared European urban heritage as the protection of Ghent, or Freiburg, Bologna or Nancy.

The question is, how do we do it?

National policy responses

The need to counter decay has been recognised for some time in all the major centres of western Europe. It was first recognised in Britain and acted upon as early as the 1950s, when the non-acceptance of the slum conditions of much of our urban heritage led to the landmark legislation in the 1957 Housing Act. This reorganised and made more effective the various strands of such legislation, which stretched back to the mid-nineteenth century. It moved the process forward, symbolically by changing the name of the process from *slum clearance* to *urban renewal* – a term borrowed unashamedly from the United States.

The results are chronicled by Gibson & Langstaff (1982), who relate the effects of the vigour of the process of clearance on the UK urban scene. The clearance of huge areas of inner-city housing and the problems of replacing this housing loss led to the creation of the, thought to be cheap, high-rise estates of the 1960s and early 1970s. The retraction from this approach, and the recognition of the value of much of the older stock, led to the policies of housing improvement. However, by the mid-1970s it became dimly per-ceived that the renewal process was more than a housing problem, and that other social factors such as skills, educational attainment and employment opportunities were also fundamental to the improvement of these urban areas. Added to this growing range of targets was the perceived need to update the circulation patterns especially to accommodate the car. Thus cities such as Leicester, Birmingham and Liverpool bear the mark of the predominantly engineering solution to the problem.

The Conservative governments from 1979 to 1997 also placed much empha-sis on the need to renew, but essentially to renew the economic *raison d'être* of cities, and with the private sector taking the lead in defining objectives and financing projects. After all, they pointed out, these cities had been created by private enterprise in the first place. The specifics of these many influ-ences, policy shifts, competing and contradictory sectoral objectives will be illustrated in the case studies. What they demonstrate is the increasingly frantic attempts to maintain the fabric of our major cities with a disjointed armoury of agencies, financial mechanisms and sectorally desired effects, which characterised British urban regeneration by the mid-1990s.

The situation in the United Kingdom has been further complicated by the ex-istence of different administrations for two of its constituent parts: Scotland and Northern Ireland. Historically these parts of the country have attempted to find their own solutions to the problems of economic marginalisation. It is no accident that the precursor of the urban development corporations in England was pioneered in the more seriously affected city of Glasgow by the Scottish Office and the local administrations in the early 1970s. The Glasgow Eastern Area Renewal (GEAR) project was born out of the need to tackle economic and social decay of a much more serious dimension than that to the south.

This process of evolution has been brought up to date quite dramatically in recent years with the publication of three seminal reports that set the scene for a new onslaught on urban deprivation and decay. Their significance is that although the first of these, *Towards an Urban Renaissance*, was writ-ten by a leading architect (Lord Rogers), it points to the complexity of urban society, and to a certain extent paved the way for the ensuing government White Paper *Our Towns and Cities: The Future*, and the volume on 'neigh-bourhood renewal'. Drawing on the lessons, and mistakes, of these volumes the Scottish Executive has commissioned its *Cities Review*, which when published is expected to take a more comprehensive view of the particular problems of the six Scottish cities.

Paradoxically, many cities in the other major industrial complexes of western Europe had arrived at a similar state of decay despite a different urban policy history. In France the path to the urban policies of the late 1980s followed a dissimilar route. Owing to France's much later industrialisation, French cities did not have industrial slum conditions to the same extent as those created in the nineteenth century in the UK. Instead France suffered from the degradation of the historic cores of its towns and cities, often of medieval origin, and the effects of uncontrolled migration to its major cities both before and after the Second World War. The latter processes made the controlling of urban growth and the improvement of conditions in the suburban rings around the cities a more critical issue. Thus the vast swathes of *pavillons* built in the Paris suburbs between the wars (Bastie 1964) were added to by the equally insalubrious *bidonvilles* in many cities. However, the national strategy, incorporated into the process of *aménagement du territoire*, had put the restructuring of French industry as a top priority, and housing and general living conditions took a back seat until the basic economic growth processes had been delivered.

Thus restructuring the suburbs to house the new industrial workers in an apparently better way through the creation of vast publicly built social housing estates became the hallmark of the era from 1950 to 1965. This process was continued through the new towns programme and then from the mid-1970s onwards through more subtle mechanisms to structure growth, such as the ZAC (*Zone d'Aménagement Concerté*) process. It was not until the early 1980s that policy makers recognised the effects of inner-city decline as industries and other users moved to the suburbs or went out of business, and measures were then put in place to tackle the problem. However, the process was essentially an application of the ZAC system to areas where the public authorities had control over the land market; major interventions in the privately owned property sector are rare.

From the late 1980s onwards in France there have been a welter of initiatives and the creation of several important bodies and pieces of legislation. These began with the *Report Dubedout* and the *Banlieue 89* programme in 1989, which were followed by the creation of the influential *Comité Interministerielle des Villes* and its supporting government department the *Direction Interministerielle des Villes (DIV)*. These latter two innovations are of considerable importance in French urban policy as they signified a recognition of the multifaceted nature of urban problems and of the need to integrate the disparate strands of urban policy if they were to be tackled (Sueur 1999). This attitude has been carried into the programme to regenerate French cities, which has resulted in the latest major legislative programme, the *Loi de Solidarité et Renouvellement urbain (SRU)* in 2001. This Act has drawn together the many initiatives of the 1990s such as *Programmes d'Insertion, Zones Franches, Les Zones Urbains Sensibles, les Zones de Redynamisation Urbaine* and *Grands Projets Urbains*, and has oriented them away from a specifically economic and physical approach to include the tackling of social exclusion as a prime objective of the new programme of *renouvellement urbain*. This policy shift will be evident when the case study of Lille demonstrates the changing emphasis of regeneration from Euralille to the Grands Projet Urbain in Roubaix.

As significant as the setting up of DIV has been the creation of the financial planning mechanism of the *Contrat de Ville*, set within the national *Contrat de Plan* structure, and which has enabled the various programmes to be planned and financed with a degree of certainty. These have been supported by the State bank, the *Caisse des Dépôts et Consignations*.

As might be expected, the history of Germany's urban and especially industrial areas was severely disrupted by war damage, and many towns were almost entirely rebuilt in the period 1945–1960. Paradoxically, therefore, the German towns do not suffer from the physical decay of age, but from a combination of the decline of their industrial base – especially in the more 'heavy' industry areas such as the Ruhr – with the need to improve housing standards in the properties built in the immediate post-war era. Indeed, the latter problem is common to all western European cities and towns. Thus urban regeneration has a more economic and social dimension to it than in the other two major countries.

The main agents in this process are the municipalities, which have been given special powers under the Federal Building Code to extend their activity beyond its original remit for slum clearance and war damage repair to wider regeneration goals. To do this they often create special redevelopment agencies, *Stadtebauliche sanierungsmafnohnohmen*. These agencies are given wide powers such as that to compulsorily acquire land in order to implement schemes: for example the STERN agency in Berlin and the STEG agency in Hamburg (EU Compendium Germany 2000).

The objectives of the regeneration process are, as with other countries, multi-targeted: to improve or replace housing stock, to provide new amenities, to provide public infrastructure, and to improve transport systems. There is, however, a strong democratic element to the German process, and at all stages from plan formulation to final implementation every possible affected person or group is involved in consultations. The regeneration programmes themselves involve land acquisition and – where necessary – subdivision, demolition of structures, changes of use and the transfer of ownership if required, and are implemented under the *B-Plan, Stadtebauliche Rahmen-plan*, but are linked to a strong *Sozialplan*, which provides measures to deal with relocation expenses and any other social effects of the programme. Other levels of government are not intimately involved in this process, but do contribute to the financing of the schemes. More recently the portion of the finances provided by the Federal (*Bund*) government can be substituted by contributions from the EU under structural fund provisions.

The cases of Belgium and the Netherlands show further variations. In Belgium, the first continental country to industrialise after the UK, much of the urban fabric in the industrial belt of French-speaking Wallonie is as degraded as in the UK. The region has also suffered catastrophically from industrial decline and the demise of its coal industry. The lack of initial public action to address these problems is in large part due to the political situation, where the issues of language and 'community' dominated Belgian politics to the exclusion of other issues. Also, in the total economic picture the growth of new industries in Flanders masked the decline in Wallonie, and the economic weight of the country moved from its traditional areas.

The federalisation of Belgium in 1990 meant that the three regions had to a large extent resolved the language issue and could concentrate on the other issues that affected them. This has enabled the Walloon government to focus its attention on the restructuring of its economy and the regeneration of its towns and cities. The Regional Planning Act of 1996 signified a major step in this process, and a comprehensive programme for regeneration has been developed and amplified by further decrees of the Regional Government in 1997 and 1998. However, the main actors are the municipalities (*communes*), which operate the statutory processes. There is a heavy emphasis on the redevelopment of 'brownfield' sites, which abound in the industrial and ex-coal-mining areas, and an equally heavy emphasis on the improvement and replacement of the older housing stock. Other objectives are to improve the commercial centres of the main towns and to introduce new services. Particular attention is given to the re-servicing of sites and to the control of land speculation. In the latter case a major problem is the withholding of land from the market until it appears that a market for the land has reappeared. This is self-defeating, as the withholding of land from development often discourages market interest, and the government and local initiatives are designed to break this vicious circle and ensure the recycling of key sites.

The *communes* are responsible for drawing up a communal dossier for urban revitalisation, which is sent to the Walloon government for approval. However, while the specifically planning or physical aspects of regeneration and housing policy are now in the competence of the regions, the federal level of government still retains a considerable influence over the more social and fiscal aspects of regeneration through its control of policies and funding for unemployment, job creation, and social benefits (EU Compendium, Belgium 2000).

The Netherlands has not suffered as much as Belgium or the UK, and rather like Germany has been able to relaunch its industrial transformation from 1945. Only Rotterdam, as a major city, was extensively damaged by the war, and this has provided a clear base for the city to benefit from its position at the focus of trade for a vast area of north-west Europe. Other major influences have been the lack of space in the Netherlands generally, and the need to use all buildable land with care and to meet a number of economic and social objectives as well as meeting other physical objectives. To begin with, the approach to spatial planning in the Netherlands is not purely national: it begins with the setting of all national initiatives within the European Spatial Development Perspectives (ESDP) framework (Spatial Plan 2000). The regeneration of Dutch towns and cities is seen as part of a wider programme of urban rebirth in north-west Europe as a whole. However, there is a strong tradition of national spatial planning, within which the strategy for urban areas is nested. More recently this has meant that the policy for regeneration has been integrated into the entire programme and legislative framework for urban planning. To deliver this programme there is an active land policy, which covers the development of local infrastructure, compulsory purchase, pre-emption of property sales and measures for the recouping of service and infrastructure costs. A main strand of the national effort is the *major cities policy*, which allocates development targets to the main urban centres in the country and identifies key projects (*steuldprojecten*) within them. These are coordinated in the national renewal policy, the *Beleid voor Stadtsvernewring* (VROM: Ministry of Housing, Spatial Planning and the Environment (2000)).

As in France there are strong mechanisms to ensure the integration of policy between the various government departments. This ensures that the major role played by the Ministry of Housing, Spatial Planning and the Environment (VROM) is integrated with initiatives by other ministries such as the Ministry of the Interior, the Ministry of Transport and the Ministry of Economic Affairs. These ministries are controlled by funding policies that integrate their activities and are administered by the central government Finance Ministry. Generally the four major cities – Rotterdam, Amsterdam, Den Haag and Utrecht – deal directly with the central government, and the smaller cities such as Breda and Tilburg deal through their provincial administrations.

Italian urban policy has seen a similar emergence of a national approach to urban regeneration. In 1995 the national government passed legislation enabling provincial and city governments to enact local laws to encourage and facilitate urban regeneration programmes. In the Lombardy region the *Programmi Integrati di Intervento* was initiated, and the city of Milan has developed its projects within this legislative framework.

The remarkable occurrence of every national government within its own constitutional limits launching a major programme of urban regeneration at roughly the same time means that the cities that have had to put these initiatives into practice have done so in a climate of Europe-wide concern with the future of our urban environment and culture. This is reflected in the initiatives taken by the EU itself to provide a common linking policy, indeed philosophy, to guide this renaissance.

The impact of the European Union

At the time of writing, the EU itself has no specific competence in the field of urban regeneration. However, it does have an effect on many of the contexts in which urban regeneration is conducted, and it has a direct input to certain key areas, such as finance. From this the slow administrative march to 'competence' may have begun.

A direct input to regeneration efforts can be seen in the contribution by the structural funds into major regeneration programmes such as URBAN. These have been targeted to cities in the previous Objective 1 and 2 (now all Objective 2) areas under the structural fund provision. Funds have also been contributed as a result of the series of specific industry-related programmes such as Rechar (coal), Retex (textiles), and more recently Konver (defence replacement). An interest in the social aspects of regeneration is also displayed by contributions made by other Directorates such as DGV to the social and economic development programmes such as those in Liverpool, and more recently there has been a contribution by DG XI (Environment) through programmes such as Discus and the Lasala project.

The issue of the health of the Union's cities and towns has become a major concern of the European Spatial Development Perspective (ESDP 2001), and its regional 'spatial vision' exercises. A derivative of these are the programmes being implemented for the INTERREG initiatives and its many subsidiary projects. There is a specific urban theme to one of the strands of these, as it is considered that the economic social and physical health of the towns and cities is necessary to the well-being of the EU as a whole. Most of the cities in our case study section lie in the north-west Europe area, which is the most urban and the most affected by economic structural change in recent years. Whether the involvement of the EU indirectly in urban regeneration via such INTERREG projects as the 'Urban Regeneration Network' (Lille 2001) and 'Living in Towns' (Fraser *et al.* 2001) will develop into the emergence of a competence in this area remains to be seen, but the argument is gaining ground that such an involvement is necessary in order to achieve the legitimate objectives of social and economic balance across the EU. This is being encouraged by other groups that have a legitimate say in European affairs: some voluntary, such as EUROCITIES or the Car Free Cities group, and some with official status, such as the Committee of the Regions. These actively encourage cooperation between cities in the exchange of ideas and practice as well as of staff.

New challenges

The process of globalisation of capital and labour markets, of investment markets and of consumer choice, whether it be for computers or for vacations, is well documented (Giddens 1999; Held *et al.* 1999; Woods 2000). Of all the factors that were outlined as contributors to the emergence of the first industrial revolution perhaps only the structures of national land tenure and land market systems remain unchanged. Thus investment in virtually every aspect of our economic society, from industry to local housing markets, is influenced by international criteria. Labour markets are now legally and illegally international. New technologies, environmental crises and emerging international forms of governance now dominate much of our society, and have had a profound disrupting effect on the cosy post-war programmes to improve living conditions for our industrial cities and our urban population conceived within a national context.

All of the major industrial countries face problems that are in part generic – the rundown of traditional manufacturing in western Europe as a whole, or the drive to raise housing and general environmental standards in older areas of cities – and are in part local or national. All have responded in a disjointed way to the new reality, reflecting the lack of cooperation within governments, between them, and between them and the other actors in the process of changing our cities.

To begin with, the first impulse was to try to recreate the past. Industrial estates blossomed on the edges of all industrial cities and most particularly in those areas where the structural changes were most severe. The *Team Valley Trading Estate* in County Durham, England (Hall 1992), is perhaps the best example of this type of initiative. By the 1980s, in all countries it had become evident that the attempt to recreate the past would not work, and that new futures would have to be found. The articulation of what these futures would be is a fundamental thread running through the regeneration process in all major cities: every city faced with the challenge could do nothing, or copy what the others had done or tried, or boldly attempt to find its own solution. As a result, many have placed their faith in new industries and information technology to drive a solution. In particular, new tertiary industries such as finance, advertising and publishing have grown as major employers.

A specific example of this switch to tertiary or indeed quaternary types of economic base is the use of educational establishments to alter and renew the older, run-down areas of cities. The great phase of university decentralisation seen throughout Europe in the 1960s is in some places being reversed, and a new population of students and associated services is seen as a possible answer to the problem of abandonment of central space. In Lille this has become very specialised with the development of campuses related to the medical facilities of the region or to scientific development, which are bringing new biotechnology industries and populations to the parts of the city where cotton mills once ruled.

However, the subtle change that has come about is that the city is increasingly being conceived as a place of *consumption*, not of *production*. This means that the city is seen less as a place where goods and services are produced for sale or transfer, and more of a place that people visit to eat out, to take part in events, to visit cultural features such as museums and concert halls, or to engage in certain types of activity. A recent seminar in Weimar, Germany, *Consumption and the Post-Industrial City* (Martikainen 2001; Miles 2001), brought to light a range of such ways of re-characterising the city. Papers on 'Consuming a cathedral' and 'Consuming youth' were typical of a series of reflections on the ways in which new users of and new uses for the space in the city could be encouraged or accommodated. They reflected the fact that, by bringing new groups to use the city, a new economy and society would replace the old, thereby ensuring the continuity of the buildings and spaces.

A recent variation of this has been the concept of the *event city*, whereby events of an international nature such as the Edinburgh Festival, or of a more local nature such as the *Braderie* (the giant antique fair in Lille), are used to stamp the character of the city and by changing its image will change its economy. The case studies will examine the extent to which such innovations are providing any long-term success in the process of re-branding essentially industrial centres. These are of course new variations on the more basic tourism industry, and in modern north-west Europe – with improving communications – cities are emerging as major tourist destinations as their cultural heritage, often neglected, is rediscovered as a possible economic asset. Every city in our study displays this trend.

All of this is currently being undertaken in a policy context that has a central theme of *sustainability*. This is recurrent in most cities as they strive not merely to 'green' their environment with parks and gardens but to extend the principle to a wider effort to make buildings and transport and lifestyles generally environmentally friendly. The extent of this range of new agendas and the effective re-branding of cities will be explored in more detail in Chapter 13.

The response to the challenge

The preceding two chapters have set out the contexts in which the exercise in renewing the cities of western Europe is being undertaken. The next stage of this work is to describe how the eight case study cities have tackled the problems posed by these dramatic changes in the economy and society of Europe as a whole. As described in Chapter 1, in order to obtain comparable pictures of this process each contributor has attempted to provide a similar analysis. From this the final chapters will make some analytical comparisons of a structural nature to discern what is common to their efforts and what is specific to the cities in question.

3

Urban Regeneration in Liverpool

Chris Couch

Over the last three decades Liverpool has probably experienced more urban regeneration than virtually any other city either in the UK or in Europe as a whole. Since 1971 the city has had to respond to a reduction in its population of about one quarter as well as the loss of more than half its manufacturing industry. Over this period Liverpool has played host to a huge variety of experiments and innovations in urban regeneration. This chapter looks at the evolution of policy in Liverpool before focusing on recent initiatives that illustrate some key aspects of British regeneration policy.

In the UK one of the first responses of government to the emerging 'inner city problem' came in 1968 with the launch of the Urban Programme: small amounts of short-term funding to support local community development projects in the inner city. Liverpool was among the first cities to benefit from the programme and more than 50 schemes were supported, including nursery classes, sports and community facilities, legal and housing advice centres and language classes for immigrants. Social development was the main aim of these early interventions.

Continuing this emphasis, in 1969 the Home Office established a series of community development projects (CDP) including the Vauxhall CDP in Liverpool. In addition to supporting a number of local projects (community education programme, community centre, neighbourhood newspaper), researchers on the project concluded that the area's problems had structural roots and resulted from external economic change and restructuring (Topping & Smith 1977). The Liverpool Inner Areas Study (1973–1977), a major study of the dynamics of the inner city, reached a similar view (DoE 1977).

By the late 1970s the government was persuaded that the main causes of inner-city deprivation were economic and structural rather than social and local in origin. This view was translated into policy in the Inner Urban Areas Act 1978 and related policy changes. Partnerships were to be established between central and local government to tackle the worst areas of urban deprivation. Unfortunately the idea arrived too late in the life of the government, which lost the election in May 1979 to a Conservative party led by Margaret Thatcher. The importance of regenerating the economy of inner urban areas was still accepted, but the approach (using local authorities as partners) was not.

The new government established *urban development corporations* (including the Merseyside Development Corporation): central government agencies with powers and resources to reclaim large swathes of urban dereliction and return them to beneficial economic uses. At the same time, in other areas of derelict land, developers were offered a more relaxed planning regime and a reduced tax burden in *enterprise zones*, including the Speke Enterprise Zone in Liverpool. Throughout the 1980s British regeneration policy put a lot of emphasis on supporting local economic development by increasing the supply of land and buildings in inner urban areas. The mechanisms used were mainly direct action by government agencies or subsidies to private developers. In either case local authorities such as Liverpool City Council were being bypassed and their role marginalised.

By the end of the decade there was growing criticism that British urban regeneration policies were too complex, with too little recognition of the role that could and should be played by local authorities with their local knowledge and long-term commitment to an area. The first response of the government was to introduce City Challenge: a programme that allowed local authorities to lead local partnerships in bidding for central government money to support regeneration projects. Liverpool was among the successful cities in the first round of bidding, winning £37.5 million to support a regeneration package for the City Centre East. Government regeneration policies for England were rationalised in 1993 when some 21 different funding streams, including City Challenge, were replaced by a Single Regeneration Budget (SRB), and the work of a number of agencies was consolidated within one organisation: English Partnerships. The SRB Challenge Fund retained the competitive elements of City Challenge but introduced greater flexibility into the bidding process. In collaboration with a range of local community and commercial organisations, Liverpool City Council made a number of successful bids for SRB funding, including the North Liverpool Partnership. (See Fig. 3.1.)

Following the return of a Labour government in 1997, urban regeneration policy has been subject to considerable review, and has been further modified.

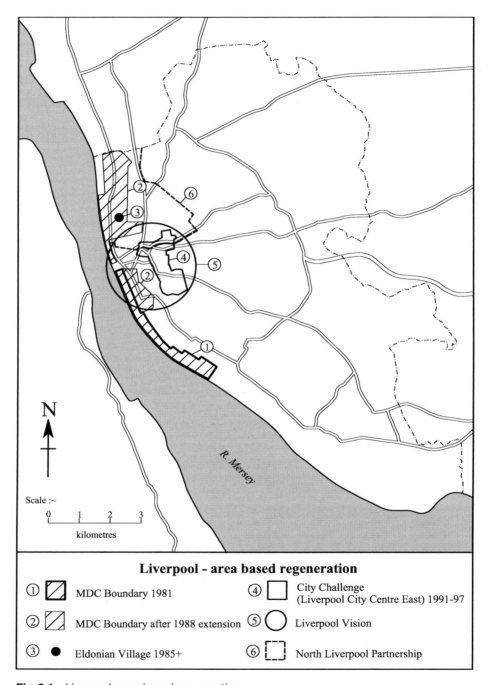

Liverpool - area based regeneration

① ▨ MDC Boundary 1981

② ▨ MDC Boundary after 1988 extension

③ ● Eldonian Village 1985+

④ ☐ City Challenge (Liverpool City Centre East) 1991-97

⑤ ◯ Liverpool Vision

⑥ ⬚ North Liverpool Partnership

Fig. 3.1   Liverpool: area-based regeneration.

Today central government responsibility for regeneration policy has been split, with the *North West Development Agency* (which is accountable to the Department for Trade and Industry (DTI)) mainly responsible for economic regeneration and business development across the region. Urban policy and neighbourhood regeneration have become the responsibility of the Office of the Deputy Prime Minister. Urban policy has been influenced by the findings of Lord Rogers' Urban Taskforce report *Towards an Urban Renaissance* (1999), and the subsequent Urban White Paper (2001). One of the most important initiatives has been the establishment of *urban regeneration companies*, intended to be single-purpose development agencies responsible for leading and coordinating the regeneration of specific areas. One such company, *Liverpool Vision*, has been established in Liverpool city centre.

A *National Strategy for Neighbourhood Renewal* was launched in 2001 with the aims of improving physical, social and economic conditions and narrowing the gap between the poorest neighbourhoods and the rest. Within this approach, *local strategic partnerships* (representing local authorities and other community and business interests) will draw up *local neighbourhood renewal strategies*, which will be supported through the Neighbourhood Renewal Fund. Additionally the New Deal for Communities (NDC) provides a focused, 10-year programme of regeneration for the most deprived areas. Kensington in Liverpool is one area to receive NDC funding (£61 million).

The city centre and docklands

The spatial extent of Liverpool city centre has remained relatively stable over many years despite a substantial decline in the amount and density of economic activity. Land use in the area is highly segregated, and there is a strong sense in which the centre comprises a series of distinct zones, each with its own predominant functions. East of the Pier Head lies the office core, centred around the Town Hall. Further east can be found the central shopping area, focused on Church Street but with extensions to the west (Lord Street), the north (Williamson Square, St Johns Precinct and Clayton Square), and the east (Bold Street). An area of restaurants, bars and clubs can be identified in Bold Street and Duke Street, extending eastwards to Chinatown, with another smaller zone around Mathew Street/Victoria Street. Cultural activities, including theatres, museums and galleries, can be found around St George's Plateau/William Brown Street, the Albert Dock, and around Hope Street, between the two cathedrals. In the extreme east of the central area, almost beyond its boundaries under some definitions, lies a higher education and health precinct containing the Royal Liverpool Hospital, Liverpool

University and parts of Liverpool John Moores University. This sprawling city centre covers a total area of around 2 km².

Formerly a major regional centre serving Merseyside, West Lancashire and North Wales for more than a century, by the 1980s Liverpool's central area was in decline. Few people lived in the city centre; office and commercial employment was falling, and the shopping centre was losing trade to new suburban retail parks and hypermarkets and to more attractive and accessible centres elsewhere in the region such as Chester. Traffic congestion was increasing, and environmental conditions were deteriorating. After some years of neglecting the issue, the city council responded in 1987 with a discussion document, the *City Centre Strategy Review*, which set out a series of issues and options. By 1993 this had been developed into a Liverpool City Centre Plan, which was subsequently incorporated into the Liverpool Unitary Development Plan 1996. This plan included policies for promoting economic development, improving transport and circulation, enhancing the living environment, and improving the general physical environment.

There have been a number of regeneration initiatives that have impacted upon the city centre. Between 1981 and 1998 the Merseyside Development Corporation was responsible for the redevelopment of the former docklands and parts of their industrial hinterland. This area included parts of the city centre adjoining the Mersey but also included other locations that came to compete with the city centre for scare commercial investment. In 1993 Liverpool was successful in winning a City Challenge bid for the Liverpool City Centre East, and in 1997 the Ropewalks Partnership was established to pursue a regeneration strategy in the Duke Street/Bold Street area, based upon a mixed-use 'creative industries' quarter. More recently a regeneration company, Liverpool Vision, has been formed in order to facilitate development and inward investment. One of the features of these regeneration programmes is the way they have developed with only limited regard to formal development plans.

Merseyside Development Corporation

The Conservative government's Local Government, Planning and Land Act 1980 provided the Secretary of State for the Environment (then Michael Heseltine) with the powers to designate areas and establish *urban development corporations* (UDC) for the purpose of area regeneration through reclaiming derelict property, encouraging industrial and commercial development, and ensuring the provision of social facilities and housing.

These central government agencies comprised a board accountable to the Secretary of State and a chief executive and staff responsible to the board. The action-oriented structure and style was more like that of a development company than a local authority. The agencies had powers to acquire, manage and dispose of land, to carry out reclamation works, and to provide infrastructure for development. They also had powers of development control within their designated area. The Merseyside Development Corporation (MDC) was designated in 1981 within an area of 350 ha comprising the former Liverpool South Docks, parts of the North Docks, and land on the Wirral side of the Mersey. In an upbeat report on its early achievements the DoE reported that:

In the MDC area £140 million of public investment has helped to reclaim 97 hectares for residential and commercial development and 48 hectares for recreation and open space; and to refurbish 135,000 square metres for housing and commercial uses, including the historic Albert Dock restoration. The MDC has also created 1,160 jobs since 1981 and 94 per cent of its contracts have been let to firms in the Merseyside area. (DoE 1988, pp. 52–53.)

However, the early years were not without their problems. The MDC was criticised for its lack of local accountability and for its poor coordination with other local agencies. In relation to one initiative, the 1984 International Garden Festival, it has been said that – despite being a tremendous success in itself – it went ahead in the knowledge that no proper arrangements had been made for the continued funding and operation of the gardens after the end of the festival. Consequently, the site was closed and mothballed: an asset lost to local people and a monument to the consequences of lack of forward planning (Couch 1990, pp. 166–167). Today, more than ten years later, apart from the selling off of further parts of the festival site for housing, little has changed. Much of the site still lies neglected and forgotten. Another criticism comes from Richard Meegan, who has suggested that one of the biggest problems faced by the MDC was that of attracting private investment in very difficult economic circumstances. The initial development strategy had to be modified to overcome these problems, with many key sites originally zoned for industrial or mixed uses being given over to housing or retail uses as the MDC gradually responded to the needs of the property market (Meegan 1993, p. 61).

But the local political situation was also having an adverse effect on inward investment by private entrepreneurs. In the mid-1980s the city council was controlled by a 'militant' Labour administration resolutely opposed to the philosophy of the MDC and its reliance on the trickle-down benefits of private investment to solve local economic problems. Such an approach alienated potential investors. Nevertheless, the city council did have a legitimate point when they complained that much-needed financial resources were being diverted to the MDC at the expense of other local needs. While the MDC was spending some £30 million on the regeneration of 11 hectares, the city council had just £37 million to spend on the other 94 790 ha of the city (Meegan 1993, p. 68).

Nevertheless, the MDC did make a significant contribution to the regeneration of the city. The Albert Dock complex opened to visitors in 1984 and became home to the Merseyside Maritime Museum, the Tate Gallery, the Museum of Liverpool Life, a hotel, offices, luxury flats, shopping, bars and restaurants (see Fig. 3.2). Most of the South Docks, between the Pier Head and the Garden Festival site, has been redeveloped with housing, offices, hotels, workshops, showrooms and a marina (see Fig. 3.3). A new station has been opened at Brunswick Dock to serve the area. To the north of the Pier Head progress has been slower, but by the late 1990s substantial development was going into the Princes Dock/Waterloo Dock area, which adjoins the city centre; and the MDC had invested heavily in the Vauxhall area.

Fig. 3.2 Liverpool: the Albert Dock and Tate Gallery.

Fig. 3.3   Liverpool: new housing and marina in the docks.

City Challenge: Liverpool City Centre East

In 1990 15 of the most deprived local authorities in the country were invited to bid for City Challenge funds of £37.5 million each. Bids were to comprise a clearly articulated aim, developed into a strategy and investment programme. They were to be prepared by local authorities in collaboration with other local partners, such as businesses and community organisations. City Challenge was startling for its recognition of the key role that could be played by local authorities (having been marginalised by the previous Thatcher government) in facilitating developments; in its overtly competitive character; in the encouragement of local partnerships; and in the clarity of thinking required in the bid itself (De Groot 1992).

The City Challenge proposal for the Liverpool City Centre East started with an attempt to demonstrate that it was a genuine 'partnership' bid from no fewer than 35 public and private sector agencies. These ranged from the city council, the Housing Corporation and other government organisations, through representatives of the universities, Anglican and Catholic churches, to the Chamber of Commerce, various private sector organisations and even Paul McCartney. Only the community sector and local residents appear under-represented. The proposal set out a 'vision' for the area:

It's a vision of enhancement, activity, partnership, participation and quality of life. New jobs will be created in growth sectors: the arts and cultural industries, the visitor business, high-tech medical and further and higher education. The magnificent architecture and townscape will be conserved, enhanced and given a new life and purpose. Run-down areas will be regenerated and integrated with the mainstream of the city's life. It's a vision of physical regeneration, people, enterprise and growth sectors and effective and sustained management. (Liverpool City Challenge 1991, p. 6.)

The vision was followed by a wide-ranging list of proposals and issues to be addressed during the five-year programme (see Box 3.1).

Box 3.1   Liverpool City Challenge Proposals

The physical vision

- A new link road (completing the Liverpool inner ring road)

- A guided light transit system that could link the area with the rest of the city centre

- The 'rebirth' of St George's Hall

- Rebuilding Queen Square 'with a quality of architecture and design in keeping with its magnificent setting'

- Bringing Lime Street Chambers and various London Road properties back into beneficial use

- Refurbishing and redeveloping the St Andrews Gardens area to provide housing and student accommodation

- Removing through traffic from Rodney Street

- Restoration of the Canning Street conservation area

- Refurbishment and reuse of major buildings in the Hope Street area (Blackburn House, the Liverpool Institute and the Philharmonic Hall) and a new urban square at the junction of Hope Street and Mount Street.

The people vision

- 'Comprehensive and sustained training'

- Increased employment opportunities for local people

- Increased provision to facilitate entry or re-entry into the labour market

- A significant improvement in the quality of life for local people through measures embracing: increased housing choice; improved residential environments; greater access to quality social, recreational, cultural and health facilities.

The enterprise and growth sector vision

- Specific measures to encourage the development of small enterprises

- Partnerships with higher educational institutions spinning off small high-tech and consultancy businesses

- Maximising the enterprise potential of change in the health service

- The development of a vibrant craft, arts and cultural industries sector

- Increased visitor business based on enhancing the area's major attractions.

The management vision

- Create innovative, locally based and effective management and maintenance

- Develop models of good practice

- Lay foundations for managing and maintaining the area beyond 1997

- Ensure the necessary level of dedicated effort from within the City Challenge partnership.

Source: Liverpool City Challenge 1991.

Only after the programme for delivering these outputs had been explained did the document offer any consideration of the problems of the area. But this was little more than a most rudimentary description of issues and a number of unsupported assertions, such as:

> William Brown Street is a series of Grade II* listed buildings housing the popular visitor attractions of the Museums, the Walker Art Gallery and the Libraries. These, together with the refurbished St George's Hall, will create a 'critical mass' of attractions to complement the Albert Dock, and encourage the movement of visitors to and from the waterfront. (Liverpool City Challenge 1991, p. 11.)

A proposed new £5.4 million highway was justified by the assertion that the need for a link road from Berry Street to Russell Street was vital for the area, but without any evidence to support such a claim. Significantly, after an inquiry, the government eventually threw out this particular proposal on the basis that it was unnecessary, and that other solutions were possible. It was claimed that the area exhibited many of the typical symptoms of inner-city decline: high unemployment, low incomes, a low skill base, derelict sites, vacant or underused buildings, and an infrastructure, roads in particular, that required considerable investment. Yet this was an area containing 18 000 jobs, five conservation areas and 892 listed buildings, where only 4000 people actually lived. Thus it could be argued that the vision was little more than a collection of unrelated proposals, based on an uncertain analysis of the problems and needs of the area. Proposals contained a strong bias towards capital investment that would benefit property development, and much less emphasis on direct attacks on deprivation among the local population. Yet this was sufficient to convince central government to commit £37.5 million to the area over the next five years under the City Challenge banner and substantially more from other budgets.

Nevertheless, as with the MDC, it is fair to say that the City Challenge team set about their tasks with some vigour and achieved a great deal, at least in terms of physical change. By the millennium, refurbishment of the public space around Pembroke Place/London Road was complete; the former Collegiate and SFX schools were being refurbished for new uses; St George's Hall was enjoying more intensive use; and Lime Street Chambers had been converted to student accommodation. The Queen Square redevelopment was complete, including a new hotel, refurbished offices for the city council, the National Museums and Galleries on Merseyside 'Conservation Centre', a public square, bus station, shops and leisure facilities. St Andrew's Gardens (inter-war walk-up council flats) had been redeveloped for a mixture of student, social and private housing (see Fig. 3.4). Numerous properties in Mount

Fig. 3.4 Liverpool: new and refurbished housing in the inner city.

Pleasant had been refurbished and converted or returned to residential use. Around Hope Street the Philharmonic Hall had undergone extensive renovation, Blackburne House had been refurbished as a women's education and technology centre, and the former Liverpool Institute had been redeveloped as the Liverpool Institute for the Performing Arts (LIPA). Further progress had been made enhancing the Canning Street conservation area. It was claimed that there had also been improvements in the perceived environment; security and reductions in crime; and in the delivery and coordination of some municipal services.

In its own evaluation of the City Challenge programme the Department of the Environment commented:

> The emphasis was on vacant and derelict (often listed) buildings rather than land. A main indicator of success for Liverpool City Challenge was bringing back into use large prestigious buildings occupying key sites in and around the perimeter of the city centre that had been unoccupied for up to sixty years. Again this was only part of the picture in a more broadly based strategy, but it was seen as a key lever to drive change in the area, to lift its image, to generate greater investment confidence, to enhance local morale and to give the economic foundations for a more people-based programme which would bring the benefits to local residents and businesses. (DoE 1996, p. 24.)

Ropewalks Partnership

The city council, working with English Partnerships, in 1994 commissioned work on a regeneration strategy for the Duke Street/Bold Street area. Regeneration of this area would fill in the gap between the city centre and City Challenge area to the east, and was to be based on a partnership between the community, the public sector and private investors. Some work was already under way in the area, and would have to be incorporated into the emerging strategy. Earlier that year Bold Street had been repaved and provided with new street furniture, and in an early project developers Urban Splash completed a mixed-use redevelopment in Concert Square soon afterwards. Following a consultation process that included a 'planning weekend', in 1997 a formal regeneration strategy, known as the *Integrated Action Plan*, was agreed between the local community, English Partnerships, Liverpool City Council, the Government Office for Merseyside, and other interested parties. Coordination of implementation was to be placed in the hands of a short-life agency: the *Ropewalks Partnership* (so named because of the area's historic associations with rope making).

The regeneration strategy built upon the range of existing businesses in the area, with an emphasis on cultural and creative industries and the night-time economy, and concentrated on three main issues: business support and training; the public realm; and priority investment areas (development projects). The general approach envisaged:

- the enlargement of Chinatown;

- the use of construction projects as employment generators;

- enhancing local business competitiveness;

- a focus on 'creative industries';

- tackling environmental degradation and poor visual appearance (perceived as a barrier to private investment);

- creating a safe and 'sustainable' local environment.

In addition, specific physical regeneration proposals included:

- Concert Square: one of the original catalytic developments in the area in the early 1990s;

- Arthouse Square: the conversion of redundant industrial premises into an arts centre, restaurants and residential uses;

- Wolstenholme Square: a new public space in use 24 hours a day;

- The Bluecoat Triangle: containing the historic Bluecoat Chambers, but with adjoining derelict land providing an opportunity to open up a new avenue between the Mersey and the city centre;

- Dukes Terrace: refurbishment of a small listed group of eighteenth century merchant's houses and back-to-back dwellings;

- Henry Street: conversion of an area of historic, largely redundant warehouses to residential and other uses.

For a further discussion of the Ropewalks Partnership see Couch & Dennemann (2000).

Liverpool Vision

One of the many proposals to emerge from the report of the Urban Task Force (UTF), *Towards an Urban Renaissance*, was a call for the establishment of *urban regeneration companies*. In response the government initially established three such companies: Liverpool Vision in June 1999, New East Manchester in October 1999, and Sheffield One in February 2000. Although these companies are not precisely based on the UTF model they do represent a new development in urban regeneration.

Liverpool Vision is a not-for-profit limited company charged with preparing and implementing proposals for the regeneration of Liverpool city centre and the major transport corridors into the centre. It was initially funded with £200 000 each annually from English Partnerships, the North-West Development Agency, and Liverpool City Council. This figure was expected to rise to an annual operating budget of around £1 million. However, the board members also include representatives from Wimpey, Tesco, Littlewoods, Liverpool Stores Committee and Maritime Housing Association. Although in 2000 the company directly employed only four professional staff, much of its work has been subcontracted to consultants.

Most of the first 12 months was spent drawing up the strategic regeneration framework, mapping out how the city centre should be developed over the next ten years. Its strategic goals are loaded with buzz-phrases like 'a high-quality safe urban environment', 'a 21st century economy', 'a world-class tourist destination', 'a premier national shopping destination' and 'inclusive communities'. (Brauner 2000, p. 21.)

The company has drawn up a strategic regeneration framework, with a number of localities identified as action areas: the Pier Head; the commercial district; Castle Street; the cultural quarter/Lime Street Station; the retail core; King's Waterfront; Hope Street. Six city-centre-wide themes support the plans for each area: a European Capital of Culture bid; movement; public realm; community engagement; reinforcing city communities; and business development. Rather than being involved in the management of individual development projects, Liverpool Vision sees its role as one of facilitating and coordinating regeneration in accordance with the strategic regeneration framework.

The idea of urban regeneration companies was broadly welcomed in a report for the Department of the Environment, Transport and the Regions (Robson & Parkinson 2000). However, the concept raises a series of questions, at least insofar as Liverpool Vision is concerned. One issue is that of the relationship between the company and the local authority. Liverpool City Council had been painstakingly preparing its unitary development plan for a number of years. This plan included proposals and policies for the city centre. It could be argued that whereas these proposals represent a balanced view of the future role and planning of the city centre in relation to the needs of the community as a whole, the proposals from Liverpool Vision, which do not precisely coincide with the UDP, do not. Liverpool Vision does include local authority representatives on its board, but they are outnumbered by others representing more sectoral private interests. Considering their proposals, it seems that property development and the enhancement of property values in the city centre are at the forefront of concerns for Liverpool Vision, whereas the relationship between the city centre and other parts of the city is, perhaps, a secondary consideration. Another concern is the lack of division of power between the local authority as a promoter of development, through its involvement with Liverpool Vision, and the local authority as an arbiter of environmental and planning standards in its role as the local planning authority.

This is a rather different situation from that originally envisaged by the UTF, who suggested that:

an Urban Regeneration Company should be capable of acting swiftly, as a single purpose delivery body to lead and coordinate the regeneration of neighbourhoods in accordance with the objectives of a wider local strategy which has been developed by the local authority and its partners. (UTF 1999, p. 147.)

Thus despite the best efforts of the city council to plan the future development of the city centre and central docklands, the influence of the private development sector has been powerful. In an economically depressed region the bargaining power of potential investors is always going to be stronger than in more prosperous regions. Nevertheless, through institutional arrangements that have established public agencies with substantial regeneration powers but limited accountability to the local population, the government has created a situation where the balance of power has shifted towards private developers to an extent almost unparalleled elsewhere in western Europe. Planning and the needs of the local community have become subordinate to the need to stimulate inward investment.

Outside the city centre the impacts of industrial restructuring and social change are just as keenly felt while the development pressures are even weaker. Vauxhall and North Liverpool are two such contrasting districts.

Vauxhall and North Liverpool

Lying immediately to the north of the city centre and abutting the North Docks and its associated industrial zone, Vauxhall developed rapidly as a mixed industrial and working-class housing area. It has been one of the most deprived districts in the whole conurbation for virtually the whole of its history. By the 1960s employment in the area was in decline. In the five years up to 1972 some 20 000 industrial jobs disappeared from the Vauxhall dockland. Tate & Lyle, one of the largest local employers, laid off 600 people in 1976 and closed its factory in 1980 with the loss of a further 1700 jobs. By 1981 the unemployment rate in the Vauxhall ward had reached 36.6%, more than twice the county average (McIntyre 1995, pp. 43–48).

It was a short step from the city council's identification of Vauxhall as one of its most deprived wards in the late 1960s to its inclusion as one of the *community development projects* (CPD) sponsored by the Home Office. In 1969 the Home Office established the CDPs with the intention of exploring solutions to poverty in areas of high social deprivation. Particular emphasis was to be placed on community participation in both the analysis and the implementation of solutions. Working on the presumption that both the causes of and solutions to urban deprivation were local, each CDP had both a neighbourhood-based action team and a linked university-based research team responsible for problem analysis and policy evaluation (Gibson & Langstaff 1982, p. 148). That research team for Vauxhall concluded:

> One of the major problems we face is the orderly regeneration of the older industrial areas such as Vauxhall ... the process of industrial change is quickening: areas are burnt out more rapidly, and social capital is wasted. Clearly we need to move away from this destructive pattern; but the problem is how to achieve this, particularly in areas like Vauxhall where the run-down has already gone so far. (Topping & Smith 1977, p. 120.)

Nevertheless there were positive local outcomes from the project, the most notable of which was the establishment of the community-based *Vauxhall Neighbourhood Council* (VNC), which continues to this day. By 1990 the VNC had embraced a policy of community-based economic development in support of a number of initiatives including a community laundry, a community transport scheme, a crèche, a driving school, and the VNC Lifeline, providing 24 hour a day support for the elderly and infirm. A separate organisation, Routes to Work, also supports enterprise and employment creation in the North Liverpool Partnership area (see below). At the end of 1999 a new Millennium Centre for the VNC was opened in Silvester Street. The organisation continues to provide free and accredited training initiatives for the local community, notably in information technology and business administration, and support services such as classroom assistants in local schools.

The Eldonians

One of the most interesting housing developments of the late 1970s was the emergence of housing cooperatives. By the mid-1980s there were about 30 cooperatives in Liverpool providing over 2000 homes. About half had been involved in new building and the rest with rehabilitation. The cooperative movement was backed and supported by the Liberal-dominated city council until the election of a Labour majority council in May 1983. The new administration was strongly opposed to the use of public funds to support cooperatives. During 1983/84 the council froze further land sales to cooperatives and municipalised several schemes that were still in the early stages of development. The District Labour Party refused to accept that there was a place for housing cooperatives in a strategy aiming to provide decent housing for everyone in need. They believed cooperatives to be elitist, exclusive and discriminatory. Against this background was founded one of the most interesting of the cooperative developments: the Eldonians.

In the late 1970s a group of people from the Portland Gardens area of Vauxhall took up the idea of forming a cooperative to develop housing as replacement for their former council tenements. Working with MIH (now River-
side Housing Association) and local architects (Wilkinson, Hindle, Halsall,
Lloyd) between 1982 and 1986 they succeeded in completing 106 dwellings
on four local housing sites. Many of the residents of Portland Gardens and the
nearby Burlington and Eldon Street tenements had been employed at Tate
& Lyle. The Eldonian Cooperative was formed with a view to redeveloping
the site to provide homes for local people needing to be rehoused as the tenements were cleared. In 1982 the derelict Tate & Lyle site was transferred to
English Estates, and after 12 months of negotiations the Eldonians obtained
an option to purchase 12 acres of the cleared site. Despite opposition from
the city council they finally gained planning permission for a cooperative
housing development on the site in 1985. This site was highly contaminated from its previous uses, and over £2 million, mainly financed through
Derelict Land Grant and the Merseyside Task Force, then had to be spent
on getting the site to a developable state. Meanwhile the residents were
working with the architects on the design and layout of the new housing
(Cowan, Hannay & Owens 1988, pp. 48–53.)

The development of phase 1 of the Eldonian Village, providing 145 homes,
was completed in 1990. The Eldonians had always hoped to extend housing
development northwards from their first site towards the Leeds–Liverpool
canal on the 'land to the north'. The extension of the designated area of the
Merseyside Development Corporation in 1988 to include much of Vauxhall
provided the opportunity to achieve this ambition. The MDC acquired and
cleared the industrial land, and phase 2 of the development, comprising 150
further homes, was funded by a mixture of public and private funds and built
by Liverpool Housing Trust on behalf of the Eldonians. Following this success there was pressure from the Vauxhall Neighbourhood Council for another housing cooperative development at Athol Village. Confidence in the
area grew rapidly, and by the late 1990s private developers were extending
the development northwards with speculative building for owner occupation. The transformation of the area was complete. What was once a series
of derelict industrial sites is now providing over 450 homes for local people
together with a mixture of community facilities including a day nursery,
community centres, a garden centre, a sports centre and community-based
businesses providing jobs for over 70 people: a true 'urban village'.

These 'Vauxhall villages' have a significance beyond their locality for a
number of reasons. First, they demonstrate the capacity of local communities, when properly supported by government agencies, to plan, design, build
and manage their own solutions to local housing problems. Second, they

illustrate the success of 'bottom-up' approaches to urban planning. None of these land-use changes or developments was proposed or anticipated in the development plans previously produced for the area. Instead, plans subsequently drawn up by local agencies (the 1990 MDC Development Strategy and the Liverpool Unitary Development Plan) have had to accommodate the consequences of the community's decisions and aspirations. Third, they are a demonstration of the success of the mixed-use 'urban village' concept as a cooperative model for future patterns of urban living. Fourth, they are a further illustration of the now widespread trend of the conversion of former industrial urban land to residential uses. By assembling large enough parcels of land the character of entire districts can be transformed (Couch 2003).

North Liverpool Partnership

Liverpool City Council's response to the Single Regeneration Budget (SRB) was substantially informed by the fact that it already had Objective One status from the European Union. The allocation of funds to the region under Objective One was determined by a strategy outlined in what was known as the *Single Programming Document*, which stated *inter alia* that:

> A special feature of Merseyside is the very sharp degree of economic and social disparities within the region. These disparities are concentrated in well-defined localities. The effectiveness of the funds will be increased by targeting resources selectively on area of need, and areas of opportunity. (Merseyside Single Programming Document, quoted in Gillespie 1998, p. 20.)

To meet this need Liverpool City Council designated 11 area-based *local partnerships* in the most deprived areas of the city. The boundaries of these areas were widely drawn and included 55% of the whole population. This may have been spatial targeting, but of the most imprecise kind. In each case the city council was to be the lead partner, with a designated senior officer providing liaison between the council and the local partnership. The overall aim of the partnerships was to improve the economic well-being and quality of life of local residents.

The formation of the local partnerships was central to the SRB Challenge Fund bidding process in Liverpool. They brought together the key public, private and voluntary agencies into the organisational structures, and formulated the area-based strategies necessary to support successful SRB bids under the DoE's Challenge Fund regulations. One such partnership was the North Liverpool Partnership, which included three districts within Liverpool's inner city: Breckfield, a predominantly residential area of private 'by-law' terraces and council housing; Everton, dominated by multi-storey council flats built to replace slums cleared in the 1950s and 1960s; and Vauxhall.

In this run-down area of social deprivation and depressed environment the North Liverpool Partnership was established between the local authority, other public agencies, local businesses and the local community, and was awarded £21.9 million of SRB funding to 'create, through effective partnership and the utilisation of the full potential of the whole community, a thriving area whose population enjoy good quality employment, education, health, housing and environment'. The grant was large by SRB standards but rather less than the £37.5 million awarded to five-year programmes for similar areas under the previous City Challenge initiative.

According to the partnership's strategy document the problems of the area were manifold. Educational attainment and aspirations were low, truancy and exclusions commonplace. Youth and long-term unemployment were endemic. There was seen to be a need for very personalised forms of basic skills training. Small local firms needed better access to sources of capital, business contracts and marketing in order to expand. Much of the housing stock was of poor quality. There were 15 former council-owned tower blocks, many in a poor state of repair, all taken over by the Liverpool Housing Action Trust. Fear of crime was a major issue. Everton Park, a large open area created by the city council on former housing land, had lacked the investment needed to make it a useful amenity and yet, with its stunning views over the Mersey and North Wales, had considerable potential for recreational development.

It was proposed to translate the strategic vision into action through a series of programmes referred to as *routes*. Routes for People developed objectives, policies and projects for education and training, provision for young people, employment initiatives, housing renovation and management, the delivery of healthcare, public transport and other quality of life issues. Routes for Business targeted the expansion of indigenous local businesses, the development of new businesses, and the attraction of inward investment. Routes to Partnership sought to develop better working relationships and coordination between the multiplicity of agencies and stakeholders within the area.

The partnership was managed by a steering group comprising representatives of local residents (six members), local businesses (six members), the public sector (six members), four ward councillors and a chair appointed by the city council. The work of the partnership was carried out by an executive team including a manager, community coordinator, two community development workers and a number of other officers.

Through the six-year strategy it was intended that the £21.9 million SRB funding would complement other public sector funds including £36 million from the Liverpool HAT, £16 million through the Housing Corporation, £12 million of European Union funding, £2.9 million from the city council, and £2.5 million from English Partnerships (NWDA). It was estimated that this investment would lever in some £43 million of private/non-public sector funding. It was anticipated that the total investment in the area over the six years would be in the order of £138 million by the end of the programme in 2002/3.

This strategy was intended to be a comprehensive and holistic attack on the problems of the area, and as such represents the continuation and development of an approach to regeneration that emerged in the thinking behind Renewal Areas (1989) and City Challenge (1991). The coordination of spending programmes by public sector agencies was a key element of the strategy, and the levering in of private investment had been an important measure of urban regeneration achievement since the early days of the urban development corporations.

Conclusions

From the early 1970s Liverpool suffered severe economic decline that led to urban dereliction, unemployment and social deprivation. The speed of the subsequent urban regeneration process has been constrained by continuing weak demand and low levels of investor confidence within the local economy. Liverpool has been overshadowed by more attractive investment opportunities (higher rates of profit) in competing locations (notably on the periphery of the conurbation and in neighbouring cities such as Manchester and Chester).

The regeneration process in Liverpool, and indeed in England generally, has been characterised both by heavy central government intervention (through, for example, the urban development corporations, the housing action trusts and highly regulated competitive bidding regimes) and by a fragmentation of responsibility among an array of public and community-based organisations. What was once the clear responsibility of local authorities has been fragmented among local councils, regional development agencies, other government organisations, registered social landlords, health authorities, short-life regeneration agencies, private companies and community organisations.

This has led to a much greater complexity in managing urban regeneration and a weakening of lines of accountability.

The city has experienced a multiplicity of regeneration programmes. As has been shown above, some of these programmes have lacked clarity in their aims and have not appeared to sit within a clear overarching regeneration framework for the city as a whole. There has only been a limited amount of coordination between programmes. Indeed, many have been competing for the same scarce investment funds. Nevertheless, the implementation of most programmes has been pursued with vigour by the personnel involved, and many have produced locally worthwhile achievements. The question is whether, in the absence of a strategic plan, they all contribute, one with another, towards a sum that is bigger than the constituent parts. Recent initiatives from central government, such as the notion of local strategic partnerships and neighbourhood renewal strategies, are intended to bring about better coordination and efficiency in programme delivery. Whether this will become a reality remains to be seen.

4

Dundee: a City Discovering Inclusion and Regeneration

Greg Lloyd and John McCarthy

Introduction

Dundee is situated on the east coast of Scotland, on the estuary of the River Tay. Its location has proved to be an important recurrent thread in the city's subsequent history and evolution. Initially its port facilities contributed significantly to the expansion of Dundee in the nineteenth and early twentieth century, when the city was established as an important industrial and trading centre. The city's industrial strength was based on manufacturing of goods based on its trading links, the availability of local agricultural produce and industry, including shipbuilding, engineering and ancillary port activities. The Dundee hinterland included high-quality agricultural land and marginal upland farming (Whatley 1991). At this time, Dundee was therefore a relatively stereotypical industrial city drawing on its hinterland and playing to its comparative advantages in a period of economic expansion. (Indeed, the city was popularised as resting on 'jam, jute and journalism'.) (See Fig. 4.1.)

In the 1920s and 1930s, however, Dundee experienced a process of relative economic decline as a consequence of the global recession, changing market conditions with falling demand for its products, a relatively outdated technological base, relatively high costs of production, and a lack of new inward investment. That process of decline, restructuring and re-configuration continues to this day. This was a significant reversal in its fortunes. In the early to mid-nineteenth century Dundee was the jute capital of the world. Its over-dependence on that product proved its eventual undoing. It has been suggested that the 'economics of the industry in the age of laissez-faire produced human suffering and physical deterioration in Dundee which has only been eradicated in the half century since the Second World War' (Whatley 1992, p. 2).

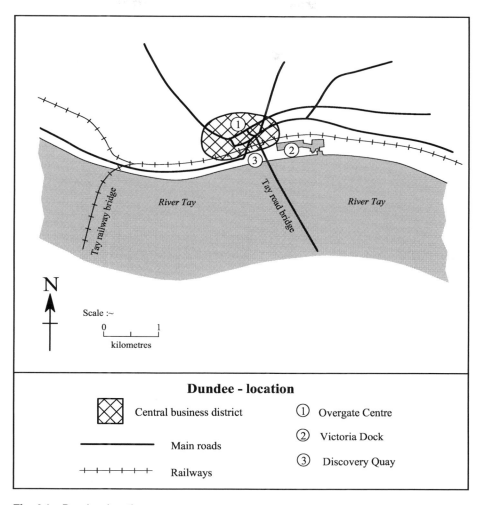

Dundee - location

⊠ Central business district	① Overgate Centre
—— Main roads	② Victoria Dock
╫╫╫╫╫ Railways	③ Discovery Quay

Fig. 4.1　Dundee: location.

Dundee continues to live with that legacy as it seeks to modernise itself.

This chapter examines Dundee as an example of a post-industrial city that is still experiencing the processes of structural, community, institutional and physical readjustment. Dundee is a relatively overlooked city, being the smallest – in terms of population and geographical space – of the principal Scottish cities. It is not perceived as part of the central belt axis, and continues to live with its image as a rugged city in decline. Yet Dundee is a city that is striving hard to define its own renaissance through institutional innovation and imaginative policies for community, cultural, economic and environmental regeneration. In effect this involves the reconstruction of the city as an important regional centre, a city of learning and discovery based on biotechnology and culture, with an outstanding quality of life. This is being grafted onto the social and community legacy of the city's past.

Historic context

Dundee's location made it ideally placed for engaging in European trade. Its early trading relations were associated with exports of hides and wool products, wine and grain imports, and fishing revenues. Dundee was established in its early period as a textile town, particularly for coarse wool cloth, plaid and knitwear. This led to the development of associated industrial processes such as dyeing of textiles. In addition, however, Dundee became an established gunmaking centre. The safety and superb location of its harbour led to its operating as an entrepôt port, bringing in timber and coal products, which were then moved onwards to other, smaller ports along the east coast of Scotland. By 1535 Dundee was Scotland's second highest-value burgh (after Edinburgh). Following the Reformation in the sixteenth century Dundee prospered, but it was eventually caught up in the uncertainties and conflicts associated with the Civil War. Thereafter Dundee faced considerable economic uncertainty, particularly with respect to contracting markets and the shift in trade to the West Coast ports. The aftermath of the 1707 Act of Union had a further deflationary effect on the Dundee city region because of its exposure to greater competition for its products. Subsequently, however, Dundee began to exploit a comparative advantage in the production of textiles, particularly the manufacture of coarse linen cloth (Whatley 1992).

The real transformation of the Dundee economy came after 1820. This was associated with the development of the jute industry, which built on its experience with the manufacture of textiles. By benefiting from the available technology, power and machines, together with a local labour market with the appropriate skills, Dundee became the jute capital of the world. Indeed the Victorian period was a highly successful epoch in the city's history: it was based on jute production, engineering, mill and factory building, shipbuilding, architecture and the arts. In 1889 Dundee attained city status. In 1894 it became a county of a city on a par with Glasgow and Edinburgh.

Notwithstanding the industrial and economic transformation of Dundee, the associated urbanisation brought with it a catalogue of social and community misery. In particular, Dundee recorded the worst indicators of social suffering in terms of mortality, housing and health. In the case of Dundee these conditions were exacerbated by the uncertainty in the jute markets. It is argued that 'the effects of periodic downturns in trade and the accompanying unemployment simply seared through the heart of what was a defence-less and poverty stricken city' (Whatley 1992, 14). This made what was to follow an even bigger challenge for Dundee.

Decline and change

By 1911 Dundee was effectively a one-industry city (Whatley 1992). It was very heavily dependent on the manufacture and trade of jute, and was vulner-able to its decline, a process that persisted to 1945. Employment in textiles and clothing remained at over 50% of the labour force. Dundee in structural and practical terms was over-specialised and over-dependent. As a conse-quence it was highly vulnerable to exogenous change, which came in the form of overseas competition, technology shifts or the imposition of tariffs in overseas markets. There were internal contradictions also, in that wages in the city were relatively very low and the costs of living relatively high. Poverty and disadvantage followed the economic downturn very quickly indeed.

The process of decline based on the contraction of jute continued in the post-war period. This was despite the early economic boom associated with national economic growth and reflationary measures introduced by West-minster. Dundee's economy reflected its over-dependence on certain manu-facturing activities. There began a process of long-term endemic decline in its traditional industrial and corporate sectors. This process of decline has characterised the Dundee economy from the 1960s to the present. The economic and corporate restructuring spilled over into the social and com-munity structures in the city: it eroded its skill base, reduced the city income level, and undermined the provision of private services and local authority community facilities (Doherty 1992).

Revival

Notwithstanding the long-term decline in the city economy, the period since 1945 also witnessed attempts to address the problems of the Dundee economy (Doherty 1992). For the purposes of this chapter, three broad phases are suggested. The first took place in the period 1945–1970, and may be char-acterised as a period of assertive planning for Dundee city and its city region. This reflected the broader emphasis on statutory land-use planning, and the attempts to integrate regional economic considerations with local planning. The second phase of intervention took place in the period 1970–1990, and had an emphasis on the physical regeneration of Dundee, with attempts to address the industrial legacy of its restructuring. The third phase of activity embraces the 1980s to the present, and may be characterised as a period in which Dundee became the focus of development agency intervention, and active partnership working in Dundee.

The first phase of intervention was concerned with *city regional planning.* Following the Town and Country Planning Act of 1947, the land-use planning framework provided an important opportunity to put in place a means of managing change in the city. The legislation reflected the mood of optimism of the age. Thus, from

> the negative and restrictive provisions of the Town and Country Planning (Scotland) Act 1932, and the Town and County Planning (Interim Development) (Scotland) Act 1943, the face of the work has changed to positive creation and inspiring endeavour. (Lyle & Payne 1950, foreword.)

In the 1950s and 1960s the Tay Valley Plan and the Dobson Chapman Plan provided the strategic context for Dundee. Both advocated a programme of improvement of working-class housing in the city centre together with the construction of peripheral housing estates. The overall aim of the Tay Valley Plan was to

> form a background for urban and rural reconstruction physically, socially and economically, which must ensue over the next 30 to 50 years in order to roll back the tide of rural decadence and urban concentration. (Lyle & Payne 1950, foreword.)

The main objectives of the Plan were:

- to ascertain the physical, social and economic advantages and disadvantages of the region;

- to demonstrate how the advantages of living in the region may be maintained;

- to secure the cooperation of the statutory planning authorities in the region, the coordination of the various schemes, and to assist these authorities to frame their proposals for development plans under the 1947 Town and Country Planning Act.

In terms of general principles, it is clear that the main problem to be addressed by the plan was the drift in population from the rural areas to the city of Dundee, and from Dundee and the remainder of the city region to England and abroad. The plan set out to reverse this drift. It acknowledged that the motivating factor of the drift was primarily economic in character, but the issue had strong social and other implications, including the impact on housing. In practical terms, the plan explicitly argued for a reduction in the population size of Dundee. It asserted that the

> fact must be faced that Dundee has reached its maximum desirable population, and in the national interests it is essential to encourage the dispersal of some of the population and industry to the smaller burghs and villages. (Lyle & Payne 1950, p. 277.)

Some observers argued for the concentration of a sizeable proportion of the projected increase in the population of the region in the city (Pocock 1968). The significance of the Tay Valley Plan was its strategic context setting for the city.

The Dobson Chapman Plan 1952 adopted a *master plan* approach for land use and the zoning of functions in Dundee. It stated:

> The primary objective of planning today is to produce an environment in which all the component parts of the area are related to each other by the regulation of land uses, and the siting and density of buildings so control-led, that all function together as a harmonious whole, and render to each and every section of the community the maximum health, amenity and convenience. To achieve this end, some form of control over development is essential, but in no way does this imply the hampering of legitimate growth. By such control, the evils of haphazard, selfish, sporadic or other ill-considered development can be effectively checked and the possibility of much wasteful expenditure of public funds on the provision of services thereby eliminated. (Dobson Chapman 1952, p. 1.)

The Dobson Chapman Plan was based on a number of general principles. First, it sought to preclude the development of Dundee beyond suitably defined limits, and therefore proposed to create a belt of open space around the periphery. Second, it sought to define zones for industrial development within the city where existing industry could be consolidated and where a limited number of new industries could be sited. Third, it proposed that residential areas should be consolidated into a series of neighbourhood units, as well as a re-planning of the central area of Dundee. Fourth, the issue of communications was assumed to require the need to secure the maximum of convenience for the residents of and visitors to the city, passing between the different component areas of the city.

Significantly, the plan considered the city of Dundee to be unique in one aspect, since it suggested that:

> An outstanding feature of the City of Dundee is the very strong feeling of corporate consciousness possessed by its inhabitants, a most important contribution to which has been the fact that, although the City is completely self-contained and possesses most forms of communal facility, it is yet of a size which allows the Dundonian to feel he [sic] is indeed a member of a cohesive community and not, as is so often the impression in many of the largest cities of Britain – certainly in Glasgow, Manchester, Birmingham and even, perhaps, Edinburgh – a member of a community so large that it is only manageable when subdivided into what are virtually completely separate and distinct sections, the inhabitants of one having little or no fellow-feeling or community of interest with those of another. (Dobson Chapman 1952, p. 19.)

The Dobson Chapman Plan highlighted the need to maintain the city as a self-contained entity, thereby precluding the extension of development beyond defined limits, and it proposed the creation of a green belt around the city as a means of achieving aims for urban containment. The Dobson Chapman Plan provided the basis for the subsequent city development plan, which was submitted to the Secretary of State in 1956, and approved in 1959. In line with the requirements of the 1947 Act, a five-year review of the plan was conducted in 1964, with a revised plan issued in 1966. Following this revised plan, however, doubts began to arise as to the continued relevance of the 1947 Act, and a new Town and County Planning Act was passed in 1969. Nevertheless, the subsequent development plan review in 1971 made no new recommendations for development planning in Dundee (Doherty 1992).

The second phase of intervention turned on the *physical renewal* of the city. This took place from the 1970s on. Attention was paid to the redevelopment of Dundee's city centre through the preparation of a local plan, which was initiated following the creation of the two-tier local authority structure (Tayside Regional Council and Dundee District Council) in 1975. Moreover, after its establishment in 1975, the Scottish Development Agency (SDA) initiated a number of immediate environmental improvement initiatives in the city. Local positive action by the key players in the city economy became an established feature of the post-war economic history of Dundee (McCarthy & Pollock 1997).

The Inner Urban Areas Act 1978 enabled local authorities to designate industrial improvement areas as the focus for positive policy action and resource allocation. In Dundee, the Blackness area of the city was identified as such an industrial improvement area. Blackness was a neighbourhood that had been an important industrial area in the inner city but had experienced a marked contraction in activity, evident in redundant properties. The Blackness Project involved the coordination of infrastructure improvements in the area; the upgrading of individual buildings and sites; the initiation of specific environmental improvements; the conversion of redundant buildings for more productive use by small businesses; the provision of new industrial units; and the provision of financial support and grants to small businesses. The Blackness Project was an important attempt to stabilise the local economy and provide a framework for area-based regeneration in the inner part of the city.

More significantly, perhaps, the Blackness Project demonstrated the potential advantages of consistency and concerted action through partnership working by the principal development bodies in Dundee. It made an important contribution to the acceptance of the partnership approach to local economic development. The immediate lesson of the Blackness Project was that coordinated, concerted action could create clear benefits for defined localities and an integrated approach to policy formulation and implementation across the city. It led to the Dundee Project, which was initiated in 1982 (Bazley 1992).

The Dundee Project was operational until 1991 as a means of addressing economic development and physical improvement in Dundee as a whole through partnership. The Dundee Project involved the SDA, Tayside Regional Council and Dundee District Council. It was initially set up for a five-year period. Its goal was to develop and diversify the city's economy and to address the city's associated physical decline (Scottish Enterprise Tayside 1991). The Dundee Project represented another important step in establishing a coordinated approach to local economic development in the city. It was part of a broader Scottish programme of economic development initiatives managed by the SDA (Keating & Boyle 1986).

An early aim of the Dundee Project was to establish an enterprise zone in the city, following the Local Government, Planning and Land Act 1980. This was achieved, and consisted of six individual sites across the city. Other urban renewal and industrial development activities were put in place, such as the Dens Road Business Development Area, which was based on environmental improvements. The Dundee Project further confirmed the advantages of the partnership approach to regeneration, and itself laid the foundations for the subsequent establishment of the Dundee Partnership.

Partnership is the principal characteristic of the third phase of intervention. The Dundee Partnership was instigated in 1991, when a formal agreement was signed between three principal partners: Tayside Regional Council, Dundee District Council, and Scottish Enterprise. Scottish Enterprise had replaced the SDA, and became responsible for the integrated delivery of economic and business development initiatives, the provision of training, and measures to secure the improvement of the environment in lowland Scotland. Scottish Enterprise Tayside (SET) is the local arm of the development body, and provides the strategic context for regeneration within Dundee.

The Dundee Partnership is an informal institutional arrangement between the three key players in the regeneration of the city's economy, and it provided a link to other organisations such as the universities, the private sector, trade unions and Scottish Homes. Scottish Homes has subsequently become Communities Scotland. The Dundee Partnership does not have executive powers of its own, nor does it have dedicated resources at its disposal. Instead, the partnership seeks – effectively by moral suasion and networking between the public and private organisations involved – to establish a common agenda for action and spending by the individual participants. It is by such means that the Dundee Partnership has been able to access the resources of constituent members deriving from their responsibilities in areas such as environmental improvement, economic development, education and social work. It can also participate through SET in the wider Scottish Enterprise network.

In 1996 there were further changes to the composition of the Dundee Partnership. These were an outcome of the Local Government (Scotland) Act 1994, which introduced a streamlined, single-tier, market-oriented enabling system of local governance. Local government reorganisation replaced the established two-tier structure of Tayside Regional Council and Dundee District Council with Dundee City Council, a general-purpose body. This authority was separated from its city region, however, which came within the jurisdiction of two other single-tier councils. In 2001 other changes were put in place as a consequence of the community planning arrangements across Scotland. The Dundee Partnership is now adapting to a changed context for partnership working in Dundee.

The Dundee Partnership laid down a *vision statement* to guide its operations and activities. The vision set out the contextual framework for the work of the Dundee Partnership, and established a common agenda for the work of the individual partners. The partnership energised the involvement of other bodies such as the Health Board and Scottish Homes, thereby rounding out the strategic foundations of the organisation. The vision expresses this in terms of key aims and tasks, identifies gaps, and sets out priorities for actions required by individual partners. In particular, it aims to recreate the city as a thriving regional shopping and service centre (for instance by improving prime and secondary shopping); as a major employment centre (for instance by meeting all land and property requirements); as a place for the realisation of potential (for instance by raising workforce skills and qualifications); as a city to be proud to live and work in (for instance by ensuring a wide range of housing opportunity); and as a city worth visiting (for instance by developing the city as a base for the wider area). Clearly, these elements are interlinked: for instance, the issue of image is a central theme that runs through several objectives of the Dundee Partnership.

Although the Dundee Partnership is concerned with the city as a whole, it also focuses on specific projects within selected localities of the city, which are considered by individual groups within the Dundee Partnership. These groups include: the Community Regeneration Group (which seeks to further the process of creating stable self-sustaining community areas); the Land and Property Group (which seeks to encourage appropriate information exchange, joint strategy formulation and coordination of joint action projects); the City Centre Group; the Tourism Group; the Enterprise and Employment Group; and the Marketing and the City of Discovery Campaign Support Group. These individual projects are multi-speed in nature, involving leadership by specific partners as appropriate, and being driven by the most relevant officers in the most appropriate partner. Moreover, leadership can change over time: the Community Regeneration Group, for example, has been increasingly influenced by Dundee City Council as part of its community regeneration strategy for the city.

Culture, partnership and regionalism

The practical outcomes of the partnership working, and the attempts to address the restructuring processes taking place in Dundee, may be seen in two parallel sets of initiatives. On the one hand, there are the interventions designed to promote Dundee as a new city, based on new industrial and technological processes. This involves the effective reconstruction of Dundee as a postmodern entity. On the other hand, there are the interventions designed to address the legacy of the city's past. These two processes of action sit alongside one another, and there are clear spillovers between them. This section examines examples of these two approaches. These are selective only, and are intended to illustrate the types of initiative taking place across the city.

First, in terms of reconstructing a new Dundee there has been an emphasis on its development through an *arts and culture strategy*. An Arts Strategy for Dundee was launched in late 1994, as the outcome of an extensive consultation exercise involving over 60 national arts organisations and the general public. The strategy set out an approach to arts and culture that would develop Dundee's status as a regional centre for the arts; recognise the role of the artist in developing and maintaining the cultural, social and economic fabric of the city; promote high standards in the creation, presentation and management of the arts; and support and develop the local arts community and develop public access to, and involvement, in the arts. Subsequently, a number of significant changes took place, including the creation of a new Arts and Heritage Department in the new unitary Dundee Council. In addition, an Arts Lottery enabled the creation of a new contemporary arts centre for the city (Dundee City Council 1997). A revised strategy located this activity within a broader city-wide regeneration strategy, by linking arts and cultural initiatives to broader corporate and related policy frameworks for planning and economic development (Dundee City Council 1997).

This approach seeks to promote the widening of access to and participation in the arts to contribute directly to the empowerment and sustainability elements of community regeneration. There is an associated programme of physical change. This includes the provision of an independent, live music venue, and the encouragement of other development proposals that have a strategic potential for the city, such as Dundee College's Dance and Theatre Centre, and expansion plans for Dundee Rep Theatre. However, of particular importance in this context is the use of the new Dundee Contemporary Arts Centre. In terms of the visual arts, crafts and design, the centre combines production and participation by providing a focal point for exhibitions as well as the creation of new work, and it is hoped that the centre will allow the recognition of the city as a major international centre for the visual arts. Using the centre as a focus, the plan also aims to create a cultural quarter around an area adjacent to the city's central waterfront.

The wider environmental aspects of the arts in terms of regeneration potential are also considered in the plan, which aims to develop the city's reputation for providing art in the environment, and to develop the role of community artists within design teams for physical regeneration areas. Reflecting the social aspects of regeneration, the plan aims to increase the awareness of, and opportunities for, participation in the arts by means of education. Finally, the plan aims to make use of a series of festivals and events to promote the image of the city so as to bring about the kind of economic and social benefits referred to above (Dundee City Council 1997).

Second, Dundee has participated in the broader national programme for *social justice*. In 1998, *social inclusion partnerships* (SIPs) were introduced. The creation of SIPs appeared to represent an attempt to reflect a specifically Scottish approach to urban policy as, in introducing the measure, the Secretary of State argued that

> Scottish circumstances differ from England in that those suffering exclusion in Scotland are disproportionately concentrated in specific communities, and there has been more experience of effective urban regeneration policies originally pioneered in Scotland and maintained in later years by local government and others. (Dewar 1998, p. 1.)

While SIPs build on established arrangements and experience of urban regeneration in Scotland, they involve a particular emphasis on seeking to prevent young people, in particular, from being excluded from participation in the economic and social mainstream. Hence the main characteristics of SIPs were to be:

● a focus on the most needy members of society;

● the coordination and filling in of gaps between existing programmes in order to promote inclusion;

● an attempt to prevent people from becoming socially excluded.

More specifically, SIPs were to

> focus more closely on promoting inclusion in our communities and preventing social exclusion from developing. As part of this refocus on prevention we will be calling on all partnerships to ensure that they are getting the early years right and ensuring that residents in their communities can take full advantage of the roll out of our plans under the Scottish Childcare Strategy. (Dewar 1998, p. 8)

Emerging agendas

History is catching up with Dundee. At the very outset of its interventions to address its problems, there was a strong emphasis on the city-region. This reflects Wannop's (1995) observation that this period is the classic vintage with respect to regional planning practice. Similarly, there was an emphasis on assertive planning practice (Ward 1994). That regional dimension was eroded in the subsequent period, and Dundee became more inward looking. This was a consequence of local government reorganisation, fragmentation of agency activity, and a fetish with boundaries linked to local government finance. Now the regional agenda is becoming more apparent again. In 2001 the Scottish Executive published its proposals concerning the future arrangements for strategic planning in Scotland (Scottish Executive 2001). This proposed to establish four city-regions in Scotland – based on Aberdeen, Dundee, Edinburgh and Glasgow – which would provide a strategic planning context for their functional hinterlands. The concept of the city-region is held to offer much in terms of contributing to a more sustainable future. Indeed, it has been asserted that each 'city-region has a unique development path, a unique set of problems, assets, and position in the regional and national context' (Ravetz 2000, p. 277). Here then may be the way forward for the future Dundee.

Conclusion

Dundee is a medium-sized city. It has a rich industrial and cultural heritage. It has undergone very deep changes as it has undergone restructuring from its traditional manufacturing and industrial activities to its modern emphasis on technology, education, medicine and science. As a consequence of this continuing transformation and adjustment it carries with it a social and community conscience as a reminder of the past. Reconciling these parallel processes is a major challenge for Dundee, yet its established experience with partnership would appear to be both an organic response to its own agenda and one that reflects broader thinking in community regeneration.

5

Urban Regeneration in Belfast

Stephen McKay

Belfast, the capital city of Northern Ireland, is infamous across the world for being synonymous with the political violence that has torn apart its society for the last 30 years. The toll of the 'troubles' has left 3700 people dead and 40 000 people injured, and has had a major impact on the political, economic and cultural life of the city.[1] This has accentuated its problems of competitiveness and social and economic disadvantage, stemming from the region's peripherality in relation to national (UK) and European cores (Adair *et al.* 1996). The management structures of the city have also been fundamentally influenced by the political situation, and are very different from those of comparable cities in other parts of the UK.

Historical background

Belfast is surrounded by hills to the north and west; the mouth of the River Lagan lies to the east. The city's Irish name, *béal feirste* ('mouth of the sand-spit'), first appeared in the fifteenth century, although the settlement dates from 1177, when the Anglo-Norman John de Courcy invaded Ulster and built a castle nearby to establish his rule over south-eastern Ulster (Bardon 1982). However, Belfast began in earnest in 1603 when the castle and lands of Belfast came into the possession of Sir Arthur Chichester, Governor of Carrickfergus, who planted the region with settlers from Devon and Scotland (Beckett *et al.* 1983). Ten years later Belfast was granted corporation status, with the right to send members to the parliament at Westminster. After 1650 the nascent town became a thriving port, although the population had only grown to 8000 by the 1750s. The city's fortunes changed with the Industrial

---

[1]For a discussion of the political history of Northern Ireland see, for example, Buckland (1981), Bew & Gillespie (1993, 1996) and Loughlin (1998).

Revolution, which, between 1770 and 1850, rapidly transformed a bustling market town into a major industrial city dependent on heavy engineering, ship building and textiles (above all, linen making). (See Fig. 5.1.)

The nineteenth century industrialisation drew in large numbers of migrants from the surrounding rural area, and introduced a significant Catholic component to what had previously been an overwhelmingly Protestant town.

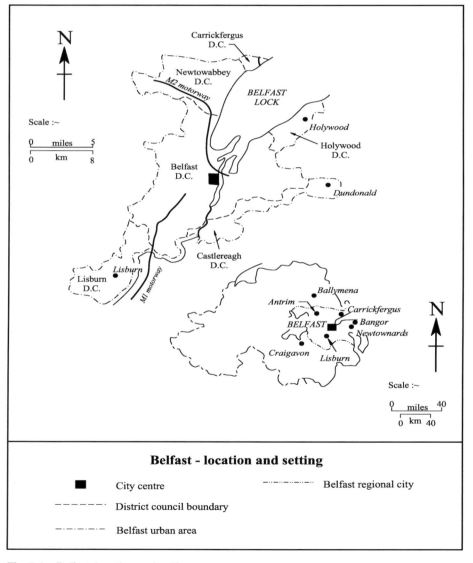

Belfast - location and setting

■ City centre   ·—··—··—·· Belfast regional city

— — — — — · District council boundary

—·—·—·—·— Belfast urban area

Fig. 5.1 Belfast: location and setting.

This influx of Irish Catholic labour was a common feature of industrialisation, not only in Belfast but also in cities in Britain such as Glasgow, Liverpool and Manchester (Boal 1995). Although all had their inter-ethnic tensions, in Belfast these 'were to prove in every way sharper, more persistent and more decisive than anywhere else' (Maguire 1993). In the period between 1861 and 1911 the population grew from 121 000 to 350 000, and although the number of Catholics increased absolutely, it is significant in that it fell proportionately.

The economy continued to thrive until the late 1920s, but ethnic tension intensified as Belfast became the capital of a newly formed province of the United Kingdom: Northern Ireland. As the economic slump of the 1930s took hold, a growing shortage of jobs increased sectarian rivalry, resulting in serious disturbances and a sharpening of residential segregation between Catholics and Protestants, the legacy of which remains today. Although prosperity returned to the city with wartime employment, and continued for some years thereafter, the decline of Belfast's key industries (shipbuilding and linen) re-emerged in the 1960s. Since then huge numbers of jobs have been lost in all aspects of manufacturing, although attempts were made to find substitutes, for instance synthetic fibres or the unhappy Delorean car manufacturing venture. Despite the attempts of the Industrial Development Board and the Local Enterprise Development Unit, Belfast's industrial base remains weak and unemployment high.

Recent population changes

There was a period of intense urban decentralisation of Belfast between 1971 and 1981, when the population fell by 416 700 to 314 300. It continued to decline throughout the 1980s, and by 1991 it had fallen to 279 200 (see Fig. 5.2). This contrasted with the trend of the previous 150 years, which had seen a progressive concentration of the Northern Ireland population in the Belfast urban region. Population decentralisation first occurred in the inner residential areas of the city and then spread towards the periphery. This pattern was not unique to Belfast: it conformed to the general UK model and that of several other major cities such as Glasgow, while Liverpool suffered a greater population loss. Although a significant degree of population movement occurred as a result of the violent political conflict, there were a number of other reasons for this population shift, for example:

● redevelopment of the inner city;

● the growth of private housing;

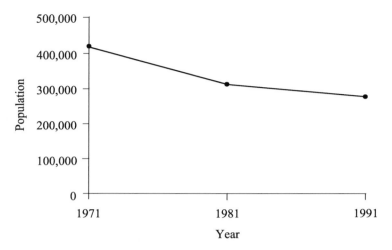

Fig. 5.2   Belfast: population change.

- a decline in mean household size;

- rising car ownership, resulting in increased commuting;

- regional policy, encouraging out-migration from Belfast.

It is difficult to anticipate accurately how population will change in Belfast in the foreseeable future. It does seem likely, however, that it will be affected significantly by a new *Regional Development Strategy* (RDS), which is being prepared for Northern Ireland to cover the period up to the year 2025 (see below). The Strategy has indicated that it will support a housing drive that will allow Belfast to hold its population at around the current level of 280 000.

In most European cities the physical setting and long-term socio-economic forces would provide an appropriate medium for understanding the institutional organisation of the urban area. In Belfast, above all else, it is recent political history that is the key to interpreting the dynamics of the city.

Political context

The institutional structures for the management of Belfast all derive from the turbulent political history of the region. Although the conflict has roots dating back centuries, the recent chapter of political violence emerged in the late 1960s with the growth of the civil rights movement protesting against discriminatory practices (particularly in employment and housing): this sparked a spiral of political crises, culminating with the UK government proroguing the Unionist-dominated Northern Ireland legislature in 1972. This action imposed direct rule, with the government at Westminster assuming full responsibility for Northern Ireland's administration.

Under this system the entire administration became the responsibility of the Secretary of State for Northern Ireland (assisted by two Ministers of State and two Parliamentary under-Secretaries), giving a centralised administration that inevitably vested civil servants with a high level of power. Most of the issues related to the administration of Belfast became the responsibility of a member of the House of Lords who had been selected not directly by any electoral mechanism, but by a cabinet whose composition is decided by a general election of the entire United Kingdom. Given the significant differences in political culture between Northern Ireland and the rest of the UK, the political issues of greatest relevance to Belfast had little resonance in the outcome of such a general election, and none of the Northern Ireland parties were represented in government. This situation was further exacerbated by a raft of quangos, covering issues such as housing and urban regeneration. With no downward accountability to the local electorate for over 26 years there had therefore been a major democratic deficit in Northern Ireland.

On Friday 10 April 1998, however, a new Northern Ireland Assembly was established as part of the Belfast Agreement reached at the multi-party negotiations, and commonly referred to as the *Good Friday Agreement*.

The Assembly, under the leadership of the First Minister and Deputy First Minister, is responsible for deciding the direction of policies and public expenditure priorities for Belfast and the region as a whole. These functions are administered through ten departments, each chaired by a locally appointed Minister and staffed by the Northern Ireland Civil Service. The departments are as follows:

- Department of Agriculture and Rural Development;

- Department of Culture, Arts and Leisure;

- Department of Education;

- Department of Enterprise, Trade and Investment;

- Department of the Environment;

- Department of Finance and Personnel;

- Department of Health, Social Services and Public Services;

- Department of Higher and Further Education, Training and Employment;

- Department of Regional Development;

- Department of Social Development.

In terms of urban management, the most significant department is the Department of the Environment. It advises the Minister on policy formulation, and provides support for a group of 11 agencies, which deliver environmental services, the most controversial being planning.

The rest of this chapter will, first, describe the existing institutions responsible for managing the regeneration of Belfast, followed by a discussion of how the city is changing as a consequence of the Good Friday Agreement.

Belfast City Council

Belfast is unique among European cities in that the local municipality has not been the main coordinator and provider of public services. The imposition of direct rule not only removed the regional tier of government from Northern Ireland, but also resulted in centralisation of local government functions such as housing and planning. Despite the formation of the Assembly there has been little change in terms of democratic accountability. Although there is a Belfast City Council (BCC), representing nearly 300 000 people, its responsibilities are very narrow, with expenditure amounting to a little over £200 per resident every year (compared with an average of £670 in England). The centralisation process has left BCC with three main roles (see Knox 1998):

- **Executive.** BCC provides a limited range of services such as street cleaning, waste management and a few regulatory functions such as environmental health and building control. Since 1992 it has been permitted to spend up to 5p in the pound for the locally raised property tax for economic development, opening up opportunities for more innovative council initiatives.

- **Representative.** Councillors are appointed to sit on a range of quangos such as the education and library boards.

- **Consultative.** The Council is regularly asked for its views on centrally provided services such as planning, roads and water.

Table 5.1   Composition of Belfast City Council.

Polictical party	Number of seats
Sinn Fein (N)	14
Ulster Unionist Party	11
Democratic Unionist Party	10
Social Democratic & Labour Party (N)	9
Alliance Party	3
Progressive Unionist Party	3
Independent	1
Total	51

N = Nationalist or Republican

The limited role left for BCC has meant that, as for other local authorities in the region (and symptomatic of the general political culture), both voting and council chamber debates have been motivated by positions predominantly on the relationship with the rest of the UK and the Republic of Ireland, rather than on the provision of local services. Since 1972 the council has been dominated by Unionist parties, who have disrupted normal council business when they have felt their hegemony to be under threat, for example following the signing of the Anglo-Irish Agreement in 1985 (Connolly & Knox 1988). In more recent years the nationalist and republican representation has increased on the council (see Table 5.1) and this, coupled with a more conciliatory stance by the main parties, made possible the election of the council's first ever nationalist Lord Mayor in 1997.

The responsibilities of the council amount to a net annual expenditure of around £63 million, with the main areas of spending being on *client services* (parks, leisure and community centres, 42%) and *health and environment services* (waste management and building control, 39%) (BCC 1998). BCC employs 2300 staff and arranges its business around six principal committees: policy and resources, contract services, client services, health and environmental services, development, and town planning. Although the planning committee is entirely a consultative rather than a decision–making body, the council has attempted to influence the future development of the city in two ways. The first is the development of a *sustainable development strategy* (BCC 1999), which reaffirms the council's commitment made by signing the Aalborg Charter (European Sustainable Towns and Cities Campaign) and defines how the city will address Local Agenda 21. While the council is introducing sustainable development principles into its own practices and undertaking a state of the environment report for the city, given its range of responsibilities, its impact can only be limited.

The second area in which the council is attempting to influence the future shape of the city is through the activities of its *development committee*, formed in 1997. Funded by the new economic development precept, the committee has primarily aimed at improving the poor image of Belfast for investors and tourists. This has included funding the regeneration of council-owned landmark sites such as St George's Market and the rehabilitation of a major brownfield site, the gasworks. Both of these projects have been undertaken in conjunction with the Laganside Development Corporation (see below). The development committee has also been instrumental in promoting an integrated marketing strategy for the city ('Bel*fast* becoming better'), developing a management plan for the city centre (BCCMSC 1999), and with a range of partners formulating a *city vision* (BCP 1999). This type of initiative has been criticised as being inconsequential in the light of the divisions and acute social and economic problems of the city. That is, they are merely 'lipstick on the gorilla' (Neill 1995; see also Neill 1999). However, this is almost inevitable, given the narrow ground of consensus between the political parties represented on the council and the limited functions it has been permitted by central government. Since the establishment of the Assembly there has been no significant change in the role adopted by the city council.

Planning

The planning system in Northern Ireland began in 1931, initially with the local authorities and New Town Commissions having responsibility for its implementation. For a variety of reasons, the old system of close local control fell into disrepute. The Belfast Regional Survey and Report of 1963 described the multiplicity of small authorities as 'an impossible impediment to the kind of broad coordinated planning and development so urgently required for the future prosperity of the Province' (Matthew 1963). The report identified various advantages of centralising the decision-making process, including greater consistency of decisions and better implementation of regional policy. This was followed in 1970 by a review of local government (Macrory Report 1970), which recommended that district councils should have responsibility only for 'local' planning matters, and that all others should be dealt with by the Ministry of Development. The White Paper to implement the Macrory Report's recommendations was published just before the imposition of direct rule in 1972. The UK government adopted the proposals wholesale – but with the significant difference that instead of the regional government taking over responsibility for the planning system, this was handed to the Ministers based at Westminster. This centralisation has led to planning being seen by many as remote, and effectively outside democratic control. This issue was addressed by the House of Commons Northern Ireland Affairs Committee (House of Commons 1996), which recommended the establishment of a non-governmental planning advisory board to oversee contentious decisions.

Broad planning policy is decided by the DoE (NI), but in 1996 responsibility for development control and area plans was handed to a 'next steps' agency, the *Planning Service*. The service operates through six regional offices ('Divisions'), overseen by a headquarters in Belfast. It functions much like the planning departments of British local authorities, with development planning and development control (including enforcement) defining the structure of the service. These activities are supported by a range of published documents, including the Planning Strategy for Rural Northern Ireland, area plans, planning policy statements, design guides, and development control advice notes.

Development control decisions are taken by the Planning Service, following consultation with the democratically elected representatives of the local authorities. In a similar fashion development plans are adopted by the Planning Service after consultation with the councils. The main legislation governing planning is the Planning (NI) Order 1991, which consolidates previous legislation. It broadly follows the system in England and Wales, the most significant difference, apart from the lack of democratic control, being that development plans are important 'material considerations' rather than of primary importance as in the rest of the UK.

By far the most significant planning division in terms of quantity of development is Belfast. Guidance for development within the urban area is provided by the Belfast Urban Area Plan 2001. In the Belfast Agreement of 10 April 1998 the government gave a commitment to make rapid progress with a new regional development strategy for Northern Ireland that will offer a framework for developing the region over the next 25 years. The draft strategy entitled *Shaping Our Future* (published in December 1998) gave Belfast a key role in creating a sustainable future for the province. One of the key strategic planning guidelines is 'to create a thriving Metropolitan Area focused on Belfast' (DoE (NI) 1988).

An aim of the draft strategy is to build on the distinctive and complementary roles of a number of component urban centres that lie outside the city limits to create a strong urban complex capable of competing in the league of European cities. To achieve this, the strategy aims to enhance the role of Belfast through measures such as improving its international image, developing a city vision process, and maintaining its role as a cultural capital. It will promote development of the metropolitan area by focusing on the use and reuse of land and buildings for housing, maximising the employment potential of the city centre, and developing tourism. A third and crucial arm of the strategy will be to improve transport along key corridors (bus and rail) beyond the metropolitan area, and to develop a comprehensive network of public transport services to link homes and jobs, particularly between areas of social disadvantage and major employment opportunities.

Housing

Housing in Belfast is controlled by a single unitary housing authority that covers the entire region, the *Northern Ireland Housing Executive* (NIHE). The executive emerged from the period of political upheaval and protest of the late 1960s. Housing was a major contributing factor to the broader political instability, as students took to the streets demanding the reform of local government, and a wider civil rights campaign pointed to poor housing conditions and the sectarian discrimination in housing administration. Proceedings were initiated when a young Stormont MP, Austin Currie, illegally occupied a council house to highlight inconsistencies in the allocation of homes, in what is now infamously known as the *Caledon incident* (Brett 1986). Subsequent to this incident, the reform of housing began, and after a series of discussions between the governments of the United Kingdom and Northern Ireland, a Joint Declaration of Principles was issued, which laid the foundation for an overhaul of many important public services (NIHE 1991). As a result, in 1971 housing was transferred from local government control to that of an entirely new single-purpose agency, the Northern Ireland Housing Executive (NIHE).

Since its inception, NIHE has built over 90 000 homes, mainly within the Belfast urban area. These homes have been accredited as being, in the main, of exceptional quality, and they make a significant contribution to the urban renewal of the city. Most significantly, however, NIHE has allocated around 300 000 homes under its Housing Selection Scheme, which ensures that those in need of accommodation are always first to receive it (NIHE 1998). The Housing Executive has never been found guilty of sectarian discrimination, and has been effectively recognised as removing religion, as far as it is possible to do so in Northern Ireland, from the housing sphere.

Urban regeneration

Given the high levels of deprivation and broad economic difficulties of the city, urban regeneration has had a high profile within Belfast over the last 25 years. Adair *et al.* (1996) suggest that, initially, regeneration programmes paralleled initiatives in England and Wales in being property led, and focused primarily on the city centre. However, a hybrid approach has emerged to meet the specific problems of Northern Ireland, as the free-market approach was blended with the need to maintain levels of public spending in a highly dependent economy. (See Fig. 5.3.)

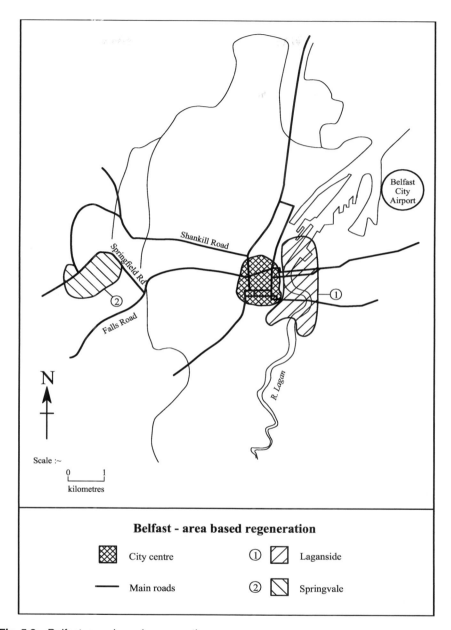

Belfast - area based regeneration

City centre ① Laganside

Main roads ② Springvale

Fig. 5.3 Belfast: area-based regeneration.

In the last decade regeneration policy, as elsewhere in the UK, has become increasingly based on partnership arrangements and geared to securing EU finances. The partnership approach has helped to integrate voluntary and community organisations with the private sector, to give the perception that policy is locally driven, essential if the city's distinctive problems are to be addressed. This is particularly important given the strength of the strong community sector, which emerged from the mid-1970s onwards, as state legitimacy broke down in many areas of the city and residents organised many of the local services for themselves. Today the Northern Ireland Council for Voluntary Action estimates that the region has 5500 voluntary organisations, community groups and charitable bodies – roughly one organisation for every 270 residents. With many of these groups concentrated in the most deprived neighbourhoods of Belfast, this community infrastructure can hopefully be used as a major asset in building a new future for the city. Regeneration activity in Belfast is focused around a number of high-profile initiatives, which are now discussed.

Laganside

Established in 1989, the Laganside Corporation has responsibility for the regeneration of 200 ha of land along the River Lagan in the centre of Belfast. Based on the model of the urban development corporations (UDCs) in other parts of the UK, Laganside has taken a property-led approach to regeneration, focusing mainly on:

- major infrastructure projects, such as the Lagan Weir (opened in 1993 at a cost of £14 million);

- marketing and image promotion (see Fitzsimons 1995);

- securing of development on individual sites.

Unlike most other UDCs, Laganside has never taken on the development control functions of the area, and whereas the last of the UDCs were wound up in 1998, it is expected to continue until 2004 – a situation unlikely to be challenged by the Assembly. Successes have included the flagship development on the Laganbank site, which encompasses the Waterfront Hall, the Belfast Hilton, and major office development such as a new Northern Ireland office for BT. A £95 million science and entertainments centre, the Odyssey Complex, part funded by the Millennium Commission, has just been completed. Attention is now increasingly being focused on the promotion of a cultural quarter around St Ann's Cathedral in an area taken in by an extension of the Corporation's boundary in 1997. Initial estimates were that Laganside would create 2000–3000 jobs, but the Corporation now estimates that, by April 2001, temporary employment of 14 000 man-years had been generated (mostly in construction), while permanent positions increased by 9000. (See Figs 5.4 and 5.5.)

Fig. 5.4 Belfast: an aerial view of Laganside and the port.

Fig. 5.5 Belfast: new apartments in Laganside.

The Springvale Initiative

In contrast to the approach adopted by the Laganside Corporation is the Springvale Initiative, a comprehensive development scheme based in some of the city's most deprived wards in the inner city in west and north Belfast, straddling both communities in an area of intense conflict. The Springvale Initiative was launched in April 1990, with the Development Scheme published in September 1991. Funding has amounted to £28 million (1991–2000) for activities covering environmental improvements and the development of a new business park, currently employing 438 people. Proposals for a new £10 million educational campus (with $5 million coming from US government) were announced as part of the package of government investment following the signing of the Good Friday Agreement.

Making Belfast Work

A further public sector regeneration initiative is Making Belfast Work (MBW), launched in 1988, following the Thatcher government's reborn interest in the inner city. MBW covers the city's 32 most deprived wards, with a brief to stimulate economic development, increase secure employment opportunities, and improve the quality of life for residents. It carries out these tasks through the funding of specific projects and coordinating the activities of central government departments. With an annual budget of £25 million, it has been relatively successful in meeting its objectives (Deloitte & Touche 1997), although previous evaluations have made criticisms in terms of its ability to coordinate government departments and the way it has involved local communities (Birrell & Wilson 1993). Since 1995 MBW has been instrumental in establishing six inter-sector local area partnerships in Belfast, creating more accountable structures, and enabling stronger community links for the implementation of regeneration projects.

The evolution of all these organisations has been dominated by the management of the sectarian conflict and the particularly pessimistic economic climate in the city. However, with the emergence of a credible peace process over the last five years, the prospects of Belfast have undergone a major re-evaluation and with it have emerged catalysts for the regeneration of the city.

Economic growth

There is much speculation as to the economic benefits of the peace process (for example see Bew *et al.* 1997), although it is broadly agreed that a more stable economic climate has facilitated and will continue to contribute to increased inward investment, improvements in local capacity, and better integration with the world economy (Gorecki 1995). Improved local governance will provide a more sustainable basis for economic policy, and savings from security spending (estimated at £530 million by Bew *et al.* 1997) will allow for public funding to be diverted to areas of deprivation. Following the impressive performance of the Republic of Ireland, long-term peace is expected to result in an increased tourist market that could generate 11 000 new jobs in Northern Ireland, with a further 7500 arising from new transnationals coming to the region (KPMG *et al.* 1995). Bew *et al.* (1997) suggest that the total private sector jobs created by the private sector would be 20 000–25 000, which needs to be offset by employment losses resulting from the winding down of security-related activity (perhaps a loss of 17 000 jobs). Therefore the peace process could result in 5000–7000 new jobs across the region.

In the wake of the Good Friday Agreement, the British government announced a £315 million economic package to build a *framework for prosperity* for a peaceful Northern Ireland. This was earmarked for increased road building, initiatives for the long-term unemployed and disabled, tax breaks for capital investment in industry, and investment in education. This underpins improved commercial confidence in the Belfast economy, which is now resulting in major private sector investment to supplement the traditionally public-sector-dominated economy. An example is the major British retailers who have only invested in the region over the last six years. During this time they have established a series of out-of-town complexes on the edge of Belfast that have had a major impact on existing town centres and patterns of car use. The economic optimism in the city is further highlighted by the growth in house prices, which traditionally have been much lower than those in the rest of the UK, but which since 1990 have increased by 7% per annum (DoE (NI) 1997), while nationally prices fell by 8%. Since 1997 the more prestigious locations located in the south of the city, such as the Malone and Stranmillis, have experienced a boom, with prices increasing at 30% per annum (Northern Ireland Property Market Analysis Project). It is anticipated that prices will continue to rise in the city over the next few years, albeit at a slightly reduced rate (RICS 1999).

The cessation of violence has provided major but less tangible benefits to the quality of life in Belfast as the city slowly regains the semblance of normality. The major security presence in the shape of army patrols and road blocks has almost all now been removed, permitting much greater freedom of movement, and this has lifted the psychological strain of living in a city under siege. In its turn this is slowly encouraging an urban culture with a greater level of investment in bars and nightclubs as people are once again venturing to the city centre in search of a good time in the evening.

Conclusion

Belfast is a city with more than its fair share of problems. De-industrialisation, peripherality, acute urban deprivation, bitter sectarian division and violent political conflict have compounded each other to produce a degraded urban society. Some of these issues are slowly beginning to be addressed. Some of the city's difficulties, such as marginality to the European core, can never be entirely overcome, and the wounds caused by the political conflict will take generations to heal. However, a new civil society is gradually emerging to help democratise and stabilise the governance of the city, and the private sector has not been slow to spot some of the opportunities of a society rebuilding itself. Little by little, things are indeed improving; Belfast is slowly getting better.

6

Lille: from Textile Giant to Tertiary Turbine

Charles Fraser and Thierry Baert

In their comprehensive review of the evolution of Lille, Paris & Stevens (2000) point to the fact that Lille is one of a very few cities that have no major river location as the root of their foundations. However, the derivation of its name, L'Isle en Flandres, indicates that it was situated on dry land among the marshes and waterways where the drier land of Artois met the low-lying Flemish plain and the tributaries of the Scheldt/Escaut such as the Deule and Lys. Its location at the very highest point of access from the sea on this network of waterways gave it an importance as a transhipment point for trade from the Low Countries into France. Even today it is the second largest river port in France.

The settlement of L'Isle-en Flandres was first noted in the ninth century, and it survived the turmoil of the Dark Ages and Viking raids to emerge as an important trading centre by the early Middle Ages. In the fourteenth century it had a population of some 40 000, which remained stable until the seventeenth century. At that time it was not the supreme city of southern Flanders that it is today. Although one of the seven major cities of Flanders it was overshadowed as a trading city by the great ports, as they were then, of Bruges, Ghent and Antwerp, as an administrative centre by Brussels, and as an ecclesiastical centre by the then French city of Tournai, location of the most prestigious cathedral in the region. To the south lay the emerging state of France with its major northern centres of Douai and Arras. Lille was therefore by its location a frontier town, changing its political allegiance from Burgundy to Flanders and to France and back again on several occasions. Its place as a city in France was finally settled with the signing of the Treaty of Aix-la-Chapelle in 1668, but it has retained – particularly in the architecture of its historic core and the 'ethnic' mix of its early population – its Flemish character.

After its capture by France in 1668 it began to expand northwards through the construction of the extension to Vieux Lille, an area of grand houses for the nobility – *hôtels* in French – to the new citadel constructed by Vauban. The fortifications were, however, not sufficient to withstand the armies of Marlborough in the War of the Spanish Succession, and much was reduced to ruin. Recaptured, Lille was finally ceded to France by the Treaty of Utrecht in 1713.

The eighteenth century saw steady growth, until by 1800 Lille had a population of around 52 000, and with two satellite towns of Roubaix (8000) and Tourcoing (12 000) it began to emerge as the centre of a textile manufacturing industry based on linen and wool as well as an important trading centre on the waterways of the tributaries of the Escaut. This growth was, however, slow compared with that achieved by the more economically 'liberal' climate of the United Kingdom. However, although the Revolution removed the remaining restrictive practices built up by the monarchy, guilds and corporations, neither Lille nor its adjacent towns of Roubaix and Tourcoing were dominated by these, and a much freer system of local capitalism led by merchant and manufacturing families was in place when the Industrial Revolution penetrated France. This family tradition persists today in companies such as Auchan and Hildar. They thus developed more quickly than other French centres, fed by a growing proletarian rather than peasant workforce, derived mainly from Flanders rather than France, and injections of investment from Paris and the Flemish cities. Importantly this process extended to the coalfield to the south, which provided the necessary energy source. Equally its growth was enhanced by the improvement of riverine and canal access to the ports of Flanders, Ghent and Antwerp. This access to overseas trade enabled the city to import cotton, which soon displaced linen and wool as the main textile product, and gave a boost to the endemic lace industry in industrial subcentres such as Armentieres. A secondary industrial focus was on industries serving the agricultural hinterland both in France and in Belgium. Metalworking was not a speciality of the Lille urban complex but again it could derive its needs from the new steel towns of the eastern coalfield in Valenciennes and from the Belgian centres such as Charleroi.

Thus by the end of the nineteenth century an industrial complex on a par with those of Britain and Germany had emerged; indeed the Lille area was the second largest textile region in the world after Manchester and south Lancashire. The population of the city of Lille had grown to 216 000, that of Roubaix to 124 000 and that of Tourcoing to 73 000 – an emerging urban complex of around 500 000 people.

The growth produced wealth, and the development of fine commercial areas and residential suburbs in adjoining communes, but also poverty and degrading urban conditions in others. The industrial city of Lille expanded mainly to the south-west in a mix of factories, mills and housing into the new suburbs of Wazemmes and Moulin. A feature of this urbanisation was the creation of *courées*, narrow pedestrian lanes with back-to-back houses and perhaps water and toilet facilities for the entire lane. A few remain as a relic of this era.

The city reached its apogee just before the First World War, during which it was occupied by the German army and suffered enormous deprivation. It never recovered its drive in the 1920s, and like many other industrial areas experienced recession and unemployment after the economic collapse of 1929. It did recover enough to maintain its position as the main industrial city of provincial France. Paradoxically, as its wealth grew through the period before the First World War, and to a lesser extent after, it began to experience the process of suburbanisation and the growth of middle-class suburbs between Lille and Roubaix/Tourcoing in communes such as La Madelaine and Mons en Bareouil.

Decline and the seeds of renewal

After the Second World War, although a measure of prosperity returned to the Lille conurbation, the traditional family business structure began to ossify, and there was a lack of investment and dynamism as there appeared to be no urgency to restructure or change an age-old pattern of industrial management undisturbed by the war. Gentle decline set in. This put the conurbation at odds with the emerging strategies of the post-war government, which was determined to assure France a place among the major industrial and technological nations of the world. During the period from 1945 to the late 1960s Lille was shaped by several major and often contradictory economic social and spatial processes:

- social and physical decay of its older industrial areas, and the decline of its traditional industries;

- spatial spread of the city to eat up land between its major urban centres and across the border into Belgium;

- redefinition of the role of the Lille urban area in France as a whole as a constituent of the national planning *aménagement du territoire* process.

The main problem in this case was that the Lille area was considered peripheral to the country and as remote from its cultural heart as the mountains of the Pyrenees. It may seem unbelievable now but *peripherality* was a major problem. The incipient decline that had set in just before the Second World War reasserted itself in the 1950s and 1960s in the textile industry in particular. However, this decline was part of a general decline in the entire Nord region's fortunes as the coal industry to the south and the steel complex in Valenciennes also declined rapidly. The decline in these traditional industries speeded up after 1970, and was particularly evident in that decade. In all, Paris & Stevens (2000) estimate that the Lille conurbation lost 130 000 jobs in textiles between 1945 and 1996. This was accompanied by huge losses in the agricultural and related sectors – some 164 000 jobs – which had a knock-on effect on the service sector in large parts of the region and in the conurbation itself. The coal industry declined from a labour force of 90 000 to nil in the early 1990s, and there were significant losses in chemicals (8000 jobs) and in metalworking (7000 jobs).

The physical manifestation of this process could be seen in the abandonment of textile factories throughout the older industrial area of the conurbation. This was allied to the accelerating decay of much of the older housing. However, unlike British cities undergoing 'slum clearance' under the 1957 Housing Act, the new workers' housing tended to be built on the periphery of the urban areas as well as in a few cleared older sites. Thus the three main centres came to acquire their own versions of the *Grandes Ensembles*, so typical of the French urban process at this time. What began to appear was a city and towns with decaying hearts. In each case this impacted on the other sectors of the inner city. Both the medieval and the seventeenth century parts of Vieux Lille were equally abandoned, and full of empty and decaying property. The main shopping and commercial core of the city was stagnant and unattractive, increasingly swamped by traffic and marked by some tasteless and scattered rebuilding, such as is found in the St Sauveur area to the south and west of the Gare Flandres.

This inner decay was accelerated by the continuing suburbanisation process that saw the spatial extent of the city increase. New construction tended to infill between Lille and the Roubaix–Tourcoing poles, and spread to the periphery of the conurbation. With it went the new shopping centres and commercial construction that increasingly relied on the car for their accessibility. To add to the physical decay of the core areas an equally unpleasant and chaotic urban structure began to form around the suburban periphery, which began to extend across the border to the Mouscron urban area of Belgium. These problems were exacerbated by the increase in migration of workers to the textile industry from North Africa, taking low-paid jobs in these declining industries. The new migrants settled in the poorer areas and posed a challenge to the local services trying to integrate them socially and culturally into French society.

A changing image in the Nord

The moves that began to reverse this process were in part planned and in part 'natural', but from the late 1960s the beginnings of a reversal of this process of decline and decay had begun. The first step came from the central government in the late 1960s. As part of the normal state planning process that includes the planning of its territory spatially, *aménagement du territoire*, the government set in motion its strategy to divert growth away from the Paris region to other centres in France, and to structure that growth both in the Paris region and in other centres. Thus the strategy of *Métropoles d'Equilibre* set out the plan for the diversion of state investment both to provincial city regions and within them. The bulk of the cities selected for Métropoles d'Equilibre status were those exhibiting signs of rapid development of the new service and technological industries, such as Grenoble and Strasbourg. Therefore Lille was an exception. Its choice was a reflection of a perceived need to invest in the renewal of the Nord region and, at the same time, a recognition of its geographic position between Paris and the major centres of growth in neighbouring European countries. (See Fig. 6.1.)

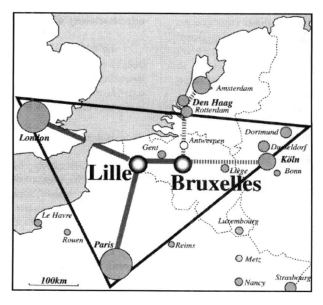

Fig. 6.1   Lille in its European context. Source: Lille after Euralille.

The local manifestation of this planning process was the designation of the new town of Lille Est, later Villeneuve d'Ascq, to act as a growth pole to attract new industries with a scientific base to the region and hence help to solve the local problems of unemployment and economic decline. However, the founding of Villeneuve d'Ascq only increased the centripetal forces operating in the region by pulling more activity away from the city core areas. A significant aspect of the plan was the specific objective of relocating various, particularly scientific, faculties of the University of Lille in the New Town to give a basis for the growth of related scientific industries, such as research and development companies. The concept was unashamedly modelled on the American university/business complex model. The result was that many buildings and sectors of inner Lille were further abandoned as almost the entire university regrouped in Villeneuve, in the *Cité Scientifique*, taking with it the staff and the students who had been part of the city's population. The effect of this was to a certain extent mitigated by the fact that the numbers of students in higher education increased dramatically in this period, and in time even those faculties left in town replaced their numbers. In all the numbers in tertiary education in the region have grown from a mere 6000 in 1946 to 145 000 in 1996 (Paris & Stevens 2000). Allied to this growth in student numbers is an additional growth in the itinerant services and research staff.

This public sector initiative did strike a chord with the private sector as it too realised the assets that the region possessed in terms of a potentially educated labour force and a location at the heart of the west European industrial area. The revival was assisted by forces that were derived from the city itself and its history as a Flemish city. The region had a long tradition of social reform derived from the tradition of social catholicism, a dominant theme in Belgian social policy, and this was marked by a degree of cooperation between private and public interests who put the city first, ahead of sectoral interests. The manifestation of this today is the existence of the *Comité Grande Lille*, a body of some 300 people representing a cross-section of Lille society, business and administration that meets every two months to discuss issues of current importance. It is no accident that the French Socialist Party was created in the city. There was thus a multifaceted series of changes to the character of the region as several parallel processes brought a new environment to the Nord and to Lille in particular.

Economic restructuring

Compared with the strenuous efforts needed to attract industry to the peripheral regions of the UK, the exercise in renewing the Nord's industrial base was more straightforward. Industries such as glass, plastics, automobiles and printing laid the base for a new industrial culture, augmented by the addition of over 400 000 new jobs in the tertiary sector alone between 1946 and 1996. A particular speciality has been the concentration of the mail order business in Roubaix, based on large companies with a national market, such as La Redoute. However, this was only a beginning, as other more recent developments have brought in a range of high-tech and tertiary industries, and have seen the continued expansion of the *métropole* as a postmodern economic centre. The key factor was the realisation that while the Lille *métropole* may have been peripheral in France, unlike other French urban areas such as Bordeaux, Toulouse and Nantes, it was in a highly favoured location in relation to the major economic regions of north-west Europe.

The Channel Tunnel

This initial planning exercise did take into account the geographic position of Lille in relation to the neighbouring European complexes, but it was essentially a national planning process. What sealed the regeneration not only of Lille itself, but also of the other centres in the conurbation and of the Nord region as a whole, was the elevation of the planning process to a specifically European level based on the construction of the Channel Tunnel, its related TGV links, and the tapping of the new benefits that were perceived as likely to flow from this infrastructural improvement.

The process began as far back as 1982, when the then French and British prime ministers, Pierre Mauroy and Margaret Thatcher, agreed to begin the construction of the Channel Tunnel. The treaty was finally signed in 1986, and the following year – after hard lobbying by the Nord region and Lille authorities – it was agreed that the link from London and Brussels to Paris should pass through Lille instead of across country. The next step was the setting up of the mechanisms to construct a new station in Lille and to capitalise on the benefits of the new link. In 1990 the *Societé d'Économie Mixte Euralille* was created, with Jean Paul Baietto as manager. From then on the rail links by TGV from Lille were gradually extended first to Paris and eventually to the rest of the network, enabling passengers to travel direct to virtually every other major French city. In 1994 the links to London and Brussels were opened and this, allied to the ability to change trains in Lille to catch TGVs to other parts of France, especially the South, meant that Lille once again resumed its historic position as the interchange town between Flanders and north-west Europe and France (Simon 1993).

Administrative reform

In 1968 administrative reforms in the French state introduced the concept of *communautés urbains*. In the case of Lille a *communauté* of 86 communes was created and a *Schéma Directeur* for the metropolitan area produced. However, this was as far as it went for some 20 years until 1989, when the *communauté* was revamped and the new *Agence d'Urbanisme et Aménagement du Territoire* was created. This set about capitalising on the incipient advantages of the city and its region, driving its economic and physical restructuring forwards. The influence of the *communauté* was further extended in 1998 as the new Schéma Directeur was extended to encompass the entire Arrondissement de Lille, a subdivision of the Département du Nord. Historic interaction with the Belgian communes, in Wallonie and Flanders across the border, has created a trans-frontier metropolis.

However, this administrative entity is only part of the total administrative structure within which the planning and especially the budgeting for the *métropole* and its regeneration takes place. Two central government bodies have an input: the national government, through various *directions régionales*, and the Département du Nord with its new powers and elected assembly, the Conseil Generale. Also, while the *communauté* and the new *arrondissement* are the creatures of its constituent communes and their elected representatives, there is also a powerful elected body in the Conseil Régionale du Nord-Pas de Calais. The relationship of these to one another and to the *implementation* agency created to deliver the strategy as part of a national directive in 1990, L'Agence de Développement et d'Urbanisme du Lille Métropole, is shown in Fig. 6.2.

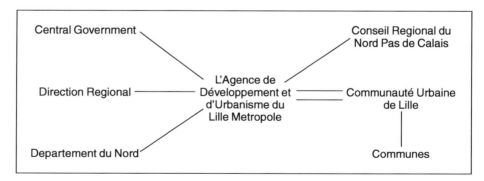

Fig. 6.2   Relationship of main regeneration agencies in the Lille Metropole.

This might seem an unwieldy structure for the planning of such a large area, but since there is clear definition of the responsibilities – the *compétences* – of each agency, conflict occurs but is manageable. More significantly, the structure gives the context for the financial planning of the various programmes, including that for the regeneration of the *métropole*. These governmental agencies and the State bank, the Caisse des Dépôts et Consignations, form the forum that agrees the Contrat de Plan and the Contrat de Ville for the metropolitan region, the *Contrat d'Agglomeration*. The physical plans set out in the Schema are thereby integrated with the financial plans of the public sector. A final important part of the jigsaw is the ability of the Agence to interact with all agencies, private and public in the metropolitan region, and to bring together the necessary ingredients to ensure the delivery of a project as conceived by the various contributors to it. Thus land, management structures and finance are all coordinated by them in an implementation process that is integrated with the spatial plan for the *métropole*.

The spatial planning context

The *communauté* has been the spatial entity for strategic planning, and the initial Schéma Directeur drawn up after its creation has recently been brought up to date: the new Schéma, *Lille Métropole en 2015,* was published in 1998. The strategy for the regeneration of the older industrial heart of the *métropole* is an integral part of the Schéma. From the outset in the first stage the areas to be regenerated are identified, *les quartiers défavorisées*, mainly in the south of the city of Lille and in the centres of Roubaix and Tourcoing. These are the areas where the major regeneration projects and the new Ville Renouvelée strategy are focused.

A major influence on the recovery of the Lille area has of course been the quality of the political and technical leadership that has worked for the *métropole* over the 25 years of its restructuring. Of particular importance has been the role of Pierre Mauroy, who has dominated the politics of the region throughout this time. As Prime Minister he was responsible for pushing for the construction of the Channel Tunnel, and as Mayor of Lille he pushed for the city to grasp the fruits of this link into the new European transport network. By doing so he had the vision to see that Lille could rediscover its historic place as the linking economic area between Britain, France and the Low Countries.

The development results

The sum of this dramatic alteration in the perception and image of Lille has resulted in several major projects that have provided the foci for lesser and more private projects to continue the process of the regeneration of the metropolitan area. (See Fig. 6.3.)

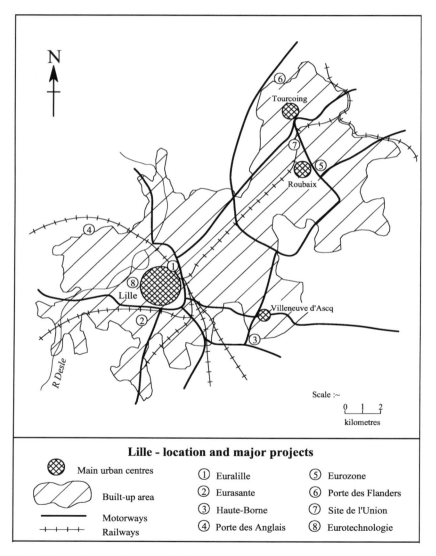

Fig. 6.3   Lille: location and major projects.

Vieux Lille

Under the direction of the national conservation agency, *Bâtiments de France*, the Vieux Lille area was declared a *secteur sauvegardé* under the 1968 Malraux Act, and from then on every effort was put into turning the fortunes of this historic area around. Certain key buildings, spaces and streets were selected for public investment, and assistance was given to the private sector to renovate property. The need was to restore business confidence in the area and to encourage resettlement of a varied population in an area that had become synonymous with squatters and down-and-outs. Several key in-fill sites have been used for social 'HLM' housing in a style that blended with the historic character of the area. The incongruous Palais de Justice built in the 1960s gives a fearful portent of what might have happened to the entire area without the conservation initiative. Major historic buildings such as the Hospice Comptèsse have been restored to their former glory, and even Lille's unfinished Cathédrale de La Treille has been completed.

Euralille

The details of the Euralille redevelopment will be outlined as one of the particular case studies, but in this general context it is noteworthy that the improvement of the stations area and Vieux Lille was the catalyst to the improvement of the main commercial streets that lie between them. Thus the Rue de Bethune and some links to the main square have been pedestrianised. The Grand Place has been transformed from a giant parking lot to one of the most lively and attractive squares in any French city, with its surrounding Flemish-style buildings and the restored seventeenth century Bourse. To the west the links have penetrated to the more formal avenues of the Boulevard de la Liberté and the Place de la République. The Palais des Beaux Arts, for so long a dull place to look at or visit, has been refurbished and is now one of France's major galleries outside Paris.

As to Euralille itself, it is a common mistake to assume that the shopping centre and TGV station, Lille Europe, are all there is to it, but as will be demonstrated it encompasses much more, and its development continues.

La Site de l'Union

This is one of the most recent sites for regeneration in the Roubaix 'Grand Projet Urbain' complex, and is described below in the Roubaix case study.

Euratechnologie

This is a technology centre project that forms part of a much bigger urban regeneration project along the banks of the river Deule. It is a site of some 40 ha of wasteland and classic industrial brownfield sites near the city centre. The aim is to attract companies from the new technology sector to the city.

The Haute Borne

This is a project for a science park on a 130 ha site adjacent to the University of Lille 1 in Villeneuve d'Ascq; it is a further development of the original plan for the area to create a modern *technopole* in the Nord region.

Eurasante

Based on the large concentration of the region's health facilities in the city – the Pasteur Institute, the Centre Hospitalier Régional (CHR), Inserm, and the medical and pharmaceutical faculties of the University – this is an economic development project that will help to give companies access to the health market. The 240 ha site has seven hospitals, three faculties, and several industrial and commercial companies working in the health field.

These projects are all now integrated into the Ville Renouvelée strategy of the metropolitan region and administered by a department of the Communauté Urbain. The strategy is both a *métropole*-wide plan to spread development throughout the urban area and a series of specific projects designed to deliver it. It draws together all aspects of regeneration such as housing policy, environmental, social and economic policies, as well as infrastructure projects and the design approaches. This is precisely the integrated approach that has been initiated in England in the Urban Policy White Paper *Our Towns and Cities: the Future*. A major factor in the success of the strategy has been the development of the *métropole*'s public transport system. The key feature of this is the development of the fully automated metro, the *VAL*. Begun in 1983, it has now been extended to the cities of Roubaix and Tourcoing and other suburban areas, and there are proposals to extend it further to connect across the border to the Belgian town of Mouscron. It is supported by improvements to the nineteenth century tramway that connects the main station, Lille Flandres, with Roubaix and Tourcoing, and by an extensive bus system.

An international profile

Other efforts to raise the profile of the city have included the bid by the city to host the 2004 Olympic Games. It was a matter of considerable local pride when Lille was chosen as France's bid city for the games. Although it did not succeed, the attempt has spurred the city to set in motion plans to improve its sporting and visitor facilities to capitalise on its new image and location. An interesting side issue is that with the emergence of the *métropole* in the French hierarchy, so too has its football team, *LOSC*, risen to be not only a French but a European team of some significance. Unfortunately its stadium is outdated, and located in the grounds around the Citadelle built by Vauban close to the central area. It is perhaps the only team in western Europe located on public grounds and sponsored by the regional council! A new stadium and sports facilities are indicated as a need in the future.

Lille will also be the European City of Culture in 2004, and this can be soundly based on the major improvements to the Palais des Beaux Arts, in the Place de la République, which is now a gallery of national standing. A strategy to stage exhibitions brought from the major centres in Paris means that these can be made available to a wider public, particularly the British, who can include them in visits via the Channel Tunnel to Lille. Visitors from Belgium and the Netherlands can also take advantage of the improved TGV service to Brussels, now only 35 minutes away. Further internationalisation of the city's role is being cultivated, and the possibility of a joint Lille–Brussels airport is just one of the imaginative ideas being mooted. Such a facility would be a mere 20 minutes from the centres of both cities, much closer than Charles de Gaulle airport in Paris, which is one hour away. A formal agreement exists between the two cities in order to further cooperation in fields such as the economy, research, culture, tourism and sport. This would enhance the dynamism of the region of Flanders/Brussels/Nord located between the big four European regions of South East England, the Paris basin, Randstad and the Rhine/Ruhr area.

Notwithstanding these mega projects and the thinking on a continental scale the city also has to address much more acute local problem areas within its boundaries. A major programme of housing renovation is proposed in its older areas, and in the Grands Ensembles, such as Lille Sud, and in central Roubaix. These are areas where migrants, especially from North Africa, have concentrated, and where social ills and unemployment are major issues. Social 'solidarity' is as important in the strategy as TGV links and cultural development. The improvement of the environment in the entire region has also vastly improved the amenities for its inhabitants. From the creation of the regional parks to detailed design schemes to improve the waterways such as the Deule and the main canals through the city, a vast programme of 'green' projects has begun to change the appearance of the *métropole* from an industrial one to an environmentally conscious one.

Case studies

From the many examples of regeneration initiatives cited above two have been selected to be described in more detail, as they not only represent the flagship projects in the metropolitan region but also demonstrate how the French approach to regeneration has evolved over the last 10–15 years.

Euralille: La Turbine Tertiere (Figs 6.4–6.6)

When Pierre Mauroy secured the Eurostar link through Lille he saw the feat as the creation of much more than a station between two major cities. The station would be only the first step in the regeneration of a vast area to the east of Lille city centre and the focus for the development of what he called a *tertiary turbine* to drive the city's economy forward into the post-industrial era. To begin with, a new line into the city had to be created, driving into the gap between the city of Lille and neighbouring areas such as La Madeleine and Fives. This area had railway lines entering from the south, but a through route was driven round the north of the city from the west and joining the

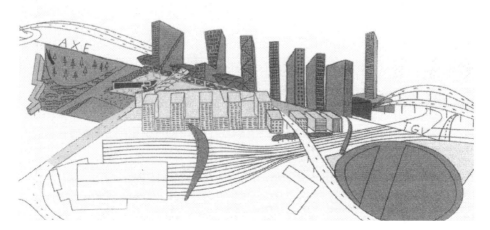

Fig. 6.4 Euralille: the concept of Rem Koolhaas. Source: Project Urban No. 20 Lille-Roubaix.

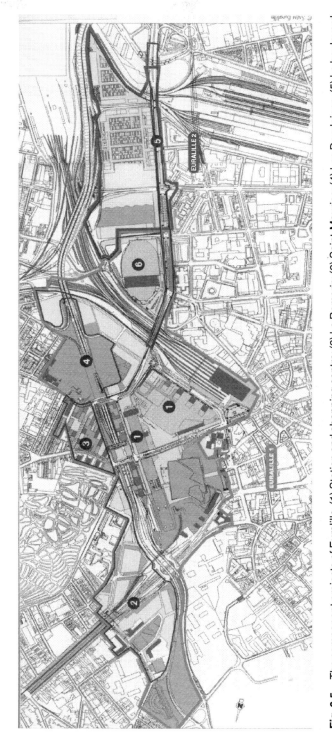

Fig. 6.5 The component projects of Euralille. (1) Station and shopping centre; (2) Le Romarin; (3) Saint-Maurice; (4) Les Dondaines; (5) Le boulevard urbain; (6) Nord-Expo. Source: Project urbain No. 20 Lille-Roubaix.

Fig. 6.6   Euralille: view.

TGV track to the south of the existing rail yards. The natural gap in the urban fabric lies along this line, the line of the old ramparts of the city that had become composed mainly of redundant railway yards and some former industrial land. In this area a site of some 73 ha was designated as the site of the first phase of the construction. The designing of the new complex was entrusted to the Dutch architect Rem Koolhaus, who brought a startlingly modern architecture to weld onto the Flemish and more conservative French character of the old city. The Euralille shopping centre, the station and the office complex with its famous 'ski-boot' are now the recognisable symbols of the new Lille.

The first phase, which is still only partly complete, centres on the new Euralille Station that links the city and the region first to Paris, London, Brussels and then beyond that to the rest of France, Belgium, the Netherlands and Germany. Above it is the main office complex, the Credit Lyonnais 'ski-boot' tower, and other office structures, and across the paved open area is the shopping centre with further offices. To the north between the Euralille complex and the emerging Romarin complex in the adjacent commune, La Madeleine, is a landscaped park. Not part of the scheme, but certainly a result of the stimulus it has given to this corner, are new offices facing

Lille Flandres Station and the renovated Caserne Souham building, which is a small congress centre used for educational purposes. To the south lies the Lille Grand-Palais exhibition centre, once detached from the rest of the city and its underground station by the peripheral motorway, but now integrated into the city as the motorway has been moved to the east of it. Under construction at the time of writing are two further office and commercial projects, St Maurice and Le Romarin. The St Maurice complex is linked closely to the station area and is a cluster of lower-level, three- to six-storey office blocks that again perform a linking function into the existing urban fabric. There is a heavy emphasis on a greener image to this area, linking it to the park area via the cemetery and the open areas around the Communauté Urbain's headquarters on the edge of La Madeleine.

The Romarin area is not in Lille but in La Madeleine, but as the entire complex is a metropolitan focus the cooperation between the two communes to integrate it into the Euralille project has been achieved without difficulty. The development will be built on both sides of the Grand Boulevard, which runs from Lille to Roubaix and forms the main axis of La Madeleine. The project will also vastly improve the infrastructure network, which at present tends to divide the area, and will not only integrate it to the Euralille focus but also to the west will improve the links to Vieux Lille and the main city centre. Green spaces and parkland will continue the green surrounding environment from St Maurice and the main park. Two other sections of the entire complex to the south of the station will complete the scheme as envisaged, but provide an *entrée* to further southerly development. The first is the second park area, Les Dondaines, partly over and partly flanking the rerouted *autoroute* to Roubaix, Tourcoing and Ghent. This will be a very formal structure of classic French design. The second and most southerly development will be the Nord Expo complex. This will continue the exhibition theme of the Grand Palais with spaces for other expositions, perhaps Lille's famous 'Braderie', and more ephemeral events. A central feature will be a new centralised administrative complex for the Nord regional government. Again the dominant atmosphere will be green, with interlinking parks and amenity spaces. The re-routeing of the main Lille–Roubaix motorway to the east of the site has meant that the existing road would be redundant. However, as part of the redesign of the area this is being turned into a tree-lined boulevard that will link the Euralille complex and the parks to the south.

As has been remarked, even then the entire regeneration process is unlikely to be complete. As part of its submission for the Olympic Games, the *métropole*, city and region envisaged the use of the continuous area of unused and derelict land that continues to stretch south to the main motorway links across the south of the city. Included in this is the redundant St Sauveur railway goods yard, which lie on a north-west to south-east axis from the Nord Expo area back into the city centre close to the Mairie. Its potential is being explored, and it may become a second regional railway station to ease overcrowding at Lille Flandres. The remaining lands provide much scope for further imaginative planning.

Euralille is perhaps one of the largest and most stimulating projects in contemporary western Europe, but how has it been achieved? What are the factors that have made it a success? To begin with, in all the literature and information gathered on the project there is little mention of a land problem. This is because there was none. Virtually all the land has been in public ownership for some time. The main source has been the land that has always been public, as it comprised the ancient ramparts and walls of the city. In the case of Lille these were not decommissioned until 1919, but they have given the city a land bank that came into its own when there was a need to drive the TGV links as close to the city as possible. The second source has been the existing network of roads and railways that have exploited this gap in the urban fabric. Allied to this has been a system of financial planning and financial provision that has ensured stability in the ability of the public authorities to follow through on their plans without depending on the vagaries of the private capital market and its speculative nature. This is based on a series of public sector contracts, from the national *Contrat de Plan* to the local *Contrat d'Agglomeration*, as well as other integrated public sector budgeting schemes. The stability of financing is derived from the existence of a public sector banking system focused on the *Caisse des Dépots et Consignations*. These and a range of other tools have been the basis for the operation of the project, and can also be seen at work in other regeneration projects in France.

From this internationally known example it is instructive to turn to a second and rather different case study in the Lille *métropole*, but one that has a similar result in terms of totally changing the image of the area and the fortunes of its inhabitants: the *Grand Projet Urbain* in Roubaix.

Roubaix: 'miser pour gagner' (Fig. 6.7)

Roubaix is the second city of the Lille *métropole*, with a population of some 100 000. It owed its existence to the textile industry. Like much of western Lille its urban fabric is a mix of housing of mixed quality woven around its now redundant factories. Close to the city centre is one of the largest *grands*

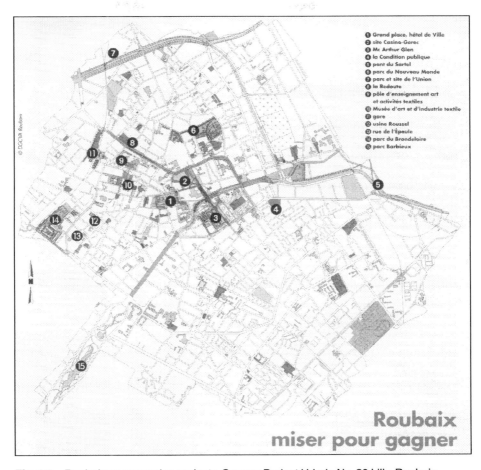

Fig. 6.7   Roubaix: regeneration projects. Source: Project Urbain No. 20 Lille-Roubaix.

ensembles of social housing built in the great post-war boom in France. Overall the city has a social housing total of some 42% of its housing stock. Socially it is a very mixed city with a large immigrant population, the most recent of whom have come from North Africa. Significantly it has an unemployment rate of some 27%. In the mid-1990s it was a city in decline, with an unattractive central area and declining services and shopping facilities. Unlike Lille it is almost peripheral to the rest of the metropolitan area, it is not connected to main rail lines or motorways in the same way, and it was poorly connected to other parts of the metropolitan area. Again, unlike Lille, it does not possess large swathes of public land upon which to base a regeneration strategy.

From such an unpromising situation the new mayor from 1994, M. Rene Vandierendonck, has brought about a remarkable change. How has this been achieved? The strategy can be summed up in the mayor's own words, *miser pour gagner* ('gambling to win'). To begin with, the entire strategy had to depend on what could be done with existing public resources to spark off a virtuous circle of reinvestment by the private sector and to bring the various actors together into an integrated team tackling the problems in a coherent way. The starting point was to improve the image of the city by upgrading those public facilities that had fallen into a degraded state. The first of these was the canal that passes through the city, not far from the centre. However, the canal was more than just a waterway because along its banks were a large proportion of the derelict factory sites that gave the poor image to the city. Tackle the canal and its borders and you begin to tackle the dereliction.

A second thrust, which has now borne fruit, was to improve the transport links both within the city and between it and the other centres in the *métropole*. A main infrastructure link has been that to the centre of Lille, served to begin with by the ancient tramway system from Lille Flandres, picturesque, quaint but hardly efficient. This has been upgraded. It has been added to by the extension of the metro to the centre of the city, reducing the time from Lille to Roubaix to 20 minutes.

Finally, despite its industrial image, Roubaix possesses some buildings of considerable architectural character, most notably the Town Hall, upon which a strategy for the physical redesign of the city could be based. The Town Hall looks onto the main square, which until recently was a parking lot surrounded by shops and other buildings that had been allowed to decay. The improvement of this square was vital to the change of image.

The unfolding strategy was based on public investment in these three major public assets, and as it evolved other initiatives were added that progressively brought in the private sector to capitalise on the potential of other assets in the city. Similar initiatives were undertaken in the neighbouring city of Tourcoing, and in 1998 under central government legislation the area became one of a few *grands projets urbains* designated in key French cities and bringing with it the security of government finance and other support to underpin the efforts of the local agencies. To this three-pronged attack some 14 other projects have been added, and these have wrought a considerable transformation in the character of Roubaix.

While it is invidious to make comparisons with the Euralille example, certain differences and similarities are self-evident. To begin with, the projects in the Roubaix area are scattered and smaller, and are a mixture of public ventures and public/private ventures where local enterprises play a part. Of the public ventures four are new parks or green spaces, something lacking in the densely built-up industrial structure. These are: the Parc du Site de L'Union, the most recent development; the Parc Barbieux, which is part of the continuous upgrade of the main boulevard link to Lille and through which the tramway runs; the Parc Bondeloire, a new creation; and the Parc du Nouveau Monde. Major upgradings and improvements are in train at several other locations: the main station; the Pont du Sartel over the canal, la Condition publique; the Usine Roussel, which now houses the headquarters of the Ballet du Nord and other dance studios; and the Rue d'Epeule.

The remaining five sites are partnerships with private agencies. Two are workshop/museum developments. The Pole d'enseignement Art et Activités Textiles is a workshop/nursery area for the regeneration of the textile industry where new manufacturers for high-quality products will start up. The Musée d'Art et d'Industrie Textile is a museum exhibition space reflecting the area's past textile heritage. Its special character is derived from the fact that it is a conversion of the former art-deco public baths restored to their former glory. The remaining three are essentially commercial ventures. One, Casino-Gerec, is the redevelopment of a site close to the main shopping centre by the Casino retail chain. The second is the revamping of the main headquarters of the La Redoute mail order chain. The last, and by far the most significant introduction, is the McArthur Glen factory outlet retail centre. This adds a new dimension to the retail facilities not only in Roubaix but also in the metropolitan area and its hinterland. The American chain was attracted by the cooperation of the city council, which provided the land for the development on a site adjacent to the city centre. In addition, a huge programme to upgrade the housing – both public and private – in the city has been launched, with a 15-year span.

The entire programme has made an impact on the job situation in the city, and 2500 jobs have been attributed to the *zone franche* (enterprise zone) status of part of the area. There is, however, an ongoing argument as to whether the new jobs are being taken up by the locals who suffer from unemployment or those who commute into work in Roubaix and live in more salubrious suburbs. To date, gentrification of the better housing in the city remains the activity of a few pioneers!

The evolution of French regeneration

Although the differences between the two projects have been shown, the key factor is that they represent two stages in the evolution of the approach to regeneration in France. Not only has the term used changed from *renovation*, with a physical or economic bias, to *renouvellement*, with a much wider scope, but also the process has moved from being one that is publicly led and managed to being a more varied and cooperative process, bringing in private and communal agencies and placing an increasing emphasis on the social and cultural aspects and on the encouragement of innovation and participation. Euralille represents the former, almost Beaux Arts style of planning, whereas the projects in Roubaix represent an altogether more sensitive and accretive approach.

In both, however, the agencies involved draw on the same basic tools and structures that have been developed in France to underpin public enterprise. An often overlooked factor is that in both cities the respective mayors and their staff had the vision to see what could be done and to develop the strategies to deliver it. In both they were backed up by an agency geared to delivery, with the skills to negotiate, coordinate and assure the finance to make things possible, and not to have to wait on that initiative coming from somewhere else.

In certain cases the need to broaden the base for management has led to the creation of management organisations called *SEMs (societé d'économie mixte)*, of which the *Société d'Économie Mixte d'Euralille* is a prime example. These bring in a range of other financial agencies such as the private banks, chambers of commerce and local agencies to an integrated team. They can also call on a range of well-honed planning tools that enable them to intervene in the land market. The main such tool is the use, where necessary, of the *ZAC (zone d'aménagement concerté)*, a process that enables the authorities to delimit an area for action and to apply within it the other tools such as the *Droits de Pre-emption*. This gives the municipality the right of first purchase of any property in the zone when it becomes available. Equally important is the willingness to use compulsory purchase, *expropriation*, where necessary in the public interest.

All of this of course requires money. It is a popular misconception that a combination of higher taxes and greater wealth gives the French state the wherewithal to underwrite this enormous financial investment. The truth is more subtle than that. The bulk of finance comes from the funds of the *Caisse des Depots et Consignations*, particularly its Urban Regeneration

Fund and its system of low-interest loans for major urban projects. This public sector bank was founded in 1816 as a *state* institution, not a *government* institution, and is answerable to the Assemblé Nationale and not to the government, the two being quite different institutions under France's constitution. It derives its funds from mutual sources such as the network of *Caisses d'Épargne* that are now a part of its structure, from the *Credit Foncier* (a formerly private mortgage bank) and from investments such as public sector pension funds. This gives it freedom from dependence on government, stability, and the ability to plan and invest in a long-term strategy linked in to national finance plans such as the Contrat de Plan and the more local Contrat de Ville ou Agglomération. The workings of the bank will be further explored below in Chapter 12 on finance mechanisms. Thus while the detailed practice evolves, the structures to assure delivery of a product and to make real changes remain timelessly constant.

Summary

The two major regeneration efforts in the Lille *métropole* have considerable differences of approach: Euralille is a large and more cohesive project based on the exploitation of large public land holdings, whereas the programme in Roubaix is a collection of different ventures requiring much more in the way of flexible cooperation between many actors, and much more consultation and negotiation. However, they are both based on certain key stable premises.

To begin with, they are both integral parts of the Metropolitan Plan, the new Schéma Directeur of 1997 and the Ville Renouvelée strategy brought in to support it. These are in accord with national strategies derived from some ten years of policy development in the field of regeneration, culminating in the Grands Projets Urbains strategies of 1998 onwards. These have been consistently backed by financial planning mechanisms, which range from the national Contrat de Plan to the local Contrat de Ville, which involve all government levels and policy areas and which are translated into action by the funding mechanisms drawing together national finance from the Caisse des Dépôts et Consignations to local contributions. Clearly the possession of much public land has been a bonus to these efforts, but as in several of the Roubaix examples there is not only a willingness to acquire land if necessary to complete a scheme but also the powers and the financial resources to do this. The actions within the ZAC areas and the use of pre-emption rights in land purchase demonstrate the ability to carry through the delivery of the planned programme.

Equally important has been the existence of powerful political figures who, backed by the Comité Grand Lille, have had a vision of how the Lille conurbation can reinvent itself given its favourable geographic location in the urban fabric of north-west Europe and the tenacity to bring it into being. They have also had the tools and agencies, managed by equally visionary staff, to back them up.

7

Rotterdam: Structural Change and the Port

Chris Couch

In many ways the recent history of urban change in Rotterdam mirrors that of Liverpool. The cities are of similar size, although Rotterdam is significantly more prosperous. Each city is a major port, and although Rotterdam is by far the larger and more successful of the two, both have experienced the effects of the revolution in shipping and port technology. In both cases this has led to the transformation of much of the former dockland areas into a post-industrial landscape of offices, retailing, tourism and leisure uses.

Within the Netherlands, Rotterdam is second only to Amsterdam in terms of size but on many economic indicators is generally considered to lie fourth in the cities of the Randstad (ring city) behind Amsterdam itself, Utrecht and Den Haag. For many years in the Netherlands there has been a concern that, if unchecked, urban sprawl from the Randstad would spill out across the surrounding countryside, especially the 'green heart' within the ring of urbanisation. Since the 1960s national policy has sought to contain overspill in a number of planned compact urban developments. By the 1980s, with growing concern about the flight of investment from inner-city neighbourhoods, the idea of compact urban development took on an additional purpose as the government attempted to promote inner-city regeneration. During the 1990s the desire to promote more sustainable cities by reducing the need for travel provided a further powerful argument for compactness in urban development (Dieleman *et al.* 1999, pp. 608, 609).

Dieleman *et al.* conclude that the policy of compact urban growth has been largely successful in its implementation over recent years. However, they are more pessimistic about the future. They identify three key factors in this success: taxation policy, which remains largely unchanged; and housing and land policies, which have recently experienced substantial change. They argue that deregulation of the housing market with much less state intervention than hitherto is leading to a situation where residential development will tend to follow households' locational preferences, and that these preferences are for lower-density living in the 'green heart'. Further, the deregulation of land policy is claimed to be leading to massive rises in the price of land earmarked for future urban growth, so pushing up the costs of development (Dieleman *et al.* 1999, pp. 618, 619). However, it is possible that these negative arguments underestimate the extent to which the market itself wishes to concentrate development within existing urban areas. The evidence from Rotterdam, below, is that the property industry still has a substantial appetite for investment in prime urban locations. Indeed, changing household structures suggest the possibility of a growing demand for 'living in the city', and the continuing redundancy of urban commercial and industrial floorspace suggests an ongoing supply of brownfield sites in search of development.

One of the effects of pursuing a policy of compact urban development and urban renewal has been to drastically reduce the rate of population decline that had characterised the city in the previous post-war years. Whereas the population fell from 687 000 in 1970 to 579 000 in 1980, it had slightly increased to 579 000 in 1990, and by 2000 had increased still further to over 593 000.

In this chapter three different sectors of urban regeneration policy are considered: first, the renewal of older inner-city neighbourhoods; second, the post-war rebuilding of the city centre and its subsequent continuous enhancement in order to maintain competitiveness; and third, the redevelopment of the former dockland south of the Maas – the Kop van Zuid. By looking at these three very different circumstances it is possible to draw out some interesting issues and aspects of the Dutch approach to urban policy. (See Fig. 7.1.)

Renewing older inner-city neighbourhoods

Ahead of national legislation, in 1974 the city council decided on a major programme of area renewal and environmental improvement throughout much of the inner city. Some 11 urban renewal areas were designated, representing more than 60 000 dwellings or a quarter of the total city. The aims of this programme were to improve housing and environmental standards while retaining the character of neighbourhoods and continuing to provide housing that was affordable by the indigenous population. Although the strategy was determined by the city council centrally, much of the detailed planning and implementation was passed down to project groups working in the renewal

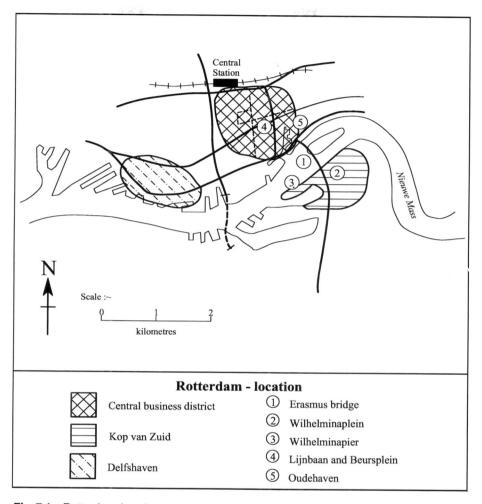

Fig. 7.1 Rotterdam: location.

areas. These groups typically comprised up to 19 people, with the majority of places being taken by community representatives and their expert advisers. The presence of these experts increased the capacity of communities to reach informed judgements on proposals and to engage in meaningful dialogue about alternative solutions. The physical locating of project group meetings within the locality, and the presence of a local majority on the group, were said to have important psychological as well as practical benefits for the participation process (Couch 1990, pp. 110–113).

By 1981 national policy had shifted away from a piecemeal approach to slum clearance and reconstruction towards a coordinated national policy of urban renewal that placed much more emphasis on housing rehabilitation. In 1985 the Urban and Village Renewal Act came into effect. Under this Act urban renewal was seen as including not only housing rehabilitation but also local environmental improvements, traffic management, and amelioration of local social problems (Teule 1998, p. 181). In this the policy reflects the same shift away from clearance and a broadening of intervention beyond the dwelling itself that was emerging in the UK, Germany and elsewhere.

Much was achieved under this housing renewal process. By 1985 more than 36 000 dwellings in Rotterdam had been improved or replaced, and many local environmental improvements had been carried out to high standards of urban design and building specification. However, it has been argued that the success of the programme was of more than local importance in that it offered a significant contribution to planning theory by demonstrating that:

> a major and sustained process of citizen participation in urban renewal can and does work to the benefit of all parties and is not something for city councils to fear but something to embrace as a way of producing better urban renewal. (Couch 1990, p. 113.)

By the 1990s this phase of activity was nearing completion, and the renewal of inner-city areas was becoming less important politically. With many of the worst areas treated, and with gradually rising affluence among the population, the government was looking to reduce its commitment both to housing subsidies and to the urban renewal process. By 1990 a national government evaluation concluded that the urban renewal programme was on schedule. According to Teule:

> After evaluating urban renewal in the past decade, the remaining activities were specified by national government, making clear the finite nature of its financial concern. According to this point of view, urban renewal policies would be finished by the year 2005. (Teule 1999, p. 192.)

But this assessment has been criticised, partly on the basis that the evaluation took inadequate account of changing housing standards, and because it overestimated the rate of housing improvement in the four biggest cities and underestimated the impact of other associated socio-economic and environmental problems in these older neighbourhoods (Priemus 2001).

Thus it seems unrealistic to assume that the government can withdraw completely from the housing renewal process. Throughout most of western Europe it is the observed case that lower-income households cannot afford the rent levels necessary to sustain high-quality housing provision. Such standards appear to be achievable only through the continued application of subsidies or the replacement of the indigenous population with a more affluent population that can afford higher rents and prices (that is, through gentrification). The situation is further complicated by the way in which socio-economic problems stigmatise some low-income neighbourhoods and dampen down any prospect of rent or price rises. Although such a situation may render dwellings more affordable in the short run, the lack of profit available from the dwelling deters longer-run investment in repairs, refurbishment and renewal, pushing the area into a further downward spiral of problems. Substantial public intervention is the only way to break this sequence. Delfshaven in Rotterdam, a problematic inner-city area, largely unscathed by wartime bombing and relatively unaffected by the urban renewal programmes of the 1970s and 1980s, illustrates such an approach.

Delfshaven

The district of Delfshaven lies to the west of the city centre, and is known colloquially to some as the 'wild west'. More than 60% of its 73 000 inhabitants are from ethnic minority groups. The population is younger and poorer than the city average and more prone to unemployment (16% compared with a national figure of 5%) (Werk voor Delfshaven). The local economy is weak; there is a high rate of out-migration, and a poor-quality housing stock. The area has also acquired a reputation for social problems, including drug abuse. Although the number of registered drug users is small, only about 200 or 0.3% of the population, the visibility of the drug users on the streets seriously damages the image of the area as well as perceptions of personal safety. In Delfshaven the problem is not so much one of dealing with the physical outcomes of economic restructuring, as in Kop van Zuid (see below), as of helping an existing community to adjust to the labour market and social changes that characterise post-industrial society. (See Figs 7.2 and 7.3.)

Despite these problems, the area is not without strengths and development opportunities. Accessibility is good, and the city's east–west metro line runs through the heart of the area, bringing most residents within a few minutes of the city centre. The science campus of Erasmus University and the main city hospital are on the eastern fringes of the area. The district itself offers a cheap location for new businesses, and the young population provides a ready workforce. There is some potential for tourism associated with the historic Voorhaven and Achterhaven, where there have been some developments of cafes, bars and specialist shops, notably in antiques and second-hand books.

Fig. 7.2   Rotterdam: Delfshaven.

Fig. 7.3   Rotterdam: Delfshaven – aerial view.

Between 1994 and 1999 the area was the subject of an URBAN programme subsidised by the European Commission. This programme envisaged a dual strategy of regeneration that would combat existing problems while exploiting the strengths and opportunities manifest in the district. The integration of economic development, social inclusion and safety measures was a key feature of the programme. The total budget of the URBAN programme for Delfshaven was in the order of €23.5 million, with 28% coming from the European Regional Development Fund, 20% from the Dutch government, 30% from the City of Rotterdam, and the remainder from private contributions. The programme sought to implement a number of measures under five main headings:

- New economic activities: business development supports; infrastructure improvements; development of tourism potential and facilities.

- Ensuring employment of local people: supporting the employment of local people in these economic activities.

- Improvements to public services and social infrastructure: security and quality of life projects to reduce drug abuse and crime; 'designing out crime'; improvements to education, training and health facilities.

- Environment: restoration of a number of neighbourhoods, squares and historic buildings.

- Communications: a series of projects aimed at improving social infrastructure and community involvement (Europa 1999).

The city council is working with the local community on a regeneration strategy for the area under the banner of *Werk voor Delfshaven* ('Work for Delfshaven'). The programme for 2000–2004 is a continuation of a European Union URBAN community initiative. The extended programme has a strong commitment to the local neighbourhoods and an integrated approach to social, physical and economic development. The responsible agency is the *Projectbureau WijkAanpak*. This agency has the task of coordinating the efforts of various organisations in the regeneration process: Delfshaven District Council; departments of the City Council, including the Department of Urban Planning and Housing; the Rotterdam Development Corporation; and the now privatised housing associations. Controlling this work is a steering group jointly led by an alderman from the city council and the chair of the Delfshaven district council. The agency itself is small. It has a staff of only seven, including a general manager; his personal assistant; managers for the social, economic and physical aspects of regeneration; and a communications manager. A budget of some Fl 36.4 million is available, of which over 80% is EU Objective 2 funding. The approach is to co-fund projects in collaboration with other public and private agencies.

On the physical side of the strategy, one of the key policies is to improve the quality of the housing stock. To achieve this, collaboration with the housing associations who own so much of the stock in the area is essential. Other proposals include improvements to the area's physical infrastructure and amenities. Economic regeneration is supported by initiatives to facilitate entrepreneurship and stimulate economic activity. Tourism- and recreation-related projects are supported around the old dock. Taking advantage of local economic specialism and linkages, investment in ICT, audio-visual and graphic design industries is being encouraged around the Van Nelle factory and the Lloyd Kwartier. As with many older inner-city areas there are too many shop units for modern needs. The policy is therefore to encourage the consolidation of retailing into selected core areas, allowing peripheral shop units to be demolished or converted to other uses.

Nevertheless, despite the good work going on in Delfshaven, in recent years the main focus of political attention has shifted towards regenerating the city centre and maintaining the competitiveness of the city in the global market place for inward commercial and industrial investment.

Rebuilding and maintaining the city centre

Badly bombed in 1940, the centre of the city was almost entirely rebuilt in the post-war period along modernist lines. Wide, straight streets separate the central area from the inner areas. The Lijnbaan, claimed to be the first pedestrianised shopping street in Europe, opened in 1953. By the 1990s it was evident that the centre needed further investment in retailing to retain its competitive position, and in 1996 more shopping space was provided in the new Beurstraverse Mall and much of the original Lijnbaan area was upgraded (see Fig. 7.4). To the west of the main shopping area the Schouwburgplein and De Doelen concert hall were completed in the 1960s. A theatre and cinema were later added, and the square was completely renovated in the 1990s as a performance and meeting place. Some of the earliest post-war offices were built in the vicinity of the Centraal Station, although much of the nearby Weena was not redeveloped for many years, with the Weenatoren, Klompenhouwer, Delftse Poort and the Unilever Building all being completed in the early 1990s. Further offices were completed along the Coolsingel and between the shopping centre and the river, for example along Blaak and around Churchillplein.

Fig. 7.4   Rotterdam: Lijnbaan.

Between the city centre and the Maas lies an area of former docklands known as the Waterstad. The closure of the docks provided the city with valuable space for the expansion of central area functions. Using mainly private capital, much of the area was redeveloped in the 1980s for commerce, leisure and residential uses.

> Commerce, much of it port-related, is a traditional activity in this quarter and was quickly re-established after the wartime bombing. But since the early 1980s the office sector has developed particularly dramatically, mainly as a consequence of investment by pension funds and insurance and shipping companies. By the 1990s over 25 000 square metres of new office space (had) been created, thus confirming the Waterstad's status as an employment node within the city. (Pinder & Rosing 1988, p. 123.)

Reflecting international trends in the changing functions of city centres and exploiting the environmental potential of former docks and quaysides, leisure uses formed a significant part of the redevelopment of this area. There are two museums (Maritime and Inland Shipping), each making use of the waterside setting, a new library, and a large indoor leisure-pool complex on the edge of the Maas. The quaysides contain numerous bars and restaurants, particularly around Oudehaven and Haringvliet. Around 2000 social and private dwellings have also been provided. A large site in the east of the area behind the Haringvliet (away from the city centre) has been given over to mainly social housing, and private housing has been built on the quaysides of the Leuvehaven (closer to the city centre) and on the Maas waterfront.

By the 1990s Waterstad was full, and developers were looking for new opportunities. If the city was to benefit from further substantial tranches of property investment more land would have to be found. This land lay across the river in the 'old south'.

Kop van Zuid

Despite the increasing importance of the market it is still reasonable to suggest that the municipalities continue to play an important role in the redevelopment of urban areas, not least as the providers of most land and infrastructure for development. According to McCarthy:

> While they hope to recoup the infrastructure costs when they sell on serviced land to developers, the subsidisation of development is frequently necessary, particularly for 'difficult' sites in urban areas. (McCarthy 1996, pp. 547–548.)

With the increasing globalisation of the economy, assisted by the creation of the Single European Market and the internationalisation of the commercial property market, competition between cities has intensified. In consequence, the last 15 years have seen a shift in emphasis in urban regeneration towards actions that improve the economic base and 'marketability' of urban areas as locations for property investment. Within the Netherlands a number of urban locations have been identified as the focal points for new development. Some have been selected as *key projects*, where planned coordinated public expenditure will lever in substantial private investment. These are intended to act as exemplars that others might follow. One such key project is *Kop van Zuid* in Rotterdam (McCarthy 1996, p. 549).

The Kop van Zuid area lies on the south bank of the Maas, opposite the city centre, adjoining the low-income neighbourhoods of Katendrecht, Afrikanderbuurt and Feijenoord. The area is known as the 'old south'. By the 1970s this part of the port of Rotterdam was redundant. The docks and adjoining warehousing and transhipment areas became vacant and derelict. Although the existing neighbourhoods had benefited from the urban renewal programmes of the 1970s and 1980s, little was done about the former dockland areas. (See Fig. 7.5.)

Fig. 7.5　Rotterdam: Kop van Zuid and the Erasmus Bridge.

By 1978 the city council was proposing that the area be redeveloped for some 4000 social housing units together with plans for building a 'red light' district in the same area. Under pressure from local residents the latter proposal was abandoned. In 1979 the Feijenoord Residents' Association prepared their own plan for social housing development in the Kop van Zuid area. During the 1980s social housing was developed in the southern parts of the area adjoining the existing districts of the 'old south'. However, by the mid-1980s, with the post-war city centre redevelopment now virtually complete, the city council was coming under pressure to find further sites to meet the continuing demand coming from the commercial property sector. Serious consideration was now being given to reusing the Kop van Zuid area, not for social housing, but to provide land for these more profitable commercial uses. In 1987 the city council began work on a new master plan for the area in collaboration with a private planning consultant: Teun Koolhaas. By 1991 the new land-use plan for Kop van Zuid had been approved by the city council. It was also accepted by the provincial government in 1993 and formally adopted by the Crown in 1994.

This bold plan to 'colonise' a redundant area with new property development opportunities has a resonance in many other cities where the service sector is expanding and traditional industries are in decline. Canary Wharf in London and La Défense in Paris are two of the largest-scale examples of this trend, but many large European cities offer similar, if smaller-scale, examples: Lille Europe; the areas around the Nord and Midi stations in Brussels; the International Convention Centre/Brindley Place in Birmingham; and La Part-Dieu in Lyon.

However, such a plan for capitalist development had to be carefully sold to a sceptical community in Rotterdam. The winning of both local and national support for the scheme is said by the Kop van Zuid project manager, P.J. Rodenberg, to have been one of the most difficult parts of the whole policy implementation process (Rodenberg 2001). Having convinced itself and the local community, the city council had to get commitment from central government to subsidise the project (the investment was too large for the city to undertake alone), and then had to get firm contracts with private developers to built the 'New Rotterdam'.

In order to facilitate redevelopment the city council had to overcome two fundamental problems with the area: the first was to improve access from the city centre to this very isolated area, and the second was to improve the image of the area as a location for private property investment. To improve access a new road bridge and a new underground station were proposed. The commitment shown by the city council in investing in these two elements was a vital prerequisite to any large-scale private property developments in the area.

After a design competition, work on the Erasmus Bridge, as it became known, started in 1992 and was completed in 1996. The bridge incorporates a roadway, bus lane and tramlines, cycle track and pedestrian walkways. The new metro station opened the following year, bringing the heart of the Kop van Zuid within 4 minutes of the city centre and 8 minutes from Rotterdam central station.

The redevelopment of the Kop van Zuid can be divided into a number of spatial elements. The metro station is contained within the Wilhelmenaplein development, completed in 1997 and containing around 150 000 m^2 of floorspace including a public 'galleria', retailing, the tax offices, customs offices, the courts of justice and further office space available for commercial letting. On an adjoining site the new 1500-seat Luxor theatre brings high culture to the area. To the south of this block the new Ichthus Hogeschool Rotterdam was opened in 2000. The college specialises in economics, communications, social work, management and legal studies.

To the west of the Wilhelmenaplein lies the flagship Wilhelmena Pier development. This thin peninsula of land between the Maas and the Rijnhaven was the historic departure point for passenger liners and the base of the Holland–America line. In one of the earliest refurbishment projects in the area, in 1993 the company's former headquarters was converted into the New York Hotel. Situated at the head of the peninsula this historic building quickly became a popular destination and a symbol for the transformation process. The Café Rotterdam and a new cruise liner terminal opened in 1997. Adjoining the hotel the 124 m high, 40 000 m² World Port Centre, designed by Sir Norman Foster, was completed in July 2000. The spectacular KPN tower (98 m high, 22 000 m²) opened in September 2000, and other large commercial and mixed-use developments are under construction or planned.

To the east of the Wilhelmenaplein, the Entrepot area is seen as a leisure area. It includes a large former warehouse complemented by new building to accommodate workshops, a market, shops, restaurants, housing and a marina. Other parts of Kop van Zuid, further from the Maas and the metro station, are given over more to housing, workplaces, retailing and social facilities for the neighbouring districts.

Not only did the Kop van Zuid master plan shift the development emphasis away from housing towards commercial development but the proportion of residential accommodation to be built as social has now fallen to only 30%. There have been other changes too. The original master plan envisaged the south exit from the Erasmus Bridge being oriented towards Laan Op Zuid, the direct route out of the city towards the A16 motorway and Dordrecht; on reflection, and in order to show that the investment had some benefits for the 'old south' residential neighbourhoods, the exit was re-oriented towards Parallelweg and Dordtselaan, the main route to the Zuidplein, the main shopping centre of the south. The master plan initially gave little support to the retention of old buildings on the site, but the success of the Hotel New York and the Entrepot refurbishment, together with a general change in attitudes, has meant that more existing structures are being retained in the later schemes. Although the whole project was conceived as a mixed-use district, the concept has been taken further with a more recent emphasis on a mixture of uses within individual building projects. The most recent building to be designed for the Wilhelmenapier, designed by Rem Koolhaas, will contain 120 000 m² of mixed commercial and residential space.

The implementation of such a large and complex project as Kop van Zuid requires the participation of numerous public and private agencies, the most important being: the Rotterdam Department of Urban Planning and Housing, responsible for land-use planning, urban design and architecture; the Rotterdam City Development Corporation, responsible for estate management and financial management; the Rotterdam Department of Public Works, responsible for civil engineering infrastructure; the Rotterdam Transportation Company, responsible for public transport; the Rotterdam Port Authority, the former owners of the land; and private developers and the local community. As with other similar major redevelopments in other cities, a single-function, short-life organisation has been established for the purposes of the Kop van Zuid project. This project organisation is led by a project manager supported by a projects office and two specialist teams: the communications team and the 'mutual benefit' project team.

The communications team is responsible for public relations and promotion, and is located in the purpose-built Kop van Zuid Information Centre within the project area. An important group is the Mutual Benefit Team. The aim of this group is to maximise the benefit to the local community of this vast investment. Mutual Benefit operates in the field of employment, and tries to establish links between job-seeking residents and the many new employers being established in the area. Additionally, the organisation aims to strengthen the local economic structure of poorer neighbourhoods, for example establishing a shopkeepers' association in Afrikaanerwijk. It also works as an economic developer, encouraging local entrepreneurship by, for example, providing managed workspaces and advice on business planning (Van den Burg *et al.* 1999, pp. 85–87).

Whereas in the UK the government has put much emphasis on the concept of leverage (the amount of private investment generated by each unit of public investment), in Rotterdam the emphasis appears to be on a much simpler profit and loss account. This is appropriate in the Dutch case because the land is in public ownership, and most of the initial infrastructure investment costs are borne by the local authorities, to whom profits return in the form of land rents and property taxes. According to Mr P.J. Rodenberg, the Kop van Zuid project manager, the account can be expressed in general terms as set out in Box 7.1.

Writing in 1996, McCarthy considered the Kop van Zuid in terms of the use of public–private partnerships; the integration of land uses within the project; and the integration of the project with the surrounding area. Today, some five years later, it is possible to make some further comments. The Kop van Zuid may have represented a sophisticated approach to partnership a decade ago, but such a mechanism seems today to be unremarkable, at least to British eyes. McCarthy, after Tweedale (1994), suggests that a negative effect of public–private partnerships may be that they lead to an over-representation of high-value land uses (such as offices, retail, and luxury housing) at the expense of social housing and community facilities. Undoubtedly there

---

Box 7.1   Kop van Zuid: a generalised picture of the financial costs and benefits to Rotterdam City Council

Cost to the City Council:

Investment in infrastructure   Fl 1.4 billion

Central government grant:

Removal of contamination, etc.   –Fl 0.3 billion

Profit from land rents   –Fl 0.55 billion

Net loss   Fl 0.55 billion

However, the total development cost, including all building carried out by private developers is Fl 5.5 billion

The local property tax income on this development, when completed, is estimated at Fl 0.5 billion per annum (or 5% of the city's total property tax income): that is, the City Council will recoup an amount equivalent to the Fl 5.5 billion net investment within 11 years.

Source: Kop van Zuid Project Office.

---

has been a shift in Dutch housing policy away from social housing provision and towards private housing. At the same time there has been a continuation of commercial investment and a growth in central area housing, leisure and tourism developments. However, these trends appear to pre-date the establishment of public–private partnerships in their modern form, and to be fairly widespread across the urban landscape. For instance, the land-use mix in the Waterstad has some similarities with Kop van Zuid but did not benefit from the same partnership arrangements. Therefore a better interpretation of the role of public–private partnerships might be that they are a mechanism for implementing the trend towards creating high-value land uses through urban regeneration, rather than being the instigators of such a trend.

Kop van Zuid appears to have maintained a high level of internal functional integration as it has developed. The city council's policy of encouraging mixed uses as part of its compact cities strategy appears to be being successfully implemented. Not only does the whole project contain a wide mix of uses but many of the larger developments, particularly the more recent ones, contain a mix of uses within the same building.

Whether Kop van Zuid successfully integrates with the surrounding area is a more problematic question. There are certainly positive indicators that the project at least tries very hard to achieve such integration. The public authorities have undertaken huge investments to connect the Kop van Zuid with the existing city centre, both through the new bridge and through the new metro station. The southern exit from the bridge has been oriented towards local traffic needs – towards the Zuidplein – rather than serving the regional road network directly. The Mutual Benefit team do try to match local people with the emerging jobs within the project. Some land uses, such as the new Ichtus Hogeschool Rotterdam, are intelligently located to encourage local people to acquire the business skills that many of the new employers in the area are likely to be seeking. The project does contain some social housing and private housing at affordable prices as well as supermarkets and other facilities serving local needs.

However, the biggest contribution made by Kop van Zuid is simply in its role as a tax base. When completed it is anticipated that the development will yield property taxes equal to about 5% of the city's total present property tax income. This is a major contribution to the income of the city that can be spent in any way and in any location that the city council see fit – for example in further infrastructure investments to maintain competitiveness or to cross-subsidise the regeneration of areas such as Delfshaven.

Conclusions

There have been two major shocks that have precipitated large-scale reconstruction in Rotterdam: the bombing of the central area in 1940, and the closure of the upstream docks during the 1970s and 1980s. Both led to major policy initiatives from government and local government agencies, involving detailed planning and massive subsidies and participation in the implementation process. In contrast, the gradual deterioration of the older inner-city neighbourhoods, with a complexity of legal interests in existing property, their indigenous population and their intricate socio-economic systems, has posed problems that require much more subtle and varied action. Although the authorities had begun to approach the problems of the inner city by means of slum clearance, it quickly became clear in Rotterdam as elsewhere in the Netherlands, by the early 1970s, that such an approach was too crude. Subsequently a more sophisticated area improvement approach was adopted.

Local economic circumstances have limited and shaped possible courses of action. Overall the West Netherland EU region has a gross domestic product per capita marginally above that of the UK as a whole but below that of South East England. Within this Rotterdam is generally regarded as trailing fourth in terms of economic growth among the cities of the Randstad. This constrains the rate at which private property developers have been willing to invest in the city. It is notable that the Weena area was not fully redeveloped until the 1990s despite its prime location between the Centraal Station and the city centre. It may be argued that there were planning problems, but lack of development pressure must have been a factor in delaying development for so long. More recently the pace of commercial development seems to have increased, and there is some evidence that the major public investments in infrastructure and environmental quality are having a beneficial effect in increasing the city's competitive position. Public investment has led to private investment. Private investment has boosted developers' confidence, and is leading to further private investment.

Similarly the regeneration of Delfshaven can only proceed at a rate that can be sustained by the local economy. Most job opportunities lie outside the district, in the city centre, docklands and industrial zones. The scope for increasing employment within the area, for example through exploiting the tourist potential of the old harbour itself, is modest. At the same time the pressures that are restructuring local retailing and service provision are unlikely to lead to employment growth. Relative growth in housing rents and prices is likely to occur only as local social and environmental problems are resolved. Private capital is unwilling to invest in districts that combine higher-than-average risk with lower-than-average rates of profit. The regeneration of areas such as Delfshaven is a complex and difficult task that generates little external private sector interest but requires external subsidy and leadership by public agencies.

8

Belgium: the Case of Wallonie

Charles Fraser and Luc Marechal

Despite its central position in western Europe, Belgium and its constituent regions have been noticeably overlooked in recent analyses of urban planning and policy. The reasons for this are complex, but may relate to preoccupation with other internal political priorities derived from its bilingual and cultural nature, which for a long period have drawn attention away from other problems such as urban and industrial decline. Since the regionalisation of the country in the 1990s the new regional governments have been able to concentrate on more pressing social issues that are of more immediate concern to their local population. In the case of Wallonie the regeneration of its industries and its towns are a paramount concern. Further, there is evidence that the new regional administration is beginning to develop approaches to regeneration that are worthy of the attention of other states and cities in this part of Europe. The region is also close to major external centres such as Lille, Brussels, Aachen, Maastricht and Luxembourg. (See Fig. 8.1.)

Historical background

Although the cities of Flanders have a history of commerce and industry (particularly textiles) going back to the Middle Ages, it was in the French-speaking part of Belgium that modern industrialisation was born. This was based in the coalfield that is part of the greater western European field, which runs from west to east from Kent through the Nord-Pas de Calais and the Sambre-Meuse valley to the Ruhr of Germany. However, although some exploitation of this coalfield occurred up to the eighteenth century, it was held back compared with the British fields by the feudal land-holding systems that gave landowners the right to exploit resources under the soil. Unlike the

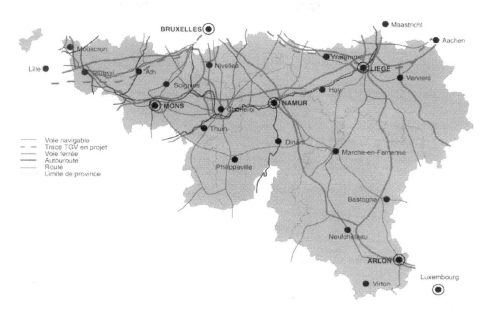

Fig. 8.1   Wallonie: location of main centres and adjacent cities.

British landowners, who – under the system of primogeniture – had acquired large holdings by European standards, those in the Belgian coalfields were small landowners, apart from the larger church holdings. Thus mines were small, near the surface, and often the source of violence as miners dug into the coal on the next property.

The problem was resolved when the region was incorporated into republican France at the end of the eighteenth century. The new regime in effect 'nationalised' the coal under a law of 1791, but gave the miners payments for the coal won on a cooperative basis. At a stroke the block to exploitation had been removed, opening up the area to the introduction of the new technologies such as the Newcomen pump engine, which had been developed in the UK, and making more extensive mining possible. With this there was a different climate for investment, and the ready capital from the banks of the Flemish towns such as Antwerp and Brussels began to flow into the burgeoning industrial areas. The Societé Générale, a bank founded by the French, was particularly influential. When the province passed to Dutch control in 1815 no change in these laws was undertaken. In 1830, when the Belgian state was set up, the cooperatives were incorporated as *sociétés civiles* and set on a more capitalistic basis.

The development of the coalfield provided the power basis for the expansion of other manufacturing industries. Iron and steel expanded as the local charcoal-based industry of the Ardennes moved into the coalfield, focusing on Liège and Charleroi, and the glass industry in which Flanders had been a European leader moved into the region and expanded considerably. Many of the entrepreneurs and engineers were British, who moved to the area bringing their expertise with them. Simultaneously the transport of the region was improved, using the substantial Sambre and Meuse rivers, which were improved and canalised in places to link the region to its traditional ports of Antwerp and Rotterdam, to the Rhine and Germany and into the French coalfield and thence to Paris. The region thus took off as the first real industrial area in continental Europe (Bruwier *et al.*; Milward 1997).

Throughout the nineteenth century this industrial base began to grow, reaping some benefits of having started after the British industries. For example, the iron and steel plants in Liège and Charleroi were larger although not more efficient than their British counterparts. However, they benefited from their proximity and links to the markets of France, the Netherlands and importantly the Zollverein (the German customs union). This gave access to the Austro-Hungarian empire and eastern Europe. By the outbreak of the First World War Belgian industry had the fastest growth in Europe and was at the forefront of technological development. The war itself, the inter-war years and the Second World War did little to alter this position. The infrastructure emerged in 1945 with the same status as it had before and with relatively little war damage to repair. A side effect was that Belgium, like Britain, did not benefit from the Marshall Plan for post-war Europe, in the belief that it was industrially and economically resilient. This was not the case, however, and although Belgium and Wallonie enjoyed the benefits of post-war consumerism the structural weaknesses in its economy had become apparent by the early 1960s, and – for the same reasons as in Britain – it became less competitive in both a global and a European context. Out-of-date plant, poor communications and to a certain extent management techniques all began to take their toll. Although supplanted by oil as the main source of power in the country, the coal industry was still a huge employer in 1950 with a labour force of around 100 000 miners, which had been swelled by the immigration of some 40 000 Italian miners in 1946. By 1970 the total had declined to 10 000, and the last mine closed in 1984.

The major industries of steel, textiles, and glass followed a similar pattern: one by one these plants closed, spreading the problems of the coalfield areas such as the Borinage into the major cities such as Charleroi and Liège. A major factor in the decline was that the finance houses of the commercial cities of Belgium, Antwerp and Brussels were now investing in the newer, smaller consumer-oriented sectors that had sprung up predominantly in the Flanders region, and the drying up of investment accentuated this downward spiral (Vandendorpe 2000).

The event that brought this impending economic crisis to a head was the loss of colonial territories in the Congo and the potential loss of the wealth created from it. This meant that, faced with calls for government investment in the declining areas and support both for the industries and for the increasing unemployed workforce, the national government was unable to respond, and indeed cut assistance to these – particularly to the mining community. This led to civil disturbances in which units of the Belgian army had to be deployed (Voye 2000). The concentration of the problem in Wallonie exacerbated the tensions between the Flemish- and French-speaking communities, which was resolved only by the adoption of the new Belgian federal constitution in 1990.

The period between the early 1960s and the mid-1980s was therefore a period of slow descent into economic extinction for much of the industrial part of the region, characterised by all the physical and social hallmarks of this process. Dereliction of old factory sites, decline in housing quality, high unemployment and other social problems created problems for the national economy and exchequer. The part of Belgium that had at one time been the powerhouse of the national economy was now the recipient of relief drawn from the new emerging industrial strength of Flanders. Its status as one of Europe's problem regions was confirmed by the classification of parts of the region as Objective 1 and much of the rest as Objective 2 in the structural fund negotiations that were concluded in the mid-1990s. The significance of this is that the remainder of the Objective 1 regions were on the remote fringes of Europe, whereas the Hainault area, which was so designated, was surrounded by the economically thriving regions of Flanders, south-east England, the Netherlands Randstad, the Ile de France and the Luxembourg/south German cities. It was an island of absolute, not merely relative, poverty in the middle of the wealthy regions of Europe. What is remarkable is that from this nadir the region has begun to fight back and tackle the range of problems with which it was faced.

A new beginning and a new programme

The analysis that was undertaken by the new Walloon regional government highlighted the need to adapt to a new industrial system that was based on small-scale activity, new sectors of the economy, and small – more local – financing efforts. An ancillary problem that was perceived as urgent was the need to prevent the peri-urbanisation of this growth and restore the heart of each of their industrial cities. This process of urban renovation in Wallonie began in the 1970s and the 1980s but was developed in the 1990s following a first decree of the regional parliament in 1990 and further decrees in 1994, 1997 and 1998. The decree of July 1994 introduced the concept of *zones d'initiatives priviligées* (ZIPs) and the instruments within them, notably the *quartiers d'initiatives* (Gouvernement Wallon 1999).

The key document is the *Code Wallon de l'Aménagement du Territoire, de l'Urbanisme et du Patrimoine*, which was totally revised in November 1997 to incorporate and expand the above measures. The code comprises four volumes, the first detailing regulations, the second general planning principles, the third the regulations for monuments and special sites, and the fourth – significantly – implementation measures. Under Article 13 of the code the *Schéma Directeur de l'Espace Régional* (SDER), a structure plan for the region, was set up. The SDER has several important functions as an instrument for planning at both the broad brush and detailed levels in the region (Gouvernement Wallon 1998; European Commission 1997). It is:

- a strategic planning instrument;

- a document to integrate various regional policies such as housing, transport and environment;

- an instrument to organise the spatial disposition of the various elements in the region;

- an instrument to integrate the region with surrounding regions, in Belgium and adjacent to it in Germany, France and Luxembourg.

In many ways the theme of regeneration seems to be underplayed in these two documents, but this is essentially because the entire programme is one directed at the regeneration of the entire region as a cohesive policy, drawing together the disparate elements of separate policies. Regeneration is specifically mentioned in Articles 167–174 of the Code.

A first strand of public action in this area is the power to service sites that have become derelict so that the private sector can bring them back into use. This has been a fraught exercise since 1978, when a previous procedure to force owners to bring their property into use was found to be unconstitutional as it was seen as a measure of forced expropriation, something that at the time the region was not competent to do. Current measures for such areas, if they are to be urbanised, rely on the preparation of plans by the

Commune, the *schémas de structure*, and these carry tacit approval for anything proposed that conforms to this plan. This problem highlights one of the characteristics of Belgian society. Historically the state was founded as a Catholic state. As a result much of its historic social policy infrastructure was predicated on antagonism to socialist values or the growth of state institutions and on a reliance on self-help and charity. Fundamental to this was a respect for private property.

The new set of procedures allows the government to adopt programmes to improve public infrastructure in urban areas to encourage the reuse of derelict areas. This applies particularly in town centres. The main measure that permits direct intervention is the creation of the ZIPs. These apply in several situations and have four basic types corresponding to four types of zone, but their common theme is that they allow *communes* to focus assistance in these areas to facilitate the upgrading of the land to encourage redevelopment. These are:

- *zones de fortes pression fonciere* (zones of pressure on the land market);

- *zones de requalification de noyaux d'habitat* (zones of housing improvement);

- *zones de quartiers d'initiatives ou sont menée des politiques integrées de revitalisation* (zones where integrated policies for revitalisation are creating new initiatives);

- *zones des cités sociales à requalifier* (social housing improvement areas).

These zones permit the authorities to service land and rebuild sewerage, drainage and access, especially in former industrial zones, *sites d'activité économique desaffectés* (SAED). In 1994, 2044 such sites were identified in a survey carried out by the University of Liège. Many of these have either been improved by local effort or dropped as non-priority. Sixty-one major sites remain for priority action, involving a total budget of some BFr1000 million (Dachouffe 2000). There is an emphasis on the facilitation of home ownership rather than the development of large social housing complexes. They also enable a programme for the renovation of town centres, large and small, to fit in with the SDER.

The significant change, however, has been to the development of a constitutional mechanism for intervention in the land market. The new powers give the regional authorities a *right of pre-emption* in land purchases in these specified areas. This can assist the region in its plans but also *communes*, housing societies, and other intercommunal public agencies. The obvious adjunct to this is that it has itinerant financial clauses, to enable purchases to be made and works to be carried out. The region has set up a new fund, the *Fonds d'Aménagement Opérationel* (article 183; CW), to finance these operations and under article 184 of the Code these provide finance for three types of action within the new zone;

● the acquisition of property;

● the renovation of property or its exterior improvement;

● the servicing of sites.

Compared with the sweeping powers normally available to an authority in France or the Netherlands these do not seem excessive or ground breaking, but in Belgium, which has a long tradition of individualism and private property rights, they are a considerable advance. They take Wallonie forward from an almost total reliance on individual efforts in the private sector to a more communal base for action. The region is now beginning to take part in the process of regenerating its considerable inheritance of urban dereliction. They have also been added to by the availability of funding for certain types of project by the addition of federal funds where constitutionally applicable for social development, and European funds since much of Wallonie was either Objective 1 or 2 under the previous European structural funds regimes and is now under the new programme Objective 2.

The process in action

Since these measures are relatively new and in many ways limited, there are no spectacular examples with which to illustrate the process of regeneration. They tend to be applied in small but effective schemes throughout the Walloon region, fitting in with the general thrust of the SDER, rather than a few major schemes. Figure 8.2 shows the scatter of the various zones and their concentration in the coalfield area along the Sambre-Meuse valley, and Fig. 8.3 shows the even more scattered nature of the location of the SAEDs.

However, particularly in the housing area, where the regional and local governments cooperate with housing societies, small but significant schemes are being developed. The new powers are also being used to facilitate more rational planning of schemes on derelict land when previously the development would have been left to the market. Two such examples in the city

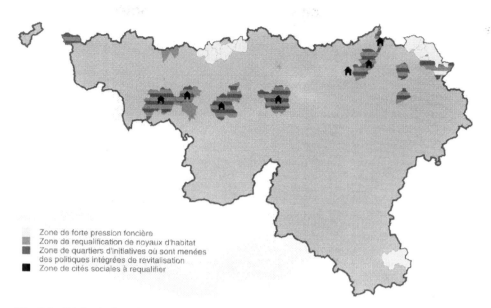

Fig. 8.2 Wallonie: location of *zones d'initiatives priviligées* (ZIPs).

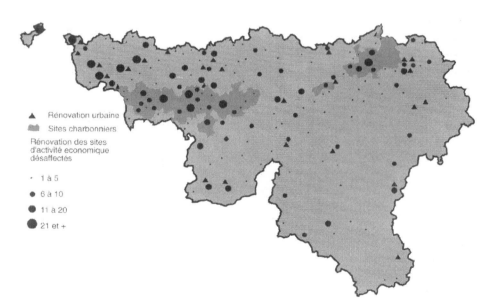

Fig. 8.3 Wallonie: location of *sites d'activité économique desaffectés* (SAEDs).

of Mons demonstrate this approach. The first is an intervention in the city centre, where a combination of wasteland and backland has been amalgamated by the city authorities and housing societies to form a large site for a development of social and private housing: the Quartier Rachot.

The second is a large site on the edge of the city centre on a combination of wasteland and vacant land between the city and the main arterial motorway serving the city. On this site a combination of public facilities, recreation complex and private ventures, cinema complex and offices is being developed in a more comprehensive manner than previously. Les Grands Prés is a significant development in the evolution of comprehensive and cooperative private/public planning in Wallonie.

Summary

Sandwiched between the Netherlands and France, both of which have long traditions of public direction and cooperative approaches to urban planning and regeneration, the case study of Wallonie, one of three Belgian regions, demonstrates how even in western Europe there are examples where a considerable amount of ground has to be made up to build the capacity to tackle the backlog of urban dereliction. Historically Belgium has a tradition of self-help or reliance on the Church, and it derives its response to the problems of poverty, unemployment and dereliction, from a quite different 'social theory' from those of its neighbours. This is changing as the population and the authorities realise that, with greater direction and guidance, the region can move rapidly to change its image and character and take advantage of its geographic location, where virtually no part of the region is more than two hours from the dynamic centres of European regeneration in the Randstad, the Lille *métropole* and the Ruhr. The region has begun the journey from being the only Objective 1 area under the old EU structural funds *not* on the periphery of the continent to being part of the post-industrial economy at the heart of Europe.

To do this it has adopted a more diffused approach than most other countries. Not only is the effort scattered geographically across the region, although there is a concentration in the older industrial areas, but also it pulls together several policy areas, housing, social policy, good physical design and infrastructure improvement in a way that is really 'joined up'. Significantly, although there has been the breakthrough in the development of new tools for public intervention in a very strongly private land market, the strategy relies on most of the traditional pillars of the social fabric of the region, such as housing societies and communal cooperation. It may be unspectacular, but as site by site and town by town a new image and confidence in the region emerges, it is effective.

9

Milan: the Bovisa District

Corinna Morandi

The historic context

Since the second half of the nineteenth century, the north-west Milan area has undergone radical changes, owing to the settlement of large firms and plants, which have continued developing until the 1970s. Initially heavy manufacturing industries established there, operating in sectors such as metal products, mechanical engineering and chemicals. Over the decades, they have been followed by small and medium-sized enterprises, which, modernising their plants, managed to survive the industrial crises that have hit Milan during the last three decades.

A discussion of the urban regeneration process in the north-west quarter of Milan means describing a situation in Milan during its transition from a city whose economy was based on manufacturing industry (with its 1800 ha of industrial plants in the mid-1970s) to a post-Fordist city – a complete change in the economic paradigm of the city. Bovisa is the most representative example of such an area in transition: it is located on the north-west boundary of Milan, and it has been progressively welded to towns of the first metropolitan belt, creating an urban continuum.

The name 'Bovisa' identifies not only a district of the north-west Milan suburbs, but also a historically relevant sector of industrial urban fabric and a peculiar urban environment, interwoven, until a few years ago, with housing, small factories, large industrial plants, goods yards, railway crossings, *trattorie* for truck drivers, and laboratories and warehouses of the Scala Theatre and the Armenia film industry complex. About 100 ha of industrial areas have been occupied by major companies such as Montedison, Sirio, Broggi Izar and Alcatel, by plants for town gas production (with their fuel depots in the near Quarto Oggiaro District), and by many other activities, mostly in the chemical and metallurgy sector. Abandonment of these plants occurred during the second half of the 1980s and has now nearly been completed. (See Fig. 9.1.)

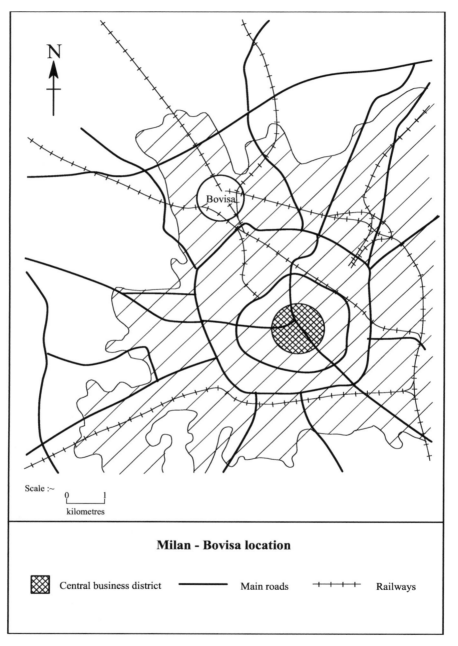

Fig. 9.1   Milan: location.

The great industrial expansion of this area was historically influenced by its proximity to a high-quality transport infrastructure. In particular, a key role has been played by Sempione Road and the historic routes towards Como and Varese, elements of the radial axis system that has historically linked Milan (centre for goods production, exchange and supply of services) to its surroundings. There, over the centuries, a productive agricultural industry had developed, relying for its productive organisation on a network of rural villages and small towns. After the Second World War that hinterland underwent an unstructured urbanisation and metropolitanisation process. Over the second half of the nineteenth century the historical main road system had been enhanced by the construction of the local railway and tramway network, which integrated the north Milan area[1] and which has been a significant support for the intense industrial, and successively residential, development of the area. Another element supporting industrial settlement has been the waterway network, crucial for the textile industry. Outposts of this manufacturing system have sprung up along these waterways according to a linear development scheme, forming centres of attraction at the correspondence with railway stations. This network of historic centres and infrastructure has provided a framework to connect industries and land, for both local and long-distance trade and commerce. The high density of stations favours the concentration of goods yards for raw materials and other goods transport to an extent not experienced in other areas of Milan.

Bovisa plays a key role in this land-use system, hosting important railway stations on the local North Milan Railways and on the east–west axis of the national highway between Venice (towards middle-west Europe) and Turin (towards France). These railway stations were formerly dedicated to goods transport only, but have lately been converted for commuters as well. Since 1870 the access to goods yards had encouraged the settlement of those pharmaceutical companies that later formed the Montecatini Group, the major Italian pharmaceutical company. In the period between the two world wars other chemical companies came along, and the area became the chemical industrial pole of Milan. Other relevant urban elements had grown in the area, oriented to stocking of raw materials, to their transformation and to energy production, such as the big fuel oil tanks of the adjacent Quarto Oggiaro District. On the Sempione Road axis stands the large, now disused, refinery of Rho, which will be redeveloped for the Fiera di Milano complex, due to be completed by 2006. The inner part of the district is dominated by gasometers, where the town gas to supply Milan was stocked until few years ago. This was produced in the industrial plants built in Bovisa at the beginning of the last century by the French company Union des Gaz. Nowadays, the leftovers of this industrial past are the main landmarks of Bovisa: vacant industrial buildings, gasometers and railway tracks shaping the area's urban morphology in a disorganised sprawl.

Since the beginning of the last century, the municipality of Milan together with major national industrial and railway companies has played a key role in defining the urban morphology and functional destination of the area, promoting the construction of the first working-class residential neighbourhoods. Subsequently, new expansions have progressively come along: first, in the period between the two world wars, south of the railway line and towards the inner part of the town; then, after the Second World War until recently, in the northern part, towards the metropolitan fringe. These development actors shaped an urban form dominated by large 'enclosures', often unconnected to each other because of the railway tracks barriers, comprising large industrial plants, combustible deposits, wide working-class residential wards, and even metropolitan facilities such as hospitals. Between these enclosures is a mixed high-density urban fabric, woven with residential areas, small craft activities and shops, forming a confused morphology based on the previous rural nuclei, and nowadays incorporated in the urban continuum.

Decline and change

Until the mid-1970s the impact of manufacturing industry decline had not become evident in Milan. This is reflected in the fact that the town planning scheme for this period not only reaffirmed the industrial destination for 1700 ha of land, but also increased industrial land use in the urban area. During the 1980s, however, the scenario changed rapidly, and in Milan as well as in the Lombard region the abandonment of manufacturing plants had knock-on effects in the settlement and socio-economic framework. In the Lombard region vacant lands amount to 2800 ha, mostly located in Milan Province (1500 ha). At the end of the 1990s Milan alone had about 500–600 ha of redundant or highly underused industrial plants. The abandonment process rapidly affected all the historic industrial areas of the city, having its epicentre along the two axes towards the outer metropolitan area, north-west from Bovisa towards Saronno and north-east from Bicocca Area towards Sesto San Giovanni. The impact of de-industrialisation is also intense both in the eastern area, owing to the closure of plants based on goods yards, and in a south-west direction, where many factories settled to use the historic canals (*navigli*).

The process of industrial plant abandonment in Milan involved different factors related to modernisation and innovation in production technology, and to the consequent reorganisation and plant relocation of manufacturing production. Major companies are also affected by changes in business strategy and by the process of internationalisation, requiring relocation of both productive plants and business centres. However, the de-industrialisation process seems more progressive and less harsh than in other European countries, proceeding through a first period of downsizing, with discarding of obsolete plants in inner-city areas, whose rent is increasing, and relocation to suburban areas. During the 1980s the period of general economic recession revealed and intensified the crisis of the manufacturing production system, causing significant job losses in the secondary sector and a progressive growth of the tertiary and quaternary sectors. (See Figs 9.2 and 9.3.)

The correct calculation of the area available for new functions, for urban reshaping and for redesign has to include 100 ha, in addition to the former industrial areas, consisting of vacant goods yards and settlements of the railway network. Moreover, they are strategically located. The peculiar structure of Milan's railway network, forming an almost continuous ring, dotted with stations for goods and passengers, has determined – owing to technology modernisation – the availability of a significant number of areas that are easily reusable, in almost central locations.

The redevelopment programmes for these large, derelict industrial sites require considerable time, owing to the difficult negotiation process between local authorities, private owners and developers, all of them constrained by

Fig. 9.2   Milan: Bovisa – derelict factory premises.

Fig. 9.3   Minal: Bovisa – vacant land.

strict urban planning instruments and by a fiscal and financial incentive system that is still ineffective and unsuitable for the purpose. Small- and medium-sized area transformation and reuse processes are more effective. Initially, medium-sized area transformation, loosely interpreting town planning regulations, led to the realisation of many business centres (almost new city 'gates' near main junctions on access roads) by the few developers that had monopolised the development process in Milan during the 1980s. Nowadays, it is interesting to look at the vast and widespread reuse process, which, in the city as a whole, is affecting small and very small estate units, well integrated into the urban fabric interstices, not only in the medium belt and in the nearby suburbs, but sometimes even in central areas. New housing, office, public and private services find here a supply of locations that are comparatively competitive with respect to new development areas. At the same time, they revive a network of interstitial areas offering, in a fashionable way, the traditional mixed character of the Milan urban milieu.

This peculiar phenomenology of Milan's industrial decline can be observed in the transformation of the north-west area, and particularly in Bovisa. There the crisis hit basic industry, a substantial presence in the area, while historic plants for the production and storage of town gas (replaced by methane gas distribution) become technologically obsolete and incompatible with the urban context. Industrial abandonment is progressive, and at the beginning of the 1990s the urban landscape of Bovisa was dominated by a succession of redundant and derelict large industrial buildings, of still active industries, and of small and medium-sized factories undergoing renovation. Railway stations were also downsized, becoming part of the vacant areas available for redevelopment programmes, although they provided difficult sites for development purposes.

In this transformation process residential land use acted as a 'binder', and stemmed the progression of urban blight. Also, after the Second World War, public housing was still a relevant element in this district. Residential blocks were refurbished, through a particular tax concession, by public funding to cooperative housing associations. These represent a typical and substantial feature of this Milan district. Conversely the facilities system was inadequate, apart from basic services such as schools. Above all, there was an almost total absence of any system of green spaces, parks or public gardens. Another peculiar element of the area was its use by many road transport companies, localised here owing to the proximity to customs and the goods yard. Following the reorganisation of the railway system and the displacement of customs, many of their depots have been left derelict, and some of them have been reused to build the first office blocks of the district.

Revival

The process that Milan has followed to create the preconditions for the conversion of medium-sized and (in particular) large distressed areas is often not straightforward, and has only recently begun its implementation phase. It has already been stated that the 1980 Milan town planning scheme restated the value of industrial land use for the city. The changing scenario of Milan's economic condition, along with the increasing number of industrial plant closures, has ignored one of the most substantial issues of the town planning scheme, the so-called preservation of industrial land use. For this reason, on the one hand the operating instructions of the town planning scheme permit the implementation of industrial conversion programmes, however widespread, sporadic and uncoordinated; on the other hand, the town planning scheme itself has been changed by many variances of this rule, involving about 50% of the total amount of vacant or nearly abandoned industrial areas.

Over the years 1985–1995 only two of the planned major conversion programmes were realised: one in the west, the Milan Fair extension with new exhibition stands built on a sector of vacant lands owned by the Alfa Romeo car plant; the other actually only a part of the technological pole (Tecnocity) planned on the Bicocca district Pirelli plant area, which is currently being vacated. Between the mid-1980s and the early 1990s attempts were made to build a programmed framework to fix some operating rules and to produce a settlement plan giving guidelines for the realisation of the great conversion possibilities of major abandoned areas connected to the railway network. One of these acts – the *Director Document for the Underground Railway Link Project* – aims to coordinate the effects of an infrastructural modernisation project with the possible transformation of abandoned or underused industrial and railway lands. The project, which is almost complete, plans to connect the national railway to the North Milan Railway through an underground link, and then realise a regional integrated railway system (SFR).

The Director Document for the Underground Railway Link has been proposed as a guideline framework, which does not give specific prescription. However, it has been followed by a town planning scheme and by some area projects that contain detailed, quantified proposals. Such area projects concern abandoned land, to be redesigned and to be allocated to new land uses, and nearby railway stations that will become junctions of the regional integrated railway system. This town planning scheme refers to the strategic plan, under discussion in Milan, that proposes the progressive transformation of the city, whose management and excellence functions are located in the dense inner centre, to a polycentric urban system supported by a strong railway network. The *Director Document for Distressed and Underused Areas*, which proposes some strategic targets and general principles for conversion, follows the same principles.

All the administrative action that has occurred since 1995 derives from the legislation for the urban regeneration programmes provided for by national and regional laws.[2] The framework for coordinating the negotiation process between public administration and the different public and private actors involved in the potential conversion of a myriad of distressed areas (370 ha of industrial areas and 93 ha of railway lands) involves a two-part process, first to outline the urban transformation areas where each specific programme will be allocated, and then to articulate two common reference schemes that orientate the operative proposals. The first of these two schemes applies to areas identified as non-strategic, with a dimension under 3.5 ha, and with a prevailingly residential land use; the second one applies to the areas identified as strategic by virtue of their dimensions and location.

Strategic area plans, which have been stalled for years, have been resumed, in an attempt to engender a new experimental approach, mediating between the establishment of town planning rules (outlining urban transformation areas, and defining quantitative standards for each specific programme), and the achievement of the desired structural, physical-morphological features for the area (according to proposals produced by the municipality containing non-binding guidelines to arrange building density, green spaces, etc). Certain interesting elements of this development process relate to three targets: first, proposing an organic system of areas, with the same set of rules for both land use and urban settlement transformation; second, introducing equalising rules; and third, 'fixing' the large units of coordinated planning, enabling the city to realise consistent programmes mainly for infrastructure building and public open space planning.

Over the last decade the Director Documents, newly introduced to mainstream Italian town planning practice and usually favouring normative and binding instruments, have not proved to be successful instruments for process implementation or for achieving coordination between public programmes (mainly infrastructure) and private investment.

However, this strategic planning approach is well developed in Milan. A recent regional law introducing the last generation of urban regeneration programmes (*programmi integrati di intervento* – 'programme integrated plans'), expressly provides for a framework document aimed at giving consistency to all these programmes. The promotion and implementation of these determines the integration of public and private resources.[3] Such a framework document, presented and discussed in Milan in 2000, replaces the polycentric city vision with a new urban settlement scheme, drawing an upside-down T: that is, the north-west/south-east axis (from Malpensa Airport Hub to Linate City Airport), with the north-east axis at right angles to it. Among the aims of this strategic scheme are increases in the supply of areas for tertiary and quaternary land uses, for research and high-technology industry, and for housing.

Only eight of the myriad of urban regeneration programmes prepared in Milan after 1995 had reached the end of the planning process by the beginning of 2000 and of the bureaucratic procedure, thanks to the formulation of a programme agreement at the end of the decade. These eight programmes involve about 180 ha, mostly former industrial areas, of which 112 ha have been allocated to green spaces and public facilities. Among the programmes that have come to implementation, two specific projects initiated the extensive regeneration process in the north-west area:

- the implementation of the second Polytechnic University urban pole on the former gasometer site in Bovisa;

- the reuse of the oil depot area in Quarto Oggiaro District.

The programme agreement is a key element for implementation of the 1990s urban regeneration programmes. It is a system introduced in the 1990s by a national law and later improved by regional Acts.[4] The programme agreement aims to develop a negotiation process between the various actors and institutions involved in any urban regeneration programme, overcoming the procedural impediments that often obstruct decision-making. The programme agreement is the first of a set of legislative Acts, promoting negotiated planning and aiming to support economic and social regeneration policies for depressed urban areas.[5]

Negotiated planning and local development incentives are the two new elements in the 1990s urban regeneration policies. Local development policies integrate central government financial and taxing instruments adopted in Italy to support structurally weak areas – such as southern Italy – and declining areas. Some of the recent legislative Acts aim to support specific programmes developed at a local level through cooperation between institutional actors and private investors.

These development policies may also apply in traditionally advanced areas, such as the Lombard region and Milan province, where the industrial crisis has caused the emergence of crisis zones. They act on innovation support, on enterprise start-ups, on human resources training and upgrading to create new jobs, and on the urban policy sector, supporting urban regeneration programmes. To implement these 'integrated' policies, specific instruments have been created or strengthened, such as development agencies, mixed companies and multi-company consortia.[6] These agencies collect different public funds, from the European Community, central and regional government, adding to the private funds coming from banks or industry. They also promote negotiation between the various actors, and develop sector or integrated programmes.

Over the last decade, after years of inactivity on the urban regeneration programmes in the north-west Milan area, Milan Polytechnic University has become a central actor in starting an effective functional and socio-economic transformation process. The Bovisa district was chosen after another possible location in the eastern sector of the city was rejected. As stated already, programmes and projects to convert vacant lands in the north-west of Milan, have been reformulated many times: from studies related to the Director Documents, to partial variations of the town planning scheme, and to inclusion of those areas within the perimeters of the urban regeneration programme. Each of those programmes or urban planning schemes stressed the need to improve the road network, which was insufficient to support any urban restructuring programme. The railway network is just the opposite:

construction of the underground railway link and conversion of the railway stations into junctions of the regional railway system (Bovisa railway station is also on the North Milan Railway and the Malpensa Express Railway) make the district an easily accessible area from the whole region by rail. Thanks to its good accessibility, the area is suitable to host high-quality and highly attractive functions. That is why Bovisa was designated as one of the poles in the town polycentric strategic plan. Good accessibility together with the availability of the former gasometers area (35 ha owned by the municipality company AEM, and 70 ha of vacant and obsolescent land, together constituting the so-called 'drop', bounded by railway tracks) has been the driving force determining the decision to locate in Bovisa one of the poles of the new Network Polytechnic, a real second polytechnic university. During the 1990s a strategic plan was developed to increase the number of polytechnic schools in the Lombard region, each characterised by an educational training programme suitable for its locality.[7]

The Polytechnic University has temporarily settled in other redundant buildings outside the perimeter of the gasometer conversion programme, beginning with this first entrenchment a process that is driving a change in the social and economic character of Bovisa. On the one hand it is a peculiar process, owing to the specificity of university function and of the actors involved, but on the other hand it is paradigmatic of the opportunities and difficulties of the abandoned area regeneration programmes. This process has highlighted the need to keep adapting a procedural and planning process to the real dynamics of transformation, which are rapid and not always predictable.

In brief, the regeneration programme for the new campus has been characterised by different development phases during the 1990s. First, the public administration delegated Milan Polytechnic University to do preparatory researches and then to prepare the detailed plan for the new campus. Second, a town planning scheme variance, regarding the totality of vacant lands inside the 'drop', was approved. Third, the inclusion of the area in the urban regeneration programmes perimeter has been realised. Finally, the municipality has approved the Second Polytechnic University project, and it has initiated the process to set up the programme agreement involving Milan Polytechnic University, the Milan municipality, the Lombard region and AEM. This phase has been complex, requiring both mediation between the expectations of the different actors involved and location of the necessary resources to solve complicated problems regarding infrastructure and the decontamination of very polluted land. Following the programme agreement, an international competition was launched to plan the new campus. Two working groups were joint winners of the competition, and they have been delegated to undertake the planning of the first part of the project, involving a large urban park and a new public transport line.

This important university site is designated to host research and production relevant to the Milan economy, such as industrial and aeronautical engineering and industrial design, and to initiate the realisation of a scientific library and a convention centre. This university should be the driving force for a wider regeneration of the north-west area, beyond the boundaries of the municipality. Simultaneously with the construction of the first Polytechnic University buildings, the construction site in the Quarto Oggiaro district has started. Here the promoter is a private company specifically formed for regenerating distressed areas, which has built a residential neighbourhood, along with some office and commercial spaces. The programme agreement envisages the construction of a large urban park, large retailing developments, a multiplex cinema and a new infrastructural line on this site, which, being connected to the new road network to the Polytechnic University, should link this area with the motorway system.

Emerging agendas

Without doubt, the role of the Polytechnic University, a relevant actor in the decision-making process (hastened by the urgent need to transfer some students from the overcrowded Città Studi, and pushed by the Minister of University and Scientific Research to build new campuses in the region), has been to stimulate and hasten the regulation of the programme agreement, by overcoming smoothly the difficulties of property transfer, cost-sharing of clean-up operations and primary infrastructure costs.

The programme agreement has been the most appropriate instrument to devise and to implement choices that had been partially outlined through the Director Documents, town planning scheme variances and urban regeneration programmes. However these have only been finally resolved by the decision of the university to build its campus in this area. North Milan Railways has not adhered to the programme agreement, diminishing the overall potential of the project as agreed by the other actors regarding the Bovisa regeneration process, driven by the new campus construction. Actually, it is contemplated that some segments of the road network essential to integrate the district in the metropolitan area should be built and connected to the adjacent districts. Meanwhile, the potential for enhancing the value of the important Bovisa station junction, well located between the campus and the area under regeneration, has not been exploited.

By contrast some other relevant programmes seem to be working in the direction of enhancing the process that has been begun. In one of these cases the decision maker is Milan municipality, which has introduced, in the museum initiatives program, the realisation – expected for the year 2002 – of a contemporary art museum inside one of the Bovisa gasometers. This project aims to give a new impulse to the creation of a sort of *industrial design culture district*, related both to the Third Architecture Faculty located in Bovisa, which offers this educational specialisation, and to the recent openings of art galleries, and studios of photography, graphics and design.

Another important location choice regards a pharmacological research centre, which, being connected with one of the original productive specialisations of the area, enhances the area's new role as a magnet for scientific research. An important effect of the Polytechnic University's location in this marginal area is the great variety and vitality of small local economic activities (commerce, personal and technical services, buildings).

A recent documented analysis has highlighted a statistical improvement in the demographic condition of Bovisa in that negative trends in population totals and ageing have reversed (Ambrosini & Rossi 2002). A first support for local economic activities has been the funds supplied by both the region and the municipality to individual enterprises or firms, aimed at improved innovation of production processes and the refurbishment of their plants. At the end of 2000, a regeneration and economic revitalisation programme for the whole north-west area had attracted European funds from the regional directorate under the Urban programme (Pasqui 2002). This prominent funding, dispensed over five years, concerns an area of 12 km^2, in whose heart are located Bovisa and Quarto Oggiaro District. For those districts the regeneration process has already started, but near them are areas suffering high rates of crime, unemployment, illegal immigration, unauthorised buildings, traffic congestion and air and soil pollution: a very depressed urban environment. The urban programme produced by the Milan municipality coordinates urban regeneration, industrial conversion, innovation programmes, infrastructural projects (such as IT wiring) and specific projects to build green spaces and to convert a monumental building into a business incubator. European funds have been augmented by extra funding from Lombard region, Milan province and municipality, and from municipal companies, with the objective of levering in additional financial resources from private actors who will participate in the projects.

Notes

1 The first section of the north-western railway network was realised in 1858 by the Austro-Hungarian government. The network was enhanced during the following decades, mostly through the action of the Ferrovie Nord Milano Company (FNM), at the beginning by means of Belgian financial investment (Corinna 1992).

2 The first set of laws that had as a main goal to facilitate the implementation of urban development programmes changing the prescriptions of local and general plans were approved by the Lombardy region (in Italy regions have legislative power in several fields, among them planning and urban regeneration) between 1986 and 1990: L.R. 3/1982 (Legge Verga) and L.R. 23/1990 (Legge Adamoli). National laws followed, meant to provide funding and to integrate public and private developers in urban renewal programmes: L. 179/1992 (Programmi di riqualificazione urbana – PRU); L. 493/1993 (Programmi di recupero urbano); and D.M. 8.10.1998, n. 1169 (Programmi di riqualificazione urbana e di sviluppo sostenibile del territorio – PRUSST).

3 L.R. 9/1999 (Disciplina dei Programmi Integrati di Intervento).

4 The origin of the Programme Agreement goes back to the mid-1980s, when this Act contributed to setting up the National Railway Company and stating funds for the South of Italy. The recent contents of the Programme Agreement are fixed in the Law 142/1990 (Ordinamento delle Autonomie Locali). In order to give effectiveness to the principle of coordination that inspires the Law, it states that the goal of the Agreement is 'to define and create works, actions or plans of actions that require a coordination between Municipalities, Provinces and Regions and the national Government or other public bodies…'. Later agreements with private subjects were added as 'second-level contracts' to the main text of the Programme Agreement. The Lombard Region Act 14/1993 states detailed rules and procedures to undertake local Programme Agreements.

5 A national law (L. 662/1996, Programmazione negoziata) sets out procedures for negotiation between public and private subjects to implement various projects aimed at improving local development programmes. Different procedures can be followed, including programme agreements (see footnote 4), *patti territoriali* and *contratti di quartiere* (specifically aimed at funding housing rehabilitation programmes), and *contratti di area* (for local employment development programmes).

6 Agencies for local development are usually public–private bodies, established to realise specific programmes of urban regeneration. A national law (L. 127/1997) inspired by the French model of the *sociétés d'économie mixte* states that major municipalities, with the cooperation of provinces and regions, can establish joint-stock companies to implement urban regeneration programmes (*società per la trasformazione urbana* – STU). One of these agencies, the Agenzia per lo sviluppo del Nord Milano (ASNM), has during recent years been leading the main transformation processes of the large industrial implantations of the north-eastern sector of the Milan metropolitan area.

7 During the 1990s a strategic plan was developed to increase the number of polytechnic schools in the Lombard region, each characterised by training suitable for the local socio-economic conditions.

10

The Ruhr: from Dereliction to Recovery

Susan Percy

The industrial heartland of Europe has historically been associated with the Ruhr region, also known as the Ruhrgebeit, in the German state of North Rhine Westphalia (NRW). The Ruhr exists as a result of the exploitation of coal deposits between Duisburg and Dortmund during the industrial revolution of the nineteenth century (Blotevogel 1998). In recent times the region has lost its industrial dominance, and has suffered from an economic crisis resulting from a severe decline in demand for its traditional products, leading to a major change in its economic base. This has resulted in a shift from steel, iron and coal production and other ancillary industries to service sector and high-technology industry. Watson (1994, p. 80) declares that the number of coal mines in the Ruhr region fell from '173 to 42 in the period 1957–78', leaving the Ruhr region suffering from high unemployment, environmental dereliction and social exclusion.

In response to this crisis the German state government of North Rhine Westphalia launched an ambitious initiative for the reconstruction of the northern part of the Ruhr, by means of an International Building Exhibition, known as Emscher Park. The initiative provides an interesting case study of the economic decline of a major industrialised area and subsequent economic, social and environmental restructuring. This regeneration process relies on comprehensive planning, strongly influenced by the international sustainable development agenda, and on place marketing and the need to change the image of the area in order to attract inward investment. As Shaw recognises in the context of the Ruhr region, 'any strategy in which economic aspects take precedence over the environment cannot work' (Shaw 2002, p. 83).

This chapter will explore the factors leading to the decline of this once prosperous region, the approaches taken to reconstruct the area, and the institutional and political context and actors and agencies involved in the process. It will discuss the social, economic and environmental impacts that are occurring, and will conclude by assessing the recovery of the Ruhr region. In doing so, this chapter examines the approaches of regional and subregional regeneration.

Background

The historical, political and administrative context of an area provides the framework for understanding contemporary change and the extent and nature of that change. In the case of the Ruhr region there are a number of factors that have shaped regeneration and environmental policy in recent years.

As a country Germany has over the years undergone geographical changes, and its development has been subject to a wide range of external influences. One of the most recent changes has involved the reunification of the country through the joining of East and West Germany, now made up of 16 federal states (*Länder*). The decentralised and federal nature of government in Germany provides for three tiers of government, the federal government (*Bund*), the individual states (*Länder*), and the local government (*Kommunes*). Planning in Germany consists, however, of four tiers (Danielzyk & Wood 1993, p. 130):

- federal regional policy (*Bundesraumordnung*);

- state planning for the area of a state (*Landesplanung*);

- regional planning (*Regionalplanung*) for small units within the larger states;

- town and country planning (*Bauleitplanung*), devised by the local authorities

The local plans comprise a land-use zoning plan (*Flachennutzungsplan*) and a binding development plan (*Bebauugsplan*).

The *Länder* and *Kommunes* are legally independent bodies, although in practice there are many interdependences between the three tiers of government in terms of political, legal and financial matters. Power is devolved down to *Länder* and local authority levels, which have their own autonomy enshrined in the Basic Law (*Grundgesetz*) of 1949 and have influence over housing, urban development, regional development and open space policies. Urban planning and regeneration are complex and decentralised activities, and as Couch points out the *Länder* 'are largely responsible and autonomous with regard to planning and development within their boundaries' (Couch 1995, p. 20). Owing to the devolution of power and autonomy there is a strong tradition of regional planning and policy and cooperation between, for example, the *Länder* and local authorities. This cooperation is strengthened by the constitution, which sets out the commitment to ensuring equal living standards across all the *Länder*. However, the equalisation of living standards across the whole country requires financial transfers between the poorest and richest *Länder*. This has significant impacts on planning and regeneration policy, as it determines the amount of money available to fund regeneration programmes (Fox 2001). Since reunification, when West Germany agreed to be financially responsible for narrowing the economic gap between eastern and western *Länder*, there has been an economic drain on many West German *Länder* including NRW.

The relatively strong political influence of the German Green Party, Die Grünen, has also shaped development policy since environmental issues have received widespread political attention and have been incorporated into regeneration programmes. Environmental policies are seen as providing a framework for economic development rather than something in conflict with economic growth (Couch 1995).

Regeneration and development in the Ruhr region

The Ruhr region or Ruhrgebeit is located in the state of NRW in the north-western part of Germany, close to the Belgian border. NRW is a highly urbanised state with a total population of nearly 18 million and is a polycentric region, with several major centres and many minor centres (see Fig. 10.1). The large towns and cities such as Cologne, Düsseldorf and Bonn orientate themselves towards the Rhine and try to dissociate themselves from the industrial image of the Ruhr (Blotevogel 1998). These urban centres market themselves as international cities distinct from the image of the Ruhr, which has been synonymous with heavy industry, a lack of economic opportunities and a poor environment. Nevertheless, the whole of the *Land* is seeking inward investment, and hence the urban centres all compete with each other for economic growth.

Within NRW there is a concentration of industry along the east–west flowing rivers Ruhr and Emscher and around their confluence with the river Rhine, which has common economic and environmental factors, enabling

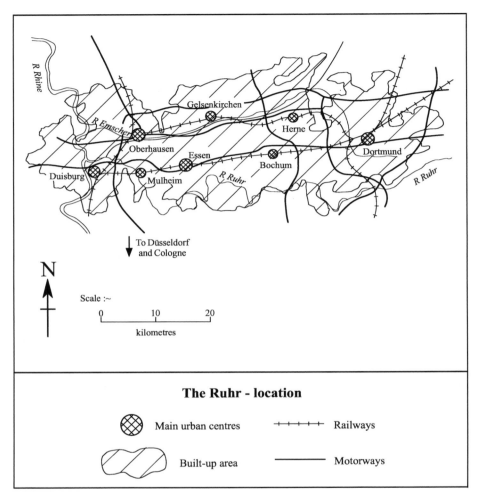

Fig. 10.1   The Ruhr: location.

the area to forge its own identity. The Ruhr region covers nearly 4450 km² with a population of 5.4 million and 11 independent cities and towns. Heavy industry (coal and steel) dominated the economic sector and hence it is as much an ideological area as it is an administrative region. Up until the 1960s the Ruhr flourished in response to a massive modernisation programme following the destruction of the Second World War. The first signs of economic crisis began to emerge in the 1950s as the demand for coal declined, domestically and internationally. This was compounded by a recession in 1966–1967, and growing international competition during the 1980s led to the traditional industries plunging into a severe and irreversible decline. Between 1958 and 1976 the number of people working in the coal industry dropped from 400 000 to 150 000 (Kommunalverband Ruhrgebeit, undated). As the traditional industries were experiencing decline, so the tertiary sector industries – financial services and electronics – were expanding, although this economic growth missed the Ruhr region and located in places such as Munich, Frankfurt and Düsseldorf (Kurpick & Weck 1998).

Owing to the past dominance of heavy industry in the Ruhr, settlement structure, environmental and employment profiles reflected this legacy. Thus the decline of these industries severely affected the region's economy, environment and society. The scale of job losses in the Ruhr region was massive: between 1976 and 1998 jobs in the iron and steel industry dropped from 180 000 to 80 000, in coal from 160 000 to 60 000, and in mechanical engineering from 80 000 to 40 000 (Bömer 2000, pp. 20–21). Not only was there severe unemployment, but this was also accompanied by a mismatch in the skills profile of the local workforce and the qualifications requirements of the new tertiary industries. These job losses were accompanied by other social problems, including the breakdown of traditional social networks, housing difficulties, and the need to retrain people from the traditional labour force. Consequently social exclusion has become a growing problem in NRW (Kurpick & Weck 1998). The area is also experiencing depopulation: between 1995 and 1999 the Ruhrgebeit saw 61 000 people leave the region (Kommunalverband Ruhrgebiet, undated).

Environmental pollution also accompanied the rise and fall of the industrial miracle, with abandoned iron and steel plants dominating the Ruhr landscape. The closure of the iron and steel plants and coal mines also left large areas of contaminated land requiring costly reclamation. Owing to the high levels of environmental contamination, regeneration policy in the Ruhr region has been tied into environmental improvement together with social enhancement. This approach to regeneration is supported by the political presence of the Green Party and is fostered through the decentralised administrative system in Germany.

Administratively the Ruhr region is covered by the State Government of NRW, various local authorities, and a regional organisation known as the *Kommunalverband Ruhrgebiet* (KVR) – the Ruhr District Association of Communities – providing a regional voice for the Ruhr. Over the last few years the KVR has concentrated its efforts on regenerating the area and on improving the environmental conditions of the region by strong promotional activities and place marketing within Germany, Europe and worldwide. *Place marketing* is a central theme of the regeneration projects undertaken in the region – the need to promote the area as a viable, clean and accessible location for new business at the heart of Europe. This approach to regeneration has had some limited success in the Ruhr, but has been blamed for the growth of undemocratic agencies and the support of prestige projects without solving associated environmental and social problems.

Over the years the NRW government has made a concerted effort to work out specific programmes to combat sectoral and regional problems of socio-economic structural change. The Ruhr Development Programme (*Entwicklungsprogramm Ruhr*) was initiated in the late 1960s and merged into the NRW Programme in 1975 (*Nordrheine-Westfalen-Programm*). The aim of these programmes was to provide a planning procedure for the development of the region based on the modernisation of the mining industry and the encouragement of inward investment. These programmes led to more infrastructure and the creation of new universities. In 1979 the Ruhr Area Action Programme (*Aktionsprogramm Ruhr*) was established to encourage urban renewal, environmental protection and technology transfer. The programme 'helped to soften the impact of job losses, but it also held back the process of restructuring and creating a new economic basis' (Kommunalverband Ruhrgebiet, undated). The Future Technologies Land Initiative (*Landesinitiative Zukunftstechnologien*) followed this programme in 1984–1988. (See Box 10.1.)

Despite these programmes the Ruhrgebiet in the 1980s still retained a poor image and had high unemployment and social problems. It was recognised that past planning initiatives and programmes were not adequately solving the region's economic and structural problems, and hence new ideas were developed that reflected a growing interest in place promotion and image transformation. These approaches reflected a shift from the urban managerial governance of the 1970s to a more entrepreneurial approach to regeneration (Hotchkiss 2002). Griffiths emphasises that entrepreneurialism is

> predicated on a competitive quest for new sources of economic development, in response to a collapsing manufacturing base and a growing internationalisation of investment flows. (Griffiths 1998, p. 42.)

In the Ruhr region there has been much effort at encouraging the development of a tertiary sector with a more flexible mode of production: as Blotevogel (1998) states with regard to NRW, 'the government now recognises that the future of the land does not rest with Fordist mass production' (p. 408). Consequently the Ruhr region, within its restructuring process, gradually began to acknowledge the area as a place of mass consumption rather than purely a production space, and saw a role for its industrial heritage in developing a new regional identity that included a cultural dimension in its economic development.

Box 10.1   Chronology of Ruhr restructuring

Year   *Event/instrument*

1950s   Ruhr coal increasingly replaced by cheaper imports and alternative fuels.

1966–1967   Recession leads to extensive closures and establishment of national economic regulation, resulting in all colliers being brought together into a single body: Ruhrkohle AG.

1968–1973   The Ruhr Development Programme (became the NRW Programme in 1975) aimed at modernising the mining industry and enhancing the mobility of land, capital and labour. Priority given to improving public transport, developing settlements and founding/extending universities.

Mid-1970s   Crisis of iron and steel industries caused by global restructuring in those industries.

1979   Ruhr Area Action Programme gave financial resources to strategically important areas, e.g. urban renewal, environment, energy and technology transfer, without a development plan. These programmes were not generally held to be a success.

1980s   Intensification of the economic crisis, especially in the Emscher subregion, made worse by the almost complete lack of alternative industries and employment types.

1984–1988   Future Technologies Land Initiative.

Late 1980s   International Building Exhibition (IBA) set up along with regional conferences.

Source: Danielzyk & Wood (1993) cited in Shaw (2002, p. 82).

By the end of the 1980s two new state approaches were developed: the *Zukunftsinitiative Montanregionen* (ZIM), which consisted of regional conferences with regional stakeholders to develop programmes to regenerate the economies of areas affected by the decline in the steel industry; and the *Emscher Park Building Exhibition*, the official title being a 'Workshop for the Future of Old Industrial Areas'. It is this latter initiative that is now explored.

Emscher Park International Building Exhibition (IBA)

The economic decline of the Ruhr region affected a vast geographical area, and the main heartland has been designated for the Emscher Park International Building Exhibition (Internationale Bauausstellung Emscher Park). The Emscher subdistrict is not an administrative unit, but is made up of collieries and steel works, many of which are now abandoned, interspersed with settlements and centred on the River Emscher. It is a conurbation between Dortmund and Duisburg, covering an area of approximately 800 km², embracing 17 cities and towns with a population of over 2 million (Knapp 1998).

In the past the planning of the Emscher subregion has been poor, dominated by industrial and economic growth with little, if any, attention paid to environmental and social conditions. The Park is therefore severely degraded, with poor housing and a weak industrial base. The landscape of the Emscher area has been largely restructured by human intervention: watercourses have been altered, hills have been formed from spoil heaps, and hollows have been left from mining. A problem for the Emscher Park and the cities therein has been one of image, of breaking the traditional perceptions that people have of areas that have a long industrial heritage.

The federal and state governments decided that the local authorities could not individually deal with the scope and extent of the problems that existed within their administrative boundaries. As a consequence the Emscher Park IBA was created in 1989 to provide a focus and framework to assist the cities and administrative districts within the Emscher region. The State Ministry of Urban Development, Housing and Transport set up the Emscher Park Planning Company in 1988–1989 to act as the coordinating body for this workshop. Its role was to encourage and evaluate proposals for regeneration projects in the Park. A key factor in the IBA programme has been the regional marketing of the area to create a new image for the Ruhr, away from that of an environmentally contaminated industrial landscape to one offering a high quality of life and suitable for the new economic sectors (Fox 2001).

Funding for the Emscher Park project has come mainly from the state and federal governments, with some from the European Union and relatively little from the private sector. The life of the project was 10 years, ending in 1999, with the fundamental aim of investing money, promoting a vision and implementing developments in the area over a relatively quick period of time (10 years) to pump-prime major structural changes in the Park. Over the lifespan of the project the IBA brought forward the development of nearly 120 projects (Brandolini 2000). The range of projects stretches from the development of large areas of derelict land right down to much smaller-scale activities such as the creation of new ecosystems or the planting of trees.

The IBA aimed to regenerate the region from a base of manufacturing and heavy industry to one of service industries through the refashioning of space as places of consumption rather than production (Fox 2001). The renewal has relied on comprehensive planning and ecological revitalisation since the IBA sees regional quality, in physical, social, environmental and cultural terms, as a key factor in improving the competitive edge of the area (Healey *et al.* 1992).

The regeneration of the Emscher Park has been taken forward by encouraging projects that foster a number of objectives, detailed below.

Economic growth and diversification

With high unemployment rates, depopulation and loss of revenue from taxation for the urban areas, much effort has been put into economic growth. The IBA has therefore aimed to attract new industry to the region through a variety of means, including creating state-of-the-art buildings with the latest technology in energy conservation and design. Recent figures show that in NRW 22% of all enterprises are environmental industries that employ 200 000 people (NRW State Government 1998). An example is the *Wirschaftswissenpark* (science park) in Gelsenkirchen on the former site of a steelworks. Most of the redundant buildings have been removed, the contaminated land has been cleaned up, and the largest solar-heated building in Germany has been constructed on the site (Kushner 2000).

The building was intended as office space for new environmental technology companies. Unfortunately, it is expensive to rent, and few private companies have occupied it; most of the building is now occupied by public institutions. The IBA has also developed subsidised industrial start-up units, and in addition to subsidising particular market sectors the scheme has strategically linked new industrial units with educational facilities offering appropriate courses.

The IBA has been active in providing suitable land for development, through, for example, the redevelopment of contaminated sites, realised by means of a process of state purchase, renovation and upgrading. The sites have then been rented out at reduced rates in order to encourage industry to the Park. For example, in Dortmund Eving a former coal mine has been decommissioned, the land has been cleaned up, some buildings have been removed, and the former mine shaft has been converted into offices, currently occupied by a practice of architects and the Research Institute for Regional and Urban Development of the Federal State of NRW (Redgrove 2002).

However, some developments are more controversial. In Oberhausen a large area of former derelict land has been redeveloped as Centro, a new regional shopping and leisure complex (see Fig. 10.2). The development is well designed and of high quality, is well served by public transport, and has generated considerable service employment. On the other hand it has also generated large volumes of additional road traffic, and had a significant impact on the functioning of nearby town centres: consequences that do not fit comfortably with the aim of the IBA to achieve 'sustainable development'.

Fig. 10.2   The Ruhr: Centro – a new shopping and leisure complex in Oberhausen.

Environmental improvement

The ecological regeneration of the Emscher River system has been one of the priorities of the Park. In the past the Emscher River and its tributaries have been used as an open sewer running throughout the Ruhr valley. Canalisation of the sewerage system has helped to clean up the Park and cut down on the amount of pollution entering the River Rhine. Another example of environmental improvement is a new housing development in Duisburg inner harbour, where reed-bed technology has been incorporated into the urban environment to filter and clean surface water runoff from the development (Fox 2001). 'Environmental improvement was deemed by the IBA planners to be a prerequisite for economic renewal on the basis that business is becoming increasingly sensitive to environmental considerations' (Shaw 2002, p. 85).

New uses for industrial monuments

The IBA has also had a programme of reusing old and derelict industrial plants and sites for cultural and recreational purposes. This has provided new opportunities for the population of the Ruhr and tourists to have access to leisure and cultural facilities that have traditionally been in short supply in the area. One of the aims behind the retention of industrial monuments and buildings was to retain links with the past and promote a strong regional identity (Shaw 2002). The former Meiderich steel works near Duisburg-Nord has been transformed into a landscape park (*Landschaftpark*), with new recreational and leisure facilities built in and around the old steel structures. At night the former steel plant is lit up by a coloured lighting display by Jonathan Park. Activities include climbing, the use of the redundant gas tower as a diving training centre, and conversion of part of the steel plant into a theatre.

Another example is the gasometer in Oberhausen, which has been converted for new uses such as arts, culture, recreation, businesses and offices (Shaw 2002). (See Fig. 10.3.)

The Zeche Zollverin (a former industrial works) in Essen has been converted into the Design Zentrum Nordhein Westfalen, an art and industrial park. 'The park includes an exhibition hall of industrial design located in a former boiler house that was remodelled by Sir Norman Foster' (Kushner 2000, p. 862).

Fig. 10.3   The Ruhr: a former gasometer, now an exhibition centre.

Landscape enhancement

The IBA has been regenerating the landscape through the development and implementation of a regional park by coordinating a regional green space system that provides an ecological backbone to the area. This has been carried out by preserving green spaces in between urban areas and enhancing some derelict sites that were left unused. The green areas have been part of a larger network of green corridors known as the Emscher Landscape Park covering 320 km², connecting the parks and green public spaces of 17 towns along the Emscher into one green corridor (Almaas 1999). The landscape improvements are 'laid out for recreational use, complete with pedestrian signage and landscaped cycle paths' (Almaas 1999, p. 13). In addition the park has a number of spectacular public sculptures, such as Jurgen Lit Fischer's *Tetraeder* at Bottrop.

Social inclusion

The enhancement of the social fabric of the area was seen to be very important, because the decline of industrial processes had led to the erosion of traditional social networks and milieus (Madanipour *et al.* 1998). With increasing social inequality, certain groups have become vulnerable to social exclusion from the formal labour market, and from social and cultural opportunities. To try and tackle social exclusion a number of initiatives have been pursued. Old housing stock has been improved and living conditions enhanced, although consultations with the local population have been minimal (Madanipour *et al.* 1998). The IBA has encouraged self-build projects for low-income groups, giving them the opportunity to achieve ownership and as an encouragement to remain in the region. According to Almaas (1999), '26 new "garden city" housing developments were planned providing 3000 new flats, of which 75% were public sector rented' (p. 14). A major problem still exists in that the economic restructuring of the area has led to skill mismatch for the existing unemployed in the region (Madanipour *et al.* 1998). Hence other initiatives have been developed involving employment and training schemes for young, long-term unemployed people. (See Fig. 10.4.)

Fig. 10.4 The Ruhr: new social housing in Dortmund.

Place marketing

A key strategy for attracting inward investment for many of the cities and towns in the Emscher Park has been through active place marketing and promotion campaigns. Duisburg, which lies at the western end of the Emscher subregion, has been regenerating its old inner harbour area, replacing derelict industrial buildings with new industries and housing developments, with public funding coming from the IBA programme. The scheme is a mix of refurbishment of existing buildings and new buildings, creating a high-quality waterfront development of new flats (private and public), commercial space and leisure facilities (Redgrove 2002). The master plan for the inner harbour was designed by Foster and Partners following an international design competition, and includes the landmark Euro-Gate office building. The redevelopment has also sought to retain aspects of the industrial heritage in an area known as the Garden of Memories. The city has put a lot of effort into transforming its image from one associated with coal, iron and steel to that of 'Duisburg on the Rhine'. It is unlikely, however, that the Duisburg inner harbour redevelopment will be fully realised for a few years, owing in part to the cessation of the IBA and the reliance now of the development on private sector investment.

The extent of recovery

In total, about DM5 billion has been spent on the Emscher Park IBA scheme, of which two thirds has come from public funds and the rest from private investors (IBA 1999). This has resulted in the successful redevelopment of a number of major old industrial sites; has reduced the development pressure on greenfield sites; has promoted a more vibrant image of the region in the minds of locals and visitors; has improved inward investment; and has assisted and supported the restructuring of the region's economic base. The IBA has also created more accessible and attractive open space in the Park, brought forward new housing schemes, and refurbished existing domestic and commercial properties.

New industry has been attracted into the Park, but not on the scale hoped. The image of the area still seems to be a constraint on relocation, and brownfield site redevelopment is hugely expensive. The impact of reunification has been felt in the project implementation: the redistribution of funding to eastern *Länder* has meant that available public money has been contracted over the project period. Thus the IBA has had a smaller project in the Park than was first anticipated, with many jobs created in the short-term world of construction reflected in the unemployment rate, which in January 2001 for NRW as a whole was 9.9% and for the Ruhr region was 12.6% compared with the national average of 8.9% (Bömer 2001).

In terms of the regeneration of the Emscher Park there are some key issues that have provided both opportunities for and challenges to the redevelopment of the subregion. These are discussed below.

Joint working

The Emscher Park project has been able to encourage informal planning to occur through joint working across and between different agencies and administrations. This horizontal and vertical coordination between various governments and departments is illustrated in the development of the Dortmund Technology Park: 'Various participants and executing agencies were involved at the Regional and State level, which formed a dense network of formal and informal interactions' (Stohr 1992). Mandanipour *et al.* (1998) go on to state: 'The neighbourhood regeneration programme of the state of NRW was characterised by the institutional emphasis of the programme targeted at transcending traditional departmental thinking and networking at the local level'.

However, the complexity of the IBA project has meant in many cases that community projects have not been encouraged: the main actors have been the local authorities and some private industry (Danielzyk & Wood 1993). In German society generally there is emphasis on legislative controls: environmental protection is highly regulated. One problem with a highly regulated society is that the public rely on the state to take responsibility for all aspects of management, and hence do not see the need for involvement. This may help to explain, in part, why public participation in the Emscher Park project has been limited despite the authorities' attempt to include public participation in their decision-making processes.

A regional tier

The existence of a tradition of strong regional planning and spatial development is an advantage in that it helps to maintain balanced growth rates and living standards between regions (Couch 1995), although in contrast Danielyzk & Wood (1993) argue that the IBA did not in fact present a regional strategy but was based more on a local perspective of neighbouring authorities' cooperation.

Environmental awareness

In Germany and NRW there has been a long-standing tradition of linking economic growth to environmental enhancement, so in the case of Emscher Park there was political support from the outset for a sustainable development approach to regeneration. However, the late 1990s saw a subtle shift in the prioritising of the environment over other issues owing to the economic pressures faced in Germany as a result of reunification. With money being diverted to the 'poorer' *Länder*, it is likely that publicly funded sustainable regeneration schemes in the region will become more limited, with emphasis in the future being increasingly placed on private funding and the use of public–private partnership schemes.

Autonomy

The decentralised nature of the German political system, coupled with the ability that each tier of government has in answering the problems of regeneration, is a distinct advantage. The autonomy of each level of government is enshrined in the constitution, enabling decisions to be taken at the most appropriate level. This has the consequence of allowing the *Länder* to implement federal decisions through local or regional regeneration strategies. Interestingly it was the *Länder* rather than the local authorities that held the power in the IBA programme through the regulatory instruments of technical standards and funding sources. In reality the *Länder* of NRW exerted power over the local authorities to accept particular projects (Danielzyk & Wood 1993), which resulted in competition rather than cooperation between different local authorities.

Cultural heritage

Kushner (2000) notes that 'communities need to identify and preserve their unique cultural heritage while creating entertaining spaces with specialised museums and parks' (p. 870). The reused buildings are seen as architectural witnesses, explaining the history of the region to visitors and attracting tourists to the area. The IBA has been proactive in building a cultural dimension into the regeneration process, which has seen the development of many projects, attracting both local visitors and tourists to the area.

However, now that the Emscher Park project has ceased, and in the absence of continuing public sector funding on the scale provided by the IBA during the ten-year project, it is unclear whether the private sector will continue to invest in the region. It is likely that inward investment will slow down, and some of the IBA's planned projects will not be realised.

Conclusion

Trying to judge whether the regeneration of the Ruhr region has been successful is fraught with difficulties, particularly as very few official policy evaluation studies have been carried out on the IBA. It is clear, however, that the scale of the task faced by the IBA and the constraints on realisation have meant that work has been carried out on only a small percentage of the land area of the Park, and fewer projects have been implemented. Nevertheless, there are discernible qualitative signs that regeneration attempts have been successful: much best practice has been recorded, and should be considered by other institutions and governments that need to regenerate large areas. For example, the IBA programme has taken a proactive and innovative stance on redevelopment by offering a holistic and regional public sector approach towards the restructuring of old industrial areas. The project has also attempted to go beyond the improvement of physical infrastructure by facilitating ecological improvement and socio-cultural innovation, and with its focus on environmental improvement and finding new uses for obsolete structures, a transformation of the Ruhr region's image can be said to have begun. The integrated and holistic manner in which a range of issues – environmental, social, economic and cultural – have been tackled is also important in demonstrating a sustainable regeneration model for other regions suffering similar problems to follow (Shaw 2002).

Note

This chapter has drawn on visits to North Rhine Westphalia run by South Bank University for postgraduate planning students. I have utilised material gathered while in Germany, and coursework completed by the students, for which I am grateful.

11

Economic and Physical Influences on Urban Regeneration in Europe

Chris Couch

This chapter considers some of the similarities and differences between the case study areas in terms of the effects on regeneration of their geographical location, economic and physical circumstances. Location has important impacts both on the causes of urban change and on decline; on the ability of places to regenerate, and on the nature of what can be achieved through regeneration. Here the issue of peripherality is central to the debate. At a more local level, the physical legacy of the past must also be taken into account. Comparison of the physical structure and character of each location shows different potentials for regeneration: in some cases the exploitation of the built heritage or landscape features, in other cases the opportunity to sweep away old and outworn premises and infrastructure.

Consideration also needs to be given to the economic circumstances of each area. The rationale for regeneration is often couched in predominantly economic terms, 'restructuring' the economy being a necessary prerequisite for physical change in the built environment. Comparisons between the case study areas reveal how responses have differed according to economic circumstances, the strength of local markets, and the degree of external subsidy.

Geographical location

Peripherality is one of the key geographical features that affect the fortunes of these cities. The three cities in the UK are particularly affected. Belfast and Dundee are both remote from the heartlands of Europe, cut off from industrial markets by the high cost and long duration of journeys. Liverpool, although less remote, has a port that was traditionally considered to be well placed for deep-sea trading but found itself poorly located to take advantage of the increasing trade between the UK and mainland Europe in recent years. Whereas Belfast is a free-standing city and has little relationship with any other urban area, both Dundee and Liverpool are interconnected with urbanised regions. Dundee is at the north-eastern apex of a triangle of Scottish cities with Glasgow and Edinburgh at the western and eastern points respectively. Within this triangle is to be found a high proportion of total Scottish economic activity, cultural and political power. Although Dundee is very much the smallest of the three cities, it is geographically close enough to this economic heartland (about one hour by train or road from both centres) to receive some benefit from this relationship. This situation can be contrasted with the location of Liverpool, 60 km to the west of Manchester. These cities have been economic competitors for more than a century, but in recent years Manchester, with a major international airport and a more central location, has emerged as the regional capital. As such it has received the benefits of economic centralisation and the growth of regional headquarters offices at the expense of Liverpool. Manchester has also benefited from strategic investments in the post-industrial economy, such as exhibition centres, conference facilities, sporting and cultural arenas, and in bidding for international events (such as the Commonwealth Games 2002).

In the past the Nord-Pas-de-Calais was perceived as being on the northern periphery of France, remote from the centres of French economic and political power. Furthermore the local economy was heavily dependent upon coal mining, heavy manufacturing industry and textiles, all of which have suffered severe decline in recent years. Today, with the arrival of the Single European Market, and as a consequence of heavy investment in road and rail infrastructure, the region finds itself in a key location at the centre of the 'golden triangle' between London, Paris and Brussels. Lille has played to this new strength in developing a place-marketing strategy that emphasises its European centrality: the new station is called Euralille and the 'eura' epithet has been subsequently used to describe and market a technology centre, Euratechnologie, and major health campus, Eurasanté. Each of the other areas (Rotterdam, Wallonia, Ruhr and Milan) is situated in a region that is close both to the economic heart of its own country and to western Europe. All are located comfortably within DATAR's 'Blue Banana'. The Ruhr and Rotterdam have responded well to the demands of the post-industrial economy, both investing heavily in environmental improvements, higher education, exhibition and conference facilities and seeing significant growth in service sector employment. Wallonia has been less successful so far, but is beginning to make some progress in coping with its enormous legacy of industrial dereliction and outworn urban infrastructure. Milan is probably the most prosperous of the case study areas, and the problems of Bovisa appear to be manageable in economic terms.

External transport connections can have an important impact on the comparative advantage of different cities for industrial and commercial investment. These cities are increasingly dependent upon commercial rather than industrial investment for economic growth. Commerce is much more influenced than industry by the quality and speed of passenger transport connections, especially inter-city rail services and the presence of an international airport serving a good range of destinations. Table 11.1 indicates the situation in each area.

Clearly there is considerable variation in the quality of external passenger connections from these areas. It is evident that the UK case study areas have significantly poorer inter-city and airport connections than their counterparts in mainland Europe. Although Liverpool benefited from investment in its local underground railway system in the early 1970s, there have been few subsequent service improvements. Two new stations have been opened within inner-city redevelopment areas since the early 1990s, but they appear to have followed rather than led the regeneration process. The Albert Dock area remains poorly served by public transport, and the north docks and adjoining Vauxhall area

Table 11.1   Passenger transport connections.

| Case study area | Quality of passenger transport connections | | Airport |
| | Rail | | |
	Regional	Inter-city	
Rotterdam	Excellent	Excellent (some HST)	Rotterdam: regional Schipol (1hr): international
Liverpool	Average	Average	Liverpool: regional Manchester (1hr): international
Belfast	Insignificant	Insignificant	Belfast: regional
Lille	Good	Excellent (HST)	Lille: regional Brussels (1hr): international Paris CdG (1hr): international
Wallonia	Good	Good	Charleroi: regional Brussels (1hr): international
Ruhr	Excellent	Excellent (HST)	Dortmund: regional Düsseldorf: international
Milan	Good	Good (some HST)	Linate: international Malpensa: international
Dundee	Average	Average	Dundee: regional Edinburgh (1hr): some international

HST = High-speed train.

Source: author.

have seen no significant public transport investment in recent years. In consequence these areas remain isolated from the central business district and other more prosperous parts of the conurbation. Nor has much progress been made at the regional scale. Connections between the Liverpool conurbation (population 1.5 million) and Greater Manchester (population 2.0 million), only 60 km away, remain reliant upon diesel trains to provide a service that is little better than it was 70 years ago. Belfast has seen some investment in its airport and in rail connections to Dublin, although the significance of the latter to the local economy is minimal. Dundee is too small a conurbation and its surroundings too sparsely populated to support any system of local public transport other than bus services. It has a local airport that maintains a rudimentary service to London and a small number of other destinations. The train service to Edinburgh and Glasgow is adequate, but slow by modern European standards and insufficient to encourage much overspill investment from those cities.

In contrast, each of the mainland European case study areas has seen substantial investment in public transport in recent years. In Rotterdam both the Delfshaven and Kop van Zuid regeneration areas are well connected to the city centre and main station by modern metro systems. These connections have been important in maintaining the attraction of Delfshaven as an accessible inner-city residential location and in promoting Kop van Zuid as a secondary commercial centre with scarcely any locational disadvantage. In the Ruhr, Lille, Wallonia and Milan, investment in local heavy and light rail systems has been seen as making an important contribution to the infrastructure necessary to support the future regeneration of the area. Such investment not only increases accessibility but often also has environmental benefits that increase the attractiveness of locations as places in which to live and work.

The strength of the regional economy

One of the key determinants of the rate at which local regeneration can be sustained without external subsidy is the strength of the regional economy. This is not to say that specific investments may not be made quite independently of the nature of the regional economy: for example investments in tourism that are aimed at customers from beyond the region, or investments in manufacturing industry that may be made in the area precisely because wage rates are low and alternative job opportunities relatively scarce. But with these exceptions regeneration can normally be sustained only at a rate that can be supported by economic conditions.

Some of the case study areas benefit from subsidies for economic development from European Union Structural Funds. Objective One funding, to support the development of lagging regions, is available to Belfast (Northern Ireland) and Liverpool (Merseyside). Objective Two funding, to support the restructuring of areas of industrial decline, is available to Dundee and the Ruhr area.

Private investment in regeneration is generally limited by the return that can be achieved on that investment. For property developers this means the rental income or capital value of completed projects. However, the question is not simply the profitability of the project but its relative profitability compared with other investment opportunities that might be available elsewhere. This applies to all market sectors, but it is most clearly evident in the commercial sector, which is dominated by the activities of a relatively small number of financial institutions that treat property investment as a commodity and are increasingly operating on an international scale. Although construction costs do vary somewhat between different locations, the main variation lies in the rent levels or capital values that can be achieved for the completed building. This makes investment in some locations much more profitable than in others.

Public investments will be limited by the willingness and ability of the state to raise taxes from households and firms. The influences here are not only the ability to pay the necessary taxes but also the political willingness to pay. For example, in September 2000 the UK government was faced with a sudden massive popular campaign against its high rates of fuel taxation. Whatever the worthy motives behind that taxation, it had reached levels that had become politically unsustainable. The politics of taxation are complex, especially at the local level, where the desire for public spending is frequently frustrated by the perceived political necessity of minimising the tax burden on local residents, who vote local politicians into and out of office, and on firms, who provide employment for local people. Indeed, a key element of enterprise zone policy in the UK in the 1980s was the exemption of firms from local taxes in order to stimulate economic development.

The regions in which the case study cities are to be found vary quite substantially in terms of economic performance, as shown in Table 11.2.

There are significant differences in terms of industrial structure between the regions. Lombardia and Nordrhein-Westfalen are somewhat more dependent upon industrial employment, and have a weaker service employment base than any of the other regions. West-Nederland has the smallest proportion of industrial employment and the highest proportion of service

Table 11.2   Regional economic characteristics.

City and region	Structure of employment (% of employees by sector 1999)			Unemployment rate 1998 (%)	GDP per capita 1997 EU15 = 100
	Agriculture	Industry	Services		
Rotterdam (West-Nederland)	2.9**	18.1**	77.1**	3.9	121
Liverpool (North-West England)	1.2	28.2	70.5	6.4	93 (74*)
Belfast (Northern Ireland)	5.0	26.5	68.5	8.8	82
Lille (Nord-Pas-de-Calais)	1.7	29.4	68.9	15.9	82
Mons (Wallonia)	2.8	24.7	72.5	13.5	88
Ruhr (Nordrhein-Westfalen)	1.8	34.3	63.9	8.7	108
Milan (Lombardia)	2.1	41.1	56.8	5.7	131
Dundee (Scotland)	2.0	25.3	72.5	7.3	97

*GDP figures in brackets are for the NUTS2 area: Merseyside.

**1994 data.

Source: *Regional Trends* No. 35, 2000, Table 2.3.

employment of any of the regions. As a consequence of these differences each of the regions has strengths in different sorts of agglomeration economies and a comparative advantage in different fields of economic activity and therefore in the types of industrial investment that it can most easily attract. All large urban areas are able to benefit from economies of scale in the provision of goods and services in both the private and public sectors: for example in transport infrastructure, higher education and training, and commercial services. However, further agglomeration economies can also be obtained depending upon the economic structure of the area. For example, the port cities of Liverpool and Rotterdam both support a much greater level of higher education in maritime studies and naval engineering than would be found in other conurbations. Liverpool also has strength in financial services, insurance and commodity trading as well as food processing and other port-related activities. The cities of the Ruhr contain specialised industrial and commercial services related to steel production and finishing; Milan accommodates a large number of firms with skills geared to the needs of the textile and clothing industries. Similarly, in the Lille–Roubaix–Tourcoing conurbation diversification from the former textile industry led to the growth of distribution and mail order companies. The physical form and structure of former mill buildings has permitted relatively easy conversion to offices, apartments and higher education, among other uses.

Some of the regions that had a traditional dependence on industrial production have found themselves lacking the infrastructure to attract modern services and high-technology activities. Furthermore, given a general trend away from industrial employment towards service employment it may well be that regions such as Lombardia and Nordrhein-Westfalen are lagging behind the others in terms of industrial restructuring. If this is so, then these two regions can expect substantial amounts of existing industrial land to become ripe for regeneration and conversion to other uses in the future.

Lombardia is the most prosperous region in terms of GDP per capita, followed by West-Nederland and Nordrhein-Westfalen. These regions have more resources to 'buy themselves out of trouble', in terms both of the tax base and of spending power within the local economy. It is in these regions that the fastest rate of regeneration might be expected. In contrast, in the relatively depressed economies of Nord-Pas-de-Calais, Northern Ireland and Wallonie the speed with which regeneration can take place is likely to be modest without external subsidy and support.

There is also a great deal of variation in unemployment rates. In general the level of unemployment tends to reflect the prosperity of the region, with the worst figures being found in Nord-Pas-de Calais and Wallonie and the best in West-Nederland and Lombardia. The figures for the UK regions seem to buck the trend to some extent. Here policy appears to have achieved reasonably high levels of employment but without correspondingly high levels of output.

Some regions have unique characteristics that influence their ability to regenerate. For example, many would argue that the regeneration of Belfast was for many years held back by 'the troubles' but that it now benefits from recent progress made with the 'peace process'. During the 1980s political conflict between Liverpool City Council and the central government led to a sharp decline in investor confidence, with a deterioration in the image of the city that took many years to repair. Lille, on the other hand, has managed to transform its image from that of a peripheral French city to that of a dynamic metropolis at the heart of Europe's 'Golden Triangle'.

The regeneration of many of these case study areas has been reliant upon special subsidies from their own national governments and from the European Union, particularly for infrastructure investment. Another tool used with some success in a number of countries is the decentralisation of state services to provincial locations. For example, Liverpool's south docks accommodate a large new office block that houses part of the UK government's customs and excise service. In other areas, notably the Ruhr and Lille, national or regional government investment in higher education has been used as a mechanism both to broaden the economic base and to improve the employability of the local workforce.

Some of these cities are regional capitals, or are in situations where there is little intra-regional competition for investment. These include Belfast, Dundee and – to a lesser extent – Lille and Milan. In other areas, such as Liverpool, the Ruhr and Wallonia, a multiplicity of competing centres dilutes the impact of inward investment. Whereas much of the office investment seeking a location in Northern Ireland is likely to end up in Belfast, similar offices seeking a location in the Ruhr could equally well locate in any one of a dozen cities (such as Duisburg, Essen, Bochum or Dortmund) with very little difference in costs or benefits.

Nearly all of the case study areas have had physical features that have influenced the nature of the regeneration process. In some areas the physical fabric left behind by previous forms of economic activity may become an asset, whereas in other areas it may be a liability. Docks and waterfronts, warehouses and textile mills seem frequently to be returned to profitable uses within reasonable budgets. On the other hand former coal mines, steel works and chemical plants are more likely to be associated with problems of contamination and spoil, with little attraction for future investors. Warehouses, mills and waterfronts can be exploited by burgeoning cultural and tourist industries, but the sheer size and frequently poor location of former mines and heavy industrial plants tend to render them useful only for further manufacturing or distribution activities.

Liverpool and Rotterdam, and to a lesser degree Dundee and Belfast, have exploited their waterfront locations. Former docks have been converted for leisure use, and the former warehouses of the last century have proved particularly adaptable and attractive locations for up-market residential accommodation. The growth in urban tourism has made these areas popular locations for 'character' hotels, museums, shopping, restaurants, bars and performance venues. In the other areas, notably the Ruhr, physical artefacts from the industrial past have been exploited for their heritage, cultural or recreational potential. Examples include the Landschaftspark Duisburg-Nord (a former steel works transformed into a country park); the Zeche Zollverien XII in Essen (a former coal mine with buildings dating from the Bauhaus era, now converted into an arts centre and museum); and the Gasometer Oberhausen (a former gasometer, now converted into an exhibition hall and viewing platform). However, the Ruhr, Wallonia and other regions also contain large tracts of former industrial land where the main post-reclamation use is wholesale or retail warehousing.

As the regeneration of these regions becomes increasingly dominated by the service sector, including retailing, cultural activity and tourism, so the quality of the local environment becomes a more important factor in attracting investment. The quality of town and city centre environments seems to be particularly important. In response, recent years have seen many of these cities spend large sums of money improving the physical quality of such centres. Virtually all now have pedestrianised shopping areas, and many have invested in new squares and public spaces as well as moving to protect heritage buildings and townscapes. Lille and Dundee stand out as being particularly successful in transforming formerly uninspiring city centres into vibrant and attractive hubs of urban activity. Rotterdam, one of the first cities to have a pedestrianised centre in the 1950s, has also had some success with a recent modernisation programme. The physical environment of these central areas seems to have a major impact on the image of the city as perceived by developers, and can be an important stimulus to further investment across the region. Table 11.3 summarises these economic drivers and their impact on regeneration.

The use of land and buildings

Over the last 50 years the processes of urban change that have taken place in most of these case study locations, aided and abetted by urban planning policies, have tended to encourage the gradual separation of land uses into different zones. In particular, the intense zoning of post-war redevelopments and subsequent slum clearance and rebuilding schemes kept housing well away from industry, with its air pollution, noise and traffic. Furthermore, ambitious highway schemes physically divided one zone from the next. By the 1970s and 1980s there had been a change of policy in favour of area improvement rather than slum clearance, and major urban highway proposals had fallen out of favour across most of western Europe. At the same time there was rising unemployment and political pressures for job creation virtually everywhere. In these 'improvement areas' the pressure to remove the remaining local industrial base diminished, and was replaced by a desire to nurture and support indigenous industrial growth. More recently, pressure from the environmental lobby has made a virtue of mixed uses, and such proposals are positively sought in many schemes.

Nevertheless, the nature of the physical relationship between residential

Table 11.3   Success rates and the economic drivers of regeneration.

City	Success of regeneration	Important influences on regeneration
Rotterdam	High	Heavy investment in city infrastructure Widespread public ownership of land and buildings Exploitation of 'waterside' location Development of flagship projects and tourism (e.g. Hotel New York) Constrained by intra-regional competition within the Randstad
Liverpool	Moderate	High dependence on EU and state subsidy Decentralised state services Growth of higher education and health sectors Exploitation of built heritage (e.g. dockland warehouses) Development of flagship projects and tourism (e.g. Albert Dock) Poor image Constrained by intra-regional competition (e.g. Manchester)
Belfast	Moderate	Northern Ireland 'peace process'/improving image High dependence on EU and state subsidy Investment in decentralised state services Exploitation of waterside potential (Laganside) Peripheral location within Europe Infrastructure investments Regional capital
Lille	High	Removal of international borders Investment in inter-city road and rail infrastructure Regional capital Investment in decentralised state services Growth of higher education, health and research sectors Exploitation of built heritage (e.g. textile mills)
Wallonia	Moderate	High dependence on EU subsidy Intra-regional competition: no dominant regional capital Widespread derelict land Poor image, limited potential for flagship/tourist projects
Ruhr	Moderate	Investment in regional infrastructure and the environment Central location within Germany High dependence on state subsidy and investment Exploitation of widespread derelict land and buildings Poor image, improving through investment in culture and sport Diverse initiatives well combined, packaged and marketed High quality in design and specification of investments Scale of industrial restructuring and dereliction is problematic
Milan	In progress	Central location within industrial heartland of Italy Proposed infrastructure investments Greening the area Growth of higher education and research sectors
Dundee	Moderate	High dependence on state subsidy Subregional capital Growth of higher education Exploitation of waterside location Peripheral location

Source: author's analysis.

areas and industry does vary from place to place. For example, many of the towns in the Emscher zone of the Ruhr developed as mining or industrial settlements. Mine shafts were often sunk in the heart of urban areas. Many of the small manufacturing firms of the nineteenth century have grown to become industrial giants on the same sites today.

The physical form of urban development also varies. In much of central Europe the tenement block is a commonly used building form. It is also known in Scotland, but is rare in England or Northern Ireland, nor is it very often seen in the Netherlands. Within the tenement areas building densities tend to be much higher than in terraced housing areas. Typically tenements are built up to four or six storeys around the perimeter of a block, leaving an inner courtyard for other uses. This leads to plot ratios (building floorspace to site area) of 2 : 1 or even 3 : 1, whereas the equivalent figure found in the terraced housing areas is around 1 : 1. The net residential density of tenement areas can be up to 500 persons per hectare compared with 180 in terraced housing areas. This building density was increased historically as the inner courtyards of tenements were taken over for additional building structures. One consequence of the use of the tenement block is that there can be a closer proximity between residential and non-residential uses than in other sorts of building form, such as terraced housing. In tenements much of the ground floor space is typically given over to shopping or commercial activities, and historically the courtyard commonly accommodated small-scale industrial premises, or workshops, with all the noise, vehicular intrusion and lack of privacy that this implies. Today many cities have policies to remove such structures and redesign the courtyards for the leisure and recreational use of residents.

A further consequence of the tenement form is less roadspace. There is physically less road frontage per household than in terraced housing areas. This makes the parking and storage of cars more problematic. When combined with high car ownership, as in parts of the Ruhr, this becomes a serious environmental issue. Because there are fewer residential streets in tenement areas, more dwellings front onto busier roads and suffer more from traffic intrusion than in terraced housing areas. The greater number and length of roads in terraced housing areas make it easier to create environmental areas and local traffic management schemes that exclude through traffic, whereas in tenement areas the solution lies more with traffic calming.

The townscape generated by tenement areas tends to feel highly urbanised. Streets are wide, with high buildings (12–18 m) rising from the back of the pavement. Most of the space between the fronts of these buildings is given over to roadways, paving or hard landscaping. Because the tenement is a much bigger building project than the terraced house they are much more likely to have been designed by an architect rather than being 'builder designed'. Thus many of these residential buildings in the Ruhr, in Milan and in Wallonie have some individual design qualities and features, so that they contribute more than just mass and shape to the street scene. These large buildings frequently combine together to form fine, well-proportioned streets. Although development may have been piecemeal, developers have usually been obliged to maintain a unity of height, form and façade. The result is often a pleasantly harmonious blend of old and new.

In the older areas of cities such as Liverpool and Belfast, dominated by terraced housing, in all but the poorest streets dwellings are separated from the pavement by small front gardens, often only 1 m deep but creating an important semi-private space. This separation, together with the smaller buildings (only 6–8 m high) and the individual variety of the houses, tends to create streets of less unity and less satisfying proportions.

The purposes for which land and buildings can be used through a regeneration process will depend upon local demand. Within central business districts the trend has been for regeneration to be concerned mainly with the modernisation of the buildings and infrastructure of the city centre, together with some intensification of use and the introduction of residential and leisure uses in property that cannot command high commercial values. Outside these areas the general trend has been for the regeneration process to result in a change of use from extractive, manufacturing or transport industries towards service industries or consumption uses. In most of the case study areas this has been the trend (see Table 11.4).

The combination of housing form and tenure can have a significant impact on the choices facing regeneration policy makers. Historically, at least from the middle of the nineteenth century, the urban working class in England were typically accommodated in single-family terraced houses. This is a very flexible building form that may be renovated, improved or converted to another use, such as retailing or commerce, with little difficulty. On the other hand the footprint of the dwelling is so small (about 4 m × 10 m including the back yard) that it is almost impossible to demolish and rebuild on a single house plot. Clearance and rebuilding has to be undertaken on a group basis (such as a whole terrace) to make any economic sense. The clearance of groups of dwellings invariably requires public intervention to be successful. Most of these dwellings were originally constructed for the private rented housing market. Gradually over the twentieth century the proportion of these dwellings in owner occupation increased dramatically, and most are now in this tenure. It

Table 11.4   Land-use changes in regeneration areas.

Case study area		Former dominant land uses	Recent investment mainly in
Rotterdam	Kop van Zuid	Docklands	Mixed commercial/residential
	Delfshaven	Residential/industrial/ commercial docks	Residential/leisure/ recreational waterways
Liverpool	City centre	Offices/retail	Offices/retail/hotels/leisure/ residential/education
	Vauxhall/Everton	Industrial/residential	Residential/warehousing
Belfast	Laganside	Industrial/docklands	Offices/hotel/leisure
	Springvale	Residential	Residential/business park/ education
Lille	Euralille	Gardens, coach station and SNCF land	Offices/retail/hotel/leisure
	Haute Borne	Greenfield	Science park
	Site de l'union	Industrial	Housing/culture/leisure
	Euratechnologie	Industrial	Technology centre
	Eurasanté	Hospital lands	Health/higher education
Wallonia	Quartier Rachot (Mons)	Wasteland/backland	Social and private housing
	Les Grandes Pres (Mons)	Wasteland	Offices, cinema, recreation
Ruhr	Various sites	Mining/heavy manufacturing industry	Offices/residential/ commercial/leisure
Milan	Bovisa	Manufacturing industry	High-technology industry/ residential
Dundee	City-wide sites	Manufacturing industry/ docklands	Light industry/commerce/ retail/leisure

Source: author's analysis.

is much more difficult and expensive for the local authorities to clear owner-occupied dwellings than it is to clear private rented dwellings.

In the early 1970s policies for the renewal of the private housing stock in England saw an almost complete movement away from clearance towards housing renovation. The reasons for this change are well documented elsewhere. They included: the increasing costs of clearing better-quality owner-occupied housing built after 1870; resident dissatisfaction with the process of clearance and rehousing, and with the perceived poor quality of alternative housing offered; and the desire to prevent further massive losses of population and the destruction of the fabric of inner-city communities. This policy has remained in place until the present, but there are emerging signs of dissatisfaction with this renovated housing stock that is leading to low demand, falling values and even abandonment in extreme cases. This is causing policy makers to rethink the treatment of older obsolete housing in future.

Conclusions

Location has a critical impact upon the ability of areas to regenerate, and on the nature of what can be achieved. Regional economic strength will boost or inhibit the regeneration process. The peripherality of some areas restricts their ability to compete in European markets. Although motorway connections are a prerequisite of modern city development, for regeneration to exploit opportunities within the service sector, especially in tourism, recreation and culture, access to good passenger rail and air services is also essential. In the case of some cities local intra-regional competition can also inhibit regeneration activity. In the worst cases there are cities suffering intra-regional competition in regions experiencing poor economic performance. Particular characteristics of local economic history and structure can have an important influence in determining the nature of future development, and local political circumstances can moderate economic regeneration for better or for worse, sometimes very significantly. The location and physical form of the inherited landscapes, structures and artefacts can also have a major impact on the potential for regeneration.

12

The Institutional and Financial Conditions of Urban Regeneration in Europe

Charles Fraser

The administration of regeneration policy is inextricably bound up with the politicians at all levels who administer it, with the traditions of the administrations they work for, and with the investment mechanisms that they operate. In each case, to make any sort of meaningful comparison some model of the framework for each must be borne in mind. Thus for each subsection there will be an attempt to ensure that like is compared with like, and that the same structure for analysis is applied to each case study.

Administrative structures

In comparing the manner in which the regeneration exercise in each case study has been administered, the following question comes to the fore: to what extent has the exercise been integrated with existing spatial planning structures, and have they been able to incorporate dealing with regeneration as part of their 'normal' approach or has it been necessary to create new organisations to deal with a phenomenon that poses problems for which they are unprepared? Taking the role played by the existing levels of government in turn, the chapter will try to clarify the success of these and identify where and how new organisations have become necessary.

National government intervention

In Belgium the federal government has no constitutional place in urban regeneration *per se*, but as it is responsible for certain national social budgets, which are often disproportionately targeted at the inhabitants of areas undergoing such planned change, it has more than a passing interest in the process. Similarly in Germany the regeneration and physical renewal processes are the 'competence' of the *Länder*, and the federal government has little involvement with them.

In Italy the national government has set a framework within which the various regions, all of which have different administrative traditions, can work with their constituent provinces and cities to execute the process at local level. In the United Kingdom (and we have explored examples from three of its constituent four parts) there is a variety of relationships between the subnational government and the UK government itself. There is a tendency to believe that the UK government plays a major role in regeneration policy, as recent publications such as the Urban Policy White Paper have been published by a central government ministry. However, what may be unclear to observers outside the UK is that such documents apply to England, or occasionally to England and Wales only, and that the Whitehall department is in fact acting as part of the administration for England only, although no de facto *English* government exists. The role of, for example, the Department of Transport, Local Government and the Regions (DTLR) (formerly DETR) is in fact to act at a subnational level. The same is true of the Scottish Executive, the Northern Ireland Executive and the Welsh Office By comparison, in France and the Netherlands the central governments have strong direct strategic involvement in the process.

Regional government involvement

Although it may be considered politically dangerous to refer to the Scottish administration in particular as 'regional', it is one of the series of government agencies at substate level in the UK that have a major responsibility for the guidance and financing of urban regeneration activity. As has been pointed out, the DTLR acts in this capacity for England, and the Northern Ireland Executive for its own province.

As yet, no English region has developed an elected assembly on a par with the Scottish and Welsh bodies, but the process of democratic devolution is heading in that direction. As intimated in the Urban Policy White Paper *Our Towns and Cities: The Future,* the aim is to devolve the funding and policy control mechanisms to the regional development authorities (RDAs), which will work in tandem with the restructured English Partnerships, which will in turn become the main agent for the delivery of urban regeneration strategies throughout England. However, so far these agencies have not played a prominent part in the regeneration effort in Liverpool. When this combination is fully operational the English regions may begin to be a motor for innovation as they try out policy and practice approaches that vary the model from the Whitehall standard one. Equally, in Belgium it is the regional government of Wallonie, in Germany the *Land* of North Rhine Westphalia, and in Italy the Lombardy region that are the key policy makers.

Unlike England, France already has two legitimate regional agencies. The first, the Direction Régional is, like regional offices in England, the regional presence of the central government and its various departments. The second is an elected regional Assembly, the Conseil Régional. In the Nord region the regional government has an important role in regeneration, but has to deal with a series of areas from the coalfields to the run-down steel towns around Valenciennes. It therefore plays a supporting role in the practical implementation of the programme for the Lille *métropole*.

The Netherlands is divided into 11 provinces, but they do not have a major role in the regeneration programmes of the four dominant cities. These tend to have direct relationships with the central government ministries, VROM and the Ministry of the Interior, which are responsible for the policy context and the financing of most of the national programme. The provinces play a more guiding role in the programmes for the smaller towns.

In Italy the regional government of Lombardy has considerable power to implement legislation from the central government, and financial powers to assist regeneration in its region, but it does not have the same power as the German *Länder*, for example.

The critical issue that distinguishes regions with an important policy role from those that are merely one of the players is the extent to which the region has the competence to legislate for itself and has some control of finance. In the case of Germany the *Land* of North Rhine Westphalia has this power. The region of Wallonie in Belgium also has this power. In the UK the case study of Dundee showed how, since the abolition of the regional tier of government, the city now works directly with the Scottish Office, which has power over regeneration devolved to it. This differentiates it from the position of Liverpool, where the regional body is still embryonic and has, to date, little devolved competence. So far the Northern Ireland Assembly is still finding its feet, but if a level of devolution can be achieved and sustained, it could become similar in its powers to the Scottish Executive. At present it does have legislative powers, but is closely monitored by the UK government through the Secretary of State's office. However, over the last 30 years of the 'troubles' the UK government's Northern Ireland Office, now evolving into the province's executive body, has been the only constant administrative agency. It is therefore the natural point of formulation of a strategy for the regeneration of the province, and working in conjunction with the NI Housing Executive produced the new regional development strategy, *Shaping our Future*, in 1998. This led in 2001 to the production of the Area Plan, which provides the framework for the regeneration process.

Overall the role of regional bodies in regeneration varies, but while they all play a key part in the regeneration process, in Germany and in the Walloon region of Belgium they are the main architects of the policies and implementation strategies, including financing for their towns and cities.

Local government

Each city region displays a different structure at the local level. In Milan and Lille there are strong metropolitan authorities that are responsible for the formulation and implementation of the planning policies and strategies for their area. Within this both have placed great emphasis on the regeneration of the run-down and derelict parts of the *métropole* as a major thrust of their policy. This is particularly true in Lille, where the Ville Renouvelée policy is guided not merely by the city of Lille but by the Communauté Urbain, and its planning agency the Agence de Développement et d'Urbanisme. In Milan the need has been for a framework to enable the need for regeneration in certain parts of the city to fit in cohesively with the normal planning process. Until the 1990s the planning process was always too slow and bureaucratic to work in conjunction with the more urgent and more swiftly moving need for redevelopment in areas such as Bovisa. Thus in 1995 the national urban regeneration programme enabled the city and regional authorities to draw up new programme-integrated plans that allowed the adoption of variance from the adopted plan. One such plan exists for the Bovisa area. Interestingly the University Politecnico, a main new occupant of the area, has undertaken much of the research for the new strategy document.

The existence of strong regional authorities and agencies in the Ruhr and Wallonie means that in these examples there is almost no need for metropolitan agencies, and in each case the string of towns that constitute their urban core work in conjunction with the regional authorities.

In the Netherlands and the UK city governments are the level at which the policy and practice of regeneration are undertaken. However, in the case of Rotterdam the city is almost *de facto* a metropolitan area on a par with the CUDL in Lille. Only in the UK is there a lack of a tradition of metropolitan government. In 1986 the existing metropolitan counties in England, which in any case had existed only since 1972 and had no great historic longevity, were abolished. Thus, in the case of Liverpool, the Merseyside Metropolitan County Council, although responsible for bringing forward the fundamental shape of an urban regeneration strategy for the conurbation, made no long-term contribution to its implementation, which was left to the city council and other agencies. The situation is similar in Dundee, where the abolition of the regional tier, again a short-lived phenomenon, means that the key authorities remain the city and the Scottish Executive. Northern Ireland is in itself so small, with a population less than the Lille or Rotterdam conurbations, that a metropolitan authority has never been deemed necessary, and the continuous objective of policy is to create a strong and viable devolved regional authority.

It is tempting to try to ascribe the success or failure of a particular city in tackling its regeneration challenge to the existence or non-existence of a regional or metropolitan tier of government with the competence and political will to tackle it. The case studies examined, however, do not point conveniently to regeneration being more successful only if a strong regional or metropolitan authority exists. The formula that seems to work is that there is a level, an authority, either national or regional, with the power and the will to drive forward a set of policies and processes for regeneration and to create the strategic context in which a more local, metropolitan or municipal, authority has an equal will and power to create and use the mechanisms to achieve the set goals within this.

In switching the spotlight from the structure to its effectiveness, four other criteria require analysis. The first has already been raised: it is the extent to which the competent authorities have been able to implement a regeneration strategy without having to develop new tools or new agencies to deliver it. The second is the extent to which a strong and visionary political machine or personality is necessary to achieve results, or whether they can be achieved by the existence of a third set of factors – the existence of a sound professional 'civil service'. The final key factor is the existence of funds and financial management structures to ensure the implementation of any proposals or plans that are devised.

Special agencies

With the exception of Wallonie, where in effect the regeneration effort has been a process of giving new tools to existing agencies, there has been a perceived need for the creation of new organisations to undertake the task. Thus the regeneration process emerging in Wallonie demonstrates that it is possible to implement a strategy without recourse to the creation of new or additional agencies, although the recent legislation enables the creation of local *societés d'économie mixte* on the French model to implement the development strategy, and such a body exists for the Grand Prés development in Mons. The case studies of the other seven cities, however, reveal a varying degree of reliance on special agencies. These, as will be demonstrated, display an equal variation in their relationship to the elected constitutional authorities, from being almost an adjunct of their administrations to being almost detached from them.

There appears to be a clear difference in the approach taken by the remaining four continental cities and the three British ones. In the cases of Rotterdam, Lille, the Ruhr and Milan, although they have developed special agencies these are closely tied to the existing government structures and have a degree of stability and continuity of purpose that distinguishes them from the mechanisms utilised in Dundee and Liverpool. The case study of Belfast, because of its particular political circumstances, demonstrates the need for agencies that are seen *not* to be tied to local politics.

In Rotterdam the plans for and the implementation of the strategy for the Kop van Zuid are undertaken by the city council although the emphasis on the regeneration of housing and social development means that it is possible for it to manage this project without major private sector involvement. The partnership that runs the project is made up almost exclusively of public sector bodies, such as the port authority, the transport authorities, the City Development Corporation and the Departments of Public Works and Urban Planning. The Delfshaven Project is more complex, however, involving local and national commercial organisations and local shopkeepers. It has its own project management team, the Projectbureau Wijkanpak.

In Lille the main organisation for the management and delivery of both the Euralille and Roubaix-Tourcoing Grand Projet Urbain has been a *societé d'économie mixte*. This body can exercise all the main powers on behalf of the city, including the right to buy land, manage investments and engage contractors. It is made up of representatives of all the government agencies that have an interest in the project, local companies, and organisations such as the chambers of commerce. It is worth noting that a chamber of commerce in France is an infinitely more powerful body, with statutory rights and powers to govern local trade and act on its behalf, than the consultative and often merely social bodies that exist in Britain. Of greater significance, however, is the Agence de Développement et d'Urbanisme, which acts on behalf of all the partners and is answerable directly to the Communauté Urbain. It has a key position as it must integrate the strategy for regeneration into the Schéma Directeur for the Lille metropolitan area.

The Bovisa Company set up in Milan to oversee and manage the redevelopment of Bovisa is a similar organisation, again closely tied into the main city and metropolitan governments.

The Ruhr presents a slightly different model in that the IBA was a unique, single-purpose, short-life agency established by the *Land* government. The IBA may at times have come into conflict with the municipal authorities in the Ruhr with regard to some of its decisions. However, as the agency was responsible for the delivery of what in essence was a series of major but targeted and time-limited projects, it by and large fitted with the wider planning strategies of the municipal authorities. The IBA was wound up in 1999 after completing much of its 10-year regeneration strategy. Completion of these tasks has now passed to new agencies.

In each of these cases the agency has been closely tied into the structures of local government and to national strategies that have had a degree of constancy over a long period of time, and this has thus added a degree of stability to their work. In Liverpool and Dundee there has been a constant change in programme and agency, which makes it difficult to discern any continuity of strategy over time in these cities. In Dundee, at least three major programmes with different emphases, different actors and different management structures have been in place over the last 20 years, from the Dundee Project in 1982 to the SIP programme now in action. The Dundee Project had a specific life term and was discontinued in 1991 to be followed by the Dundee Partnership. The former was dominated by public agencies at three levels; the latter involved a wider range of institutions, including university, housing agencies, the port authority and health boards, in an 'informal institutional arrangement'. The great weakness of this arrangement was the fact that the Dundee Partnership had no executive powers, these being held by the constituent members. Only Scottish Enterprise Tayside had a subsidiary agency, the local enterprise company, with the power to implement the agreed strategy. The current SIP programme appears to put the emphasis more on grassroots agencies at community level and in the arts.

In Liverpool the evolution of programmes and agencies has been even more complex and, to the observer, confusing. Thus there has been an evolution from the urban development corporation model – the Merseyside Development Corporation (MDC), set up in 1981 – through City Challenge and the Liverpool Vision, to the Single Regeneration Budget and its 11 local partnerships, not forgetting the Garden Festival. At each stage there has been a different managing model and a changing mix of partners. The emphasis has varied from an attempt to engage the private sector to lever in funds, as with the MDC, through to an emphasis on community involvement and local engagement in the process. The city council and other public agencies such as the government regional office, originally for Merseyside and now for the North-West, have all been major players, but at times they were considered peripheral and at others key guides to the process. Thus the MDC was so detached from local government that there was serious conflict between it and them. Under the SRB, and more recent programmes such as Liverpool Vision, the local authorities of Merseyside have become more central to the process.

In both Dundee and Liverpool there has been instability in the very structure of local government itself. In Dundee the abolition of the regional tier of local government in 1996 meant that a new relationship had to be forged between the city council and the Scottish Office at a time when, as Lloyd and McCarthy note in Chapter 4, a productive city–region–state cooperation had developed. The weakening of local institutions and the strengthening of central ones has continued with the creation of the Scottish Parliament, and the new operative SIP programme is very much driven by the Scottish Executive.

The ad hoc nature of the managing bodies, and the constant reliance on bodies that parallel local government but are not really part of it, also reflect a peculiarly British propensity that goes back to the creation of the New Towns. Indeed the urban development corporations are a natural evolution of the New Town management model. One cannot, however, include Belfast as being an example of this, as the situation there is unique, and local government has not in effect been operative until very recently. The creation of regeneration bodies that were detached from local politics was necessary if any movement was to be achieved at all. Thus the Laganside Corporation was based on the English UDC model, and it has set the process in motion in reverse by beginning to set up local bodies that have become absorbed into the local administration and have brought local people on both sides of the community into the process of regenerating their community. If the 'peace process' survives and grows then a more 'normal' set of actors and processes will evolve.

Political processes

Although it would be the wish of most professionals engaged in regeneration to see the process as a technical one, the case studies demonstrate the extent to which the process is entangled with the political strategies and personalities in certain cities. The Belfast example is perhaps the most special of these in that regeneration is a technically developed process that is part of a wider process to bring peace, stability and a 'normal' political process to that city. It cannot be argued that the political conflict in Liverpool has been on a level to compare to that of Belfast, but it was the climate of endemic political instability and militancy created in the city in the 1970s that dissuaded investors from investing in the city and thereby fed the spiral of decline. It was thus perhaps not desirable, but certainly inevitable, that in order to turn things around the regeneration process would have to be driven by other levels of government and the private sector. The UDC was thus a product of this reaction by the Thatcher government to the perceived inability of local government to deliver any strategy for change. Over the intervening period there have been gains for the city, and the political process has returned to a more 'normal' pattern, but the deep-seated social and economic problems of the Liverpool conurbation still remain acute, and the initial criticisms that the UDC, for example, was no more than window dressing on a decrepit shop that would not tackle the profound decline of the city, remain unanswered.

In the case of Lille there is a constant debate that the city would not have embarked on the path to its phenomenal redevelopment and emergence as a major French and European region had it not been for the fact that the then mayor, M. Pierre Mauroy, was also the French prime minister. This neglects the fact that had he not had the vision to see the potential for Lille to recapture its historic place as the key city at the centre of three economically powerful European regions – South East England, Brussels-Flanders and the Ile de France – either someone else would have, or the advantages of this central location would have created another response to regenerate the city and capitalise on its potential.

In Belgium it was the alteration of the constitution that altered the focus of the three regions of the country from the language issue that had dogged its post-war history to the problems internal to each region. Thus in Wallonie the focus of regional activity has moved to the regeneration of one of the most derelict regions in western Europe.

To a certain extent the situation in Dundee is almost parallel to this, as the devolution of the competence for issues surrounding regeneration has passed to the Scottish Parliament, and it is now freer to develop initiatives from a Scottish viewpoint. The recent SIP programme is an example of this.

These major shifts in the political scene are important, and often are the headline-grabbing issues. However, they mask a more subtle change in the political reality of most countries: the slow change of emphasis to more socially and community-oriented programmes. This is most evident in Lille, where the two projects described represent almost two eras in the evolution of French regeneration policy. The more diffused programme in Roubaix is much more reactive to local needs and community groups than the almost *beaux arts* grand design of Euralille. Similar shifts are detectable in Liverpool and in Dundee. In the latter case the new Scottish Executive programme, SIP, is explicitly socially oriented. In Northern Ireland a similar shift from the major 'flagship' type of project to a more diffused social and economic orientation on policy is emerging. The Laganside complex may be the venture that changed the perception of Belfast as a city for investors, but the more community-based emphasis of the Springvale initiative and the Making Belfast Work programme may produce long-term benefits in a more unspectacular way.

The major renewal and rebuilding of central Rotterdam has brought in massive private investment to the commercial heart of the city, and by contrast in both Delfshaven and Kop van Zuid the emphasis is much more on the involvement of the local community in the process of regeneration. In the Walloon legislation there is no explicit role for local and community groups, and this is to a great extent due to the fact that their involvement is implicit in the entire regional strategy. To date, the more social and local community involvement in regeneration strategies has not played a major part in the programmes evolving in Milan.

Financial structures

In attempting to make a meaningful comparison between the patterns of financial investment displayed by the cities examined in the case studies it is necessary to begin to construct some form of typology of the investment systems encountered. In each case there are similar factors evident, in that each has a source of funds in the beginning and these funds are channelled through a range of fundholders, managers and investors, who may in turn invest some or all of their funds in renewal projects. These fundholders can range from large international investment companies with a very commercial agenda, as befits the private sector, through to entirely public agencies such as the central finance ministries in each country, who are investing some of their taxation revenues in the regeneration process. Equally, in every case there are examples of large players in the process and smaller, more local ones.

The important assessment of these from the point of view of the comparison being attempted is to illustrate what the balance of these investments is in the projects and cities examined, and to draw out the differences in the sources, processes and investors and their motivation. Put simply, the funds that are drawn on originate as savings or investments by a range of agencies, stretching from the profits of a giant multinational company to the small savings of individual citizens. These may be 'invested' voluntarily – for example into banks or pensions – or involuntarily into taxes. There is thus a flow of funds that end up in certain types of agency, who make them available for regeneration. They can be divided into three types of investment source: public, commercial, and investment by 'mutual' (that is, intermediate types of) agency. Examples of all three have been evident in the case studies. A typology of these is given in Table 12.1.

Public funds

Of considerable importance are the various public funds that are invested by a range of public actors. In the context of western Europe the EU Structural funds are an important source of investment, and several cities are in areas where funds under the old Objective One and Two were available from programmes such as URBAN. However, funding is obtainable under other programmes not explicitly applicable to the case study cities. Susan Percy, in Chapter 10 on the Ruhr, points to the use of environmentally targeted programme such as the Lasala project and Discus. These were specifically targeted at cities where regeneration was a prime policy aim. The Hainault area of Wallonie, Liverpool and Belfast as Objective One areas all received 75% of funding for certain projects, and much of the rest of Wallonie, Dundee, Lille and certain areas of Milan all received funds under Objective Two, where 50% of funds are paid. As these funds have begun to have an effect on the cities, and with recent and potentially far-reaching changes to the structural funds being proposed, it is likely that this source of funding will decline in importance in the future.

In every city regeneration programme, and in most national programmes, central governments are major investors in schemes. The exceptions are in Germany, where this role is undertaken by the *Länder*, and in Belgium, where it is undertaken by the regional governments. Such funding is usually directed at the aspects of a project that have a non-commercial nature, whether infrastructure improvement, land clearance, investment in transport networks, or social benefits to the resident population. There has been considerable controversy over this funding in recent years, and it is under threat as the EU perceives it to be a barely concealed subsidy to the private sector. It is argued that, by undertaking the works that a private investor would not undertake and then passing or selling land on at a cut price to the

Table 12.1 Patterns of investment in case study projects.

Source of funds		Belfast	Dundee	Liverpool	Rotterdam	Lille	Wallonie	Milan	Ruhr
Public	*European Obj 1*	***		***			***		
	Obj 2		***						
	National subventions	***	***	***		***	***	***	***
	National agencies	NI Hsg Exec	Scot Enterprise	Hsg Corp	***	***		***	***
	Regional funds	NI Exec				***	***	***	***
	Local taxes	***	***	***	***	***	***	***	***
Mutual	*Local savings banks*					Caisse d'Epargne			
	Building societies		***	***					
	Mortgage banks					Credit Foncier			
	National mutual funds					Caisse des Despots			Sparkassen
	Lottery/charity	***	***	***					
	National savings								
Private	*Pension funds*								
	Personal investments/ISAs								
	International investment	***				***			
	National banks	***				***			
	Property development funds	***	***	***			***	***	

Key   ***   Funding source recorded
      Main funding agent in script

private sector, governments are providing an illegal subsidy and causing un-
fair competition with areas where the private sector might feel it economically feasible to undertake such work themselves. Obviously, if the land or
facilities remain in public hands this does not occur to the same extent.

The future of this 'gap funding' is in doubt, but if it is outlawed entirely then
this would seriously endanger the entire regeneration effort, which is aimed
at bringing areas that have become economically unviable back into public
and commercial use. Without this assistance, private investment capital
will go to those areas where such remedial work is unnecessary. Taken to its
logical conclusion all public assistance to 'distressed' areas and to populations in difficulty would have to cease, and those regions that are *at present*
enjoying economic buoyancy would continue to expand at their expense.
This is contrary to several of the EU's other policies, such as the Spatial Vision documents and the European Spatial Development Perspective, which
seeks to ensure sound, viable, balanced growth for all the cities and towns in
the Union. It also runs counter to much of the social policy, which aims to
provide employment opportunities and training for populations at a disadvantage due to the decline of their former prosperity. In short, it runs counter
to the 'market' philosophy that sees the structural funds as a subsidy in the
first place. The entire issue has been referred back to the Commission to be
resolved as part of the continuing agenda for future presidencies.

The combination of EU structural funds and national or regional investment
has been crucial to the process of regeneration, as evidenced by the cities
analysed; it is crucial to the continued success of the process of revitalising
Europe's urban heritage. Complementing the EU structural funds are a series
of contributions from the national or regional governments charged with the
responsibility of steering urban regeneration policy.

The position is perhaps most complicated in the United Kingdom, where
four slightly variable models operate. We have looked at three of them.
In England the main national subvention was until recently channelled
through the Single Regeneration Budget (Barlow & Hill 1995), but in the
time since its introduction in 1994 this has undergone several mutations.
The main change is that it has been combined with other budgets and is administered by the regional development agencies, which are better placed to
respond to the needs of each region. The focus of central control in Whitehall
has therefore moved from the DTLR to the Treasury, which apportions the
funds to the regions. The RDAs are assisted by English Partnerships, which is
charged with supplementing these funds with additional private sector funding. This process is a great advance on the earlier one whereby the budget was
a competitive one managed from London.

One of the main suppliers of funding for the housing component of any scheme is the Housing Corporation. This body, originally set up in 1964, has also mutated to become the main channel for government funds for the voluntary housing sector. These funds are usually also supplemented by mutual funds from building societies or by private investment.

In Scotland, Northern Ireland and Wales the pattern and process are very similar, although the agencies are different. In Scotland, public investment in places such as Dundee comes from the Scottish Executive, Enterprise Scotland, Scottish Housing and the local authorities. In Northern Ireland, direct government investment comes through the Northern Ireland Development Agency. This funding is mainly for capital investment in infrastructure, land clearance and assembly, and environmental improvement.

In Wallonie, finances come mainly from two levels. The first is derived from the regional level, the Fonds d'Aménagement Operational, and their 'credit' budget. These pay for 50% of site purchase and 100% of remedial works such as demolition, drainage and sewerage, and landscaping. The second is derived from special grants to *communes*.

In the Netherlands, regeneration funding is derived from the Stadtsverneuwingsfond, which is a constituent of the financial provisions of the national spatial plan and, in the case of a city such as Rotterdam, is channelled directly to the city. Funding for smaller cities is managed by the provincial authorities. These funds can be supplemented from local funds, which may be derived from sale of land or borrowing – that is, a type of mortgage based on the security of land or project value. If the proposed use has no return in terms of value the project can be subsidised. In the Netherlands there are several schemes whereby local authorities may raise their own finances, for instance through *battbelasting* (a betterment levy) if it demonstrated that a landowner derives benefit from public works, and through section 42 of the Spatial Planning Act where a landowner makes a contribution to infrastructure cost. These are applied where private land is brought into a major scheme and the owner is perceived to benefit from public initiatives.

In France the public funding of regeneration projects is built into the budgets of the various government levels involved through the long-term budgeting mechanisms of the Contrat de Plan. These may be programmed for the entire life of a project and give long-term stability to the financial planning process. They are backed up by funding from other public (but not government) sources.

In the German process of regeneration the costs are usually split between the three levels of government: federal, *Land* and municipal. However, currently all three, perhaps more so at municipal level, are financially constrained, and there is an emerging trend in seeking funds from other sources. In the case of Emscher Park much of the funding came from *Land* government. At local level public subsidies and tax incentives for private development are available for regeneration projects. For instance, municipalities are permitted to levy a tax on the increase in value of land that results from the giving of permission to develop. This is called *Auchleichsbetrag*; however, it is not widely used and is difficult to collect, as the basis for calculation is often difficult to establish.

A similar pattern of government subventions and direct investment from the central, provincial and local governments was evident in the Bovisa scheme in Milan.

Mutual funds

The question of when 'public money' is not synonymous with government money is one that arises in examining some of the funding sources for regeneration in France, Belgium and Germany. In France the main source of funding to back up government money comes from the Caisse des Dépôts et Consignations, and it is often considered that this is merely another form of government funding. The reality is more subtle and more interesting than this.

The Caisse des Dépôts et Consignations is a public bank, founded in 1816, with the express objective of saving and investing small savings on behalf of the public into projects and infrastructure for their benefit. It is administered by committees appointed by the people's representatives: that is, the Assemblé Nationale or the state, *not* the government. One has to understand that, under the French constitution (all of them through time!), the role of the state, which is permanent, is different from that of the government, which is temporary. The reason for the founding of the bank demonstrates this. After the Napoleonic Wars, when the wealth of the country had been expropriated by the government to prosecute these wars, carrying on a long tradition, the French public demanded of their representatives that an organisation be set up to manage public funds drawn from their savings that was not controllable by the government and therefore liable to be misused. The Caisse was the answer. It was joined in 1859 by the Credit Foncier, a private mortgage and property bank that funded public ventures and was also outside the control of government. Its founding reason was similar to that of the Caisse in that the French public and state wished to avoid a repeat of the misuse of private funds that had occurred when Baron Hausmann raided them to pay for his reconstruction of Paris, a process that nearly bankrupted the city and much else. The Credit Foncier was absorbed into the Caisse in 1996 following financial difficulties. The second remarkable fact about the Caisse is that it derives its funding from a variety of savings by the general public, *not* from taxes or similar impositions. Chief among those are the savings that are deposited in the small local savings banks, the Caisses d'Épargne, which were recently absorbed into the Caisse des Dépôts structure. A major secondary source of funds is public sector pension funds.

The result of this mechanism is that a considerable amount of money belonging to the public is invested on their behalf in public works and is outside of the control of governments, which come and go. Savers and investors are guaranteed a return that is held constant by the state management committee. This is possible because the long-term nature of both savings and investments and the historic build-up of funds means that the Caisse can smooth out the vagaries of the economic cycle, although it has in recent years had difficulties in maintaining this control. The obvious threat to it would come from any internationalisation of the savings and investments industries in France and from the effect of competition from ostensibly more rewarding places for small investment. The Caisse does have a private bank that can work with agencies outside France, and currently this is in discussions with similar agencies in Wallonie and in Germany to set up a wider network. The flow of funds into the bank is shown in Fig. 12.1.

What is important is that the Caisse has begun to develop a special regeneration fund, which is used to finance public investments in major regeneration efforts, and was a fundamental contributor to the schemes in Lille and Roubaix. It is also the main financial supporter of the social housing HLM network. Figure 12.2 shows the flow of funding from the Caisse into regeneration. One of the noteworthy aspects of this is the section of the fund that is earmarked for co-investments with the private sector (Caisse des Dépôts, Information 2000).

The negotiations with Walloon and German agencies are relatively easy, as in both countries there are agencies that are similar. In Wallonie there is a network of small local *caisses d'épargne*, and in Germany a network of local and state savings banks, the *Sparkassen* and *Landsparkassen*. The latter also have a tradition of investment in public works in conjunction with state and local governments

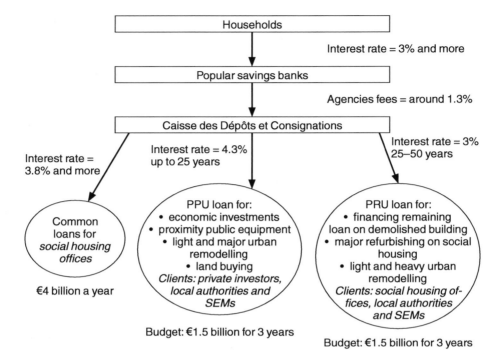

Fig. 12.1   Caisse des Dépôts et Consignations: participation in financing urban regeneration – loans to corporations. PPU = *Prêt Projet Urbain* = loan for urban project; PRU = *Prêt Renouvellement Urbain* = loan for urban regeneration. Source: Working Party on Urban Regeneration in North West Europe, unpublished seminar paper.

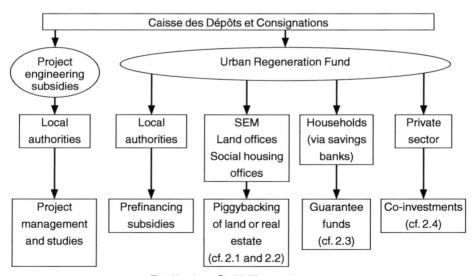

Fig. 12.2   Caisse des Dépôts et Consignations: participation in financing urban regeneration – investments. Source: Working Party on Urban Regeneration in North West Europe, unpublished seminar paper.

No such 'intermediate' sources of funding for regeneration were referred to or have been identified in Italy or in the Netherlands. In the UK generally this sector has traditionally been occupied by the building societies and by local branches of the Trustee Savings Bank, but the latter was absorbed into a commercial bank, Lloyds, and the building society movement has become divided into (a) large societies that effectively operate as commercial mortgage banks and (b) smaller, local societies that operate only in the home loans business. However, some funds have been forthcoming from this sector for social or 'affordable' housing, and small local building societies are sometimes constituent members of SRB partnerships, funding the housing component.

A final non-commercial source of funds in the UK is the National Lottery. Funds from this are used for communal and cultural ventures that are often integral to the social development aspects of major regeneration schemes. Couch refers to such investment in Liverpool (Chapter 3), and Lloyd and McCarthy in Dundee (Chapter 4). In Belfast the Millennium Commission has made a major investment in the Odyssey complex.

Other agencies that have been recorded as making a contribution to regeneration funding are local chambers of commerce. These have been constituent members of the management organisations, the *société d'économie mixte* in Lille and the SRB in Liverpool. Although representing the business sector they are not explicitly involved for direct financial gain but rather to ensure a better investment and commercial climate for business as a whole.

Commercial finance

This is the third main source of funding for regeneration, but the involvement of the commercial sector varies between the examples shown and between them and cities and towns where returns on city redevelopment are easier to achieve. All of the cities, with the exception of Rotterdam and Milan, are in areas of economic difficulty and, as has been demonstrated, it has been necessary to contribute massive amounts of public funding to reconstruct the infrastructure, communications and social dynamism to enable the private investor to engage in sometimes risky projects. There is therefore a quite logical tendency for such investment to be in ventures that bring some return for shareholders and where the risk is cushioned by acting in partnership with the public sector and other actors in the process. Such partnership is particularly encouraged in England, where the public sector is under-financed (Bailey, Barker and McDonald 1995).

In the Netherlands, towns and cities are empowered to enter agreements with a private developer, but no extra funds from central government are provided, except for housing projects (*Living in Towns*, South Bank University 2001). Similarly in Wallonie, although the main actor is the *commune* there is a strategy to involve the private sector, and it is expected that, for every single unit of contribution by the public sector, two will be raised from the private sector. There are certain aids to the private sector, such as tax breaks.

It is the objective of many cities to attract international investors. A good example is the McArthur Glen retail development in Roubaix. In Rotterdam, although there is much international investment in the central area of the city, there has been none in the two regeneration areas studied. The Hilton hotel group has invested in Belfast.

The attraction of major national developers and institutions has been more important to the cities under analysis, such as the Credit Lyonnais investment in the 'Ski Boot' in Lille. The levering in of commercial funds has been a central objective of UK policy for many years, but the ratio of private to public is critical. Making an area attractive for the private sector may bring massive commercial investment in places such as London or Paris, but it is more difficult in peripheral areas. In Liverpool, for example, for a demonstrated public investment of nearly £100 million, the expected private sector investment was only £43 million. For all its success it is discernible that most of the investment in the Lille *métropole* is public and that, McArthur Glen apart, private investment is small scale and local by comparison.

Summary

At the outset of this volume the task that was set was to attempt to bring out the differences and similarities between systems, with a view to identifying structures that worked better than others and principles that might be universally applied.

There has been a search for the 'ideal structure of government' for the delivery of effective regeneration strategies. The only conclusion that can be drawn from the cases reviewed is that such a structure is a chimera. No constitutional arrangement as such will deliver success. The magic ingredient is often provided by history, not by constitutional guarantee. In Lille, for example, the influential Comité Grand Lille is derived more from the city's Flemish history than from its French history, yet the towns and cities of Wallonie are having to construct new structures to tackle their regeneration problems.

What is important in guaranteeing some degree of success is stability of direction, of financing and of organisational cohesion.

In respect of financing, the key is not whether there are high direct taxes but how much is guided from a variety of sources into underpinning regeneration, and whether this is acceptable to both the main public and private financiers. The existence of stable semi-independent sources of funds in France and Germany, and increasingly in other continental examples, works as a conduit for investment because it is left alone, indeed encouraged, for this purpose by finance ministries and is not raided as a source of further capital by the private and commercial sector. The spread of 'globalised' free markets in capital and savings threatens these protected but accepted financial processes and organisations. From the point of view of the policy objectives of the EU and many of its constituent members to retain and enhance Europe's urban culture their retention is vital.

13

New Agendas

Susan Percy

In this new millennium there are new challenges for planning and regeneration schemes in response to changes in social trends (cultural and political), heightened awareness of environmental issues, economic changes associated with globalisation, and a desire for development to be more sustainable.

This chapter recognises the diverse responses to regeneration that the cities and regions studied illustrate due, in part, to the diversity of national structures and local circumstances. Nevertheless, there is clearly a discernible set of *new agendas* that are influencing strategies and the success of regeneration programmes in different localities. Although this chapter focuses on new agendas, in some cases these agendas are not new but have recently taken on more prominence and importance in regeneration programmes, and have been relabelled or reframed.

The first question to ask is: what are these new issues that old industrial areas in Europe are having to deal and cope with? These new agendas have in most cases evolved out of the necessity to deal with factors that are common to all the case studies. These include a fundamental restructuring of the economic base, unemployment, social segregation, and environmental degradation, coupled with the globalised nature of financial markets and the sustainable development movement. In this chapter an attempt is made to draw out some of these issues and processes and provide examples from the case studies to illustrate these new agendas.

Globalisation and place marketing

The globalisation of society has led to increased mobility of capital and to 'an intensification of competition among localities' (Knapp 1998, p. 381). In the last few decades global restructuring of industries has occurred, which has exacerbated the decline of old industrial areas that economically have legacies of heavy industry, older manufacturing and port-related industry, with the control of capital now more concentrated and centralised at national and international levels (Loftman & Nevin 1995). As old industrial areas have declined they have sought new sources of wealth, particularly in tertiary and quaternary activities. In order to attract inward investment, and footloose capital, areas that were once renowned as places of production have had to reinvent themselves as places of consumption. Since investment flows have an international dimension this has meant that regions and cities have had to compete with each other to secure new sources of wealth: consequently the attributes of the location have become important. This has meant that place promotion and marketing strategies have become increasingly important parts of regeneration strategies. As Smyth (1994) points out, 'The purpose of marketing a city is to create strategies to promote an area or the entire city for certain activities and in some cases to "sell" parts of the city for living, consuming and productive activities' (p. 2). Furthermore, 'The emphasis of place marketing is increasingly redefining – or reimaging – each individual city in ways which fit with dominant perception of urban success' (Cochrane & Jonas 1999, p. 145).

In examining place marketing strategies, Ward (1998) notes a number of policy ingredients, which include flagship/prestige developments, trade fairs, public art, sporting events, and cultural facilities. Some of these elements are evident in the case studies, as the following sections explain.

Prestige projects

Many of the urban regeneration initiatives explored in this book have included the development of prestige and flagship projects to encourage physical and economic renewal in certain areas. Prestige developments are high-profile, large-scale developments that are capable of attracting inward investment and promoting new urban images (Loftman & Nevin 1995). Well-known examples include Birmingham's International Convention Centre and the National Indoor Arena and Canary Wharf office complex in London's docklands. Local flagships are smaller-scale projects that primarily stimulate growth within an urban area and change local perception about a particular locality (Loftman & Nevin 1995). There has, however, been much debate about the role of flagship/prestige developments in achieving broader urban policy goals, and it is not the intention here to rehearse these debates. (For a discussion of the usefulness of flagship projects in the urban regeneration process see, for example, Hambleton 1990 and Brownhill 1990.) What is quite clear is that, in certain cities and regions, the prestige and flagship project approach has been used as a vehicle for physical urban regeneration: examples of such projects include shopping centres, waterfront developments, heritage parks, office complexes, convention centres and leisure facilities.

Examples from the cities studied where the regeneration programmes have developed prestige and flagship projects include the Duisburg Inner Harbour in the Ruhr. In this case the redundant docks are being redeveloped to create a spectacular mixed-use waterfront development, incorporating residential, commercial and recreational aspects.

> The winning masterplan was designed by Foster and Partners following an international competition, which itself was a global marketing opportunity. The plan includes new constructions, including the landmark "Euro-Gate" office building and the refurbishment of pre-existing warehouses. (Fox 2001, p. 12.)

In Liverpool the Albert Dock development is another example of a prestige project, and the Liverpool Vision is a response to place marketing. In Rotterdam the 'key project' of Kop van Zuid on the south bank of the Maas has been a focal point for new commercial development, with the intention of levering in private investment through planned, coordinated public expenditure. The plan for the area focused on new property development opportunities to transform the area into the 'New Rotterdam'. Interestingly, central government has had to subsidise the project, as the city authority did not have the resources to underpin the redevelopment. Also important in imaging the city was the Wilhelmena Pier project, which includes the World Port Centre, again designed by Sir Norman Foster. In Belfast an integrated marketing strategy has been used called 'Belfast becoming better', and much of the regeneration effort has been in improving the image of the city. This has been done through projects such as the Waterfront Hall and Belfast Hilton in the Laganside area of the city.

Cultural facilities

Central to many areas undergoing regeneration is the development of cultural facilities, tourist projects and public art. Hall (2000) recognises that:

> Culture is now seen as the magic substitute for all the lost factories and warehouses, as a device that will create a new urban image, making the

city more attractive to mobile capital and mobile professional workers. (p. 640.)

Consequently culture, arts and entertainment are becoming more central to the regeneration of many cities. Take for example Newcastle–Gateshead, with a huge steel angel and an art gallery converted from a flour mill, recently named as one of the world's top creative cities (Ward 2002).

Cultural regeneration is becoming more prevalent as part of regeneration strategies, with cities such as Liverpool and areas such as the Ruhr asserting their cultural independence. Many cities are promoting cultural developments such as building museums, concert halls, sports arenas and art galleries. Tourists visiting monuments, attending performances and exhibitions all help to have a positive effect on the economy, and it is argued that a new creative class is emerging in many cities, which contributes to economic productivity (Ward 2002), although there is concern that there is over-optimism about the effectiveness of culture in stimulating economic growth. Cultural revitalisation can also help to promote civic identity and improve the image of a particular area – what Griffiths (1995) refers to as *city boosterism*.

Examples of culturally led projects include the Dundee Discovery Point and the Overgate Arts Centre, developed in 1994 and backed up by the city's Arts Action Plan, linking into the city-wide regeneration strategy. In Liverpool there is the world-famous Cavern and the Tate Gallery. Lille will be the European City of Culture in 2004, based on the renewal of the Palais des Beaux Arts, a gallery of international reputation. The Ruhr has made great use of its industrial past, by celebrating its industrial heritage through the creation of industrial monuments. Examples include the former steelworks at Duisburg Nord, now a recreational and leisure facility, and the use of public art and sculptures throughout the Emscher Park.

New industries and links to education

Economic growth opportunities have shifted from manufacturing industry to high-tech sectors, and often these new industries are clustered together and have strong links to educational institutions. 'There are many indications that, increasingly, urban economic growth seems to emerge from fruitful cooperation between economic actors, who form innovative complexes of firm and organisations' (van den Berg *et al.* 2001, p. 185). The attraction of new industry has been a fundamental goal of all the cities and regions studied, with some degree of success in most cases. These high-tech activities have often been attracted to particular locations where there are links with government-supported scientific institutions, ties with the scientific community and professional associations, and interactions between the business community and educational institutions. Other important factors include accessibility and highly trained labour forces, with quality of education and training fundamental to creating a skilled and well-motivated workforce.

Old industrial areas can benefit from growth in sectors such as biotechnology, medical services, information technology, environmental technology and media industries. In Dundee there is, for instance, medical excellence in the Ninewells hospital, along with a technology park attracting high-technology industry. In the Ruhr, Dortmund's technology park adjoins Dortmund University, which is a centre for science, technology and research. Interestingly, before the Second World War there were no universities in the Ruhr; today, however, there are large and respected universities at Essen, Bochum and Dortmund as well as a number of specialist institutes of higher education and research. It is the combination of the university and technological knowledge that technology-based companies find attractive, making the Ruhr very strong as an environmental technological area.

In Liverpool, the biotechnology industry is growing, and Liverpool University is opening a new biosciences centre to promote spin-off companies and local economic growth. In Lille there is the Eurotechologie project, and there has been an expansion of the city's universities, which has resulted in the spin-off growth of scientific industries. In Milan the development of the second polytechnic university in the Bovisa district has been key to the regeneration of the area through the encouragement of research in engineering and industrial design, which has been highly relevant to the economy.

Social exclusion

Poverty and inequality issues have for many years been on the urban policy agenda; now, however, the language used and understanding have changed to embrace the concept of social exclusion (a broader notion than poverty), which 'emphasises the way people are closed out of social, economic and political mainstream of society' (Fernie 2002, p 185). Social exclusion covers issues such as unemployment, homelessness, debt, low educational attainment, and exclusion from services and social networks. 'Social exclusion is therefore historical, what is new are explicitly defined social inclusion programmes, designed, in part, to alleviate social exclusion' (Fernie 2002, p. 185).

The case studies clearly demonstrate that social exclusion is a problem for many old industrial areas. In the UK, for example, the government has set up the Social Inclusion Unit, and many regeneration programmes have social inclusion policies explicitly stated as fundamental to the renewal programmes. In general, social inclusion policies aim to widen employment and training opportunities, encourage public participation in society, and build up skills and confidence within the local community – in other words to build up social capacity within the community.

Examples where socially inclusive policies have been evident include the SRB partnership in North Liverpool, which developed strong links with the local communities. The SRB funding has encouraged local partnerships between public and private agencies, local business and the community in order to promote employment, education, health, housing and environment. Equally, the New Deal for Communities programme in Kensington in Liverpool has social inclusion as a key aim. The Vauxhall Neighbourhood Council in Liverpool has striven to encourage community-based economic development through various initiatives including training, a community transport scheme, and a community laundry project.

In the Delfshaven district of Rotterdam much emphasis in the renewal strategy is given to helping the existing community to adjust to new labour markets and social changes associated with post-industrialism. For example, in the Werk voor Delfshaven strategy, the city council is working alongside the local community on a regeneration strategy that has a strong commitment to local neighbourhoods and an integrated approach to social, physical and economic development.

In Dundee there are SIPs, which build on the past experience of urban regeneration but particularly focus on the inclusion of young people in society and the economy through, for example, out-of-school learning projects and projects to strengthen community capacity. Belfast's initiative Making Belfast Work includes securing employment opportunities in the most deprived areas of the city.

New alliances and partnerships

There is a recognition that regeneration approaches need to be holistic and integrated to be able to tackle the problems of areas, and in order to facilitate inward investment there has been increasing cooperation and working between local interested parties. In the Ruhr this has been between public authorities, scientific institutions and technology centres (Knapp 1998). In other cases there has been an establishment of cooperative structures (working groups) and cooperative procedures (consultation), and the desire to explore new forms of democracy. Effective regeneration needs the knowledge, skills and resources of the public and private sectors and local communities. There is also a move away from *government* towards *governance*: that is, a shift in modes of policy making and implementation away from the formal power held by local authorities and other state organisations towards open networks of cross-sectoral partnerships. In practice this translates into the broadening of stakeholder involvement, the facilitation of knowledge, and the building-up of trust (Cars *et al.* 2002).

In the Liverpool context new alliances and partnerships are evident in the Liverpool Vision urban regeneration company set up in the city centre as a single-purpose development agency that leads and coordinates the regeneration of the area. The company has drawn up a strategic regeneration framework, and facilitates regeneration within the overall regeneration framework. Interestingly, although the company coordinates and facilitates regeneration projects, it has paid little regard to the formal development plans. New initiatives such as local strategic partnerships drawn from local authorities and the community and business sectors will develop local neighbourhood renewal strategies. In an experiment funded through the Merseyside Health Action Zone, Liverpool City Council is also working with local primary care trusts, energy suppliers, and the police and fire services in a new holistic approach to housing renovation. This initiative is aimed not only at improving housing conditions but also at access to welfare benefits and standards of health and safety (Couch & Fitzharris 2002).

In Dundee, partnership working is also a central element of recent regeneration schemes, as illustrated by the Dundee Project, which involved the Scottish Development Agency, Tayside Regional Council, Dundee District Council and the business community in an initiative to develop and diversify the city's economic base and renew areas of physical decline. The Dundee Project was superseded in 1991 by the Dundee Partnership, made up of Dundee District Council, Tayside Regional Council and Scottish Enterprise (replacing the Scottish Development Agency). This partnership has been a way of securing informal coordination of the priorities of the partners and providing links to other organisations including the private sector.

In the Ruhr the creation of the IBA represented a fundamental shift in planning in the region. The IBA's aim was to revitalise the Emscher Park through the creation of collaborative partnerships with the local authorities, private practice, citizens and other interested parties. Furthermore, the IBA programme was coordinated by the Emscher Park Planning Company, owned by the state of NRW, with a building exhibition group approving the projects for the exhibition. This group was made up of members of the state departments, and local authority representatives from participating towns. 'The IBA was thus carried out under the auspices of a corporation rather than an authority' (Fox 2001, p. 14). In reality, however, the state government gave IBA projects funding priority, provided that ecological, social and architectural standards were met. This meant that many local authorities in need of state money often accepted a particular project through 'forced cooperation' (Fox 2001).

The renewal process *renouvellement* in Lille has become much wider in scope and more embracing, bringing together private, public and community interest. In Milan the Programme Agreement has been another useful vehicle for coordinating different agencies and groups in the urban regeneration process.

Promoting sustainability

Despite a multitude of definitions of sustainable development, what it means and how it might be implemented, the concept at least 'is increasingly assuming a central role in urban policy across Europe – not just for environmental policy, but also as a guiding principle for economic, social and cultural policies' (Gibbs 1999, p. 265). Sustainable development is a key aim of EU policy and is embedded in the EU Fifth and Sixth Environmental Action Programmes. At the European level there are various sustainable development projects, including the Sustainable Cities and Towns Campaign and Sustainable Cities and Towns Charter, also known as the Aalborg Charter. In addition, there are sustainable development strategies for individual member states, and there is generally therefore widespread support for the principles of sustainable development to underpin and shape urban development and regeneration initiatives.

Sustainable regeneration seeks to bring together environmental sustainability, economic efficiency and social needs – not an easy task, and one that has inherent contradictions. Nevertheless, many of the regeneration programmes examined have recognised the increasing importance of environmental sustainability as a new way of solving some of the problems, as it is becoming clear that, to attract new sources of wealth, then the city or region must have a good, clean environment. In the Ruhr:

> a central focus of the IBA projects has been environmental enhancement, not only through brownfield cleanup but also through the application of ecological planning principles to all projects from infrastructure improvements to housing developments to the creation of business and technology parks. (Fox 2001, p. 9.)

Clearly there has been strong re-imaging of the Ruhr, away from an environmentally degraded landscape towards a green and environmentally clean region. The IBA has spent a lot of time and effort cleaning up contaminated sites, converting redundant and disused buildings, and developing a landscape park. Likewise, the Dutch have a more rounded and holistic approach to sustainable development incorporated into planning policy and urban development programmes. In Rotterdam, for example, since the 1980s there has been an emphasis on compact urban development, and this has translated into inner-city regeneration initiatives, the use of brownfield sites, and heavy investment in subway extensions, tram lines, cycle routes and pedestrian safety. In Lille there has been the creation of the regional parks, and other green projects (such as river and canal improvements) felt to be important to help change the image of the area from that of an industrial one to that of a post-industrial city with good environmental credentials.

It is clear from the case studies that some cities and regions have developed proactive and integrated approaches to sustainable development, whereas others merely pay lip service to the concept through, for example, rhetorical policy statements. In other instances sustainable development policy goals, although not explicitly stated, are incorporated into programmes through social and economic initiatives and the cleaning up of the physical environment.

Conclusions

Taken together, these new agendas for urban regeneration are influencing current practice, and will certainly shape future approaches. The key issues to emerge include:

- the importance of the globalised economy on a city's or region's approach to regeneration;

- the need to promote an attractive image of the area;

- the increasing competition between cities and regions;

- the importance of long-term local partnerships;

- the integration of sustainable policy goals in regeneration programmes;

- the potential of culturally led renewal;

- the benefits of linking new industries to educational and research institutions;

- the need to build in social inclusion policies and foster social capital.

Some of the new agendas have been imposed on cities and regions from global changes in society and the economy and from international support for sustainable development. Other new agendas are more about developing appropriate, flexible and responsive forums for developing and delivering regeneration projects. These new agendas are maturing and becoming more central in regeneration schemes across Europe and will, with time, have increasingly positive impacts for the communities involved. It is clear that regeneration must be more than merely physical renewal, and through the new agendas growing scope exists to deliver on social, economic and environmental issues in a more integrated and responsive way.

14

Review

Charles Fraser, Chris Couch and Susan Percy

It was not the intention of this book to conduct a comprehensive analysis of the regeneration process across Europe or to produce any pan-European 'theory' of regeneration. The process is too dynamic, too swift moving and too unpredictable for that. Our purpose was to examine a series of case studies of urban regeneration in a selected number of European countries, and to consider what similarities and differences emerged. Equally the case studies do not reflect the entirety of national policy developments, and therefore in both the introductory chapters and the discussion chapters we have attempted to put them in their wider context in order to make some general points about the purposes and nature of urban regeneration in Europe.

We have attempted to bring to a wider audience some greater knowledge of the practice and achievements of urban regeneration in some major cities in their attempts to reshape their future. There is much talk, often inaccurate, about what has been achieved, and how. Until quite recently there was a lack of any comprehensive comparative analysis of what was happening in different European cities, although in the last few years various EU-funded projects have been published, such as the Urban Audit, the INTERREG llc project 'Living in Towns', and the recently produced *Compendium of Spatial Planning Systems*. In addition there are a growing number of independent academic studies by such authors as Newman & Thornley and the late Richard Williams. This volume is an attempt to contribute towards this literature.

In addition to being a conduit for passing on a more comprehensive picture of what is happening in certain cities, our three discussion chapters attempt to make some comparisons of critical factors shaping urban regeneration and emerging policy agendas in different countries. These are intended to form a basis for further exploration of the similarities and differences between the national situations and policies and their improvement through an ongoing process of comparison and transmission of policies from one country to another. This is one of the key purposes of international comparative research in public policy, as identified in Chapter 1.

A number of salient points emerge from the case studies and discussion. To begin with, urban regeneration is now a major activity in every country looked at, and in most others. This was not the case even 30 years ago. From being a field of policy that relied purely on national bases of theory and practice it has increasingly become internationalised. Urban theory is international. Learned journals such as *Town Planning Review* and *Urban Studies* are as likely to contain analyses of urban change and policy in one European country as another. Similarly, decades of ministerial visits and academic exchanges have led to a blurring of national policy characteristics as each nation borrows and tests ideas that have originated elsewhere. The development companies, architects and engineers who are responsible for many of the flagship regeneration projects mentioned in our case studies operate on an international scale, bringing their 'standard' products and approaches to any situation.

Regeneration has also become a major concern of the European Commission, for a variety of reasons. As long ago as 1990 the Commission's Green Paper on the Urban Environment (CEC 1990) called for the improvement of urban environments, reuse of derelict land, and higher urban densities in order to limit urban sprawl: in other words, urban regeneration. Several directorates of the Commission, such as Regional Affairs (DG16), Environment (DG11) and Social Policy (DG5), have each begun to develop an interest in the future of Europe's urban areas, both through specific programmes such as URBAN and through more general policy documents such as the ESDP, which has a clear focus on the importance of maintaining Europe's urban fabric as an economic, social and cultural imperative. Several of the case study cities demonstrate how these programmes and their funding are contributing to Europe's urban renaissance.

This European context is now beginning to pull together the various national efforts that have begun separately in quite different ways and for quite different reasons. Each national programme has its roots in quite different *social theories* (McConnel 1976), and this makes comparison difficult. In Belgium the Walloon programme is embedded in a social theory based in its traditions of self-help and charity, yet it is moving towards a more conventional European model where the state has a greater role in policy formulation and funding. In France the programme fits into the *dirigiste* philosophy of the French state, but as the differences between the Euralille and Roubaix case studies illustrate, regeneration agencies are now beginning to work more closely with the private sector, and are looking to UK practice as a model for new financial investments. In the UK itself the political process of devolution has enabled the development of new initiatives and the formulation of a variety of approaches in England, Scotland, Wales and Northern Ireland. This increasingly plural process in the UK is likely to stimulate innovation and make regeneration programmes more locally effective, although still working in partnership with private investors.

As knowledge of the practices in other countries becomes more widespread the rigidities of national 'ways of doing things' will be further eroded. The effect of the emergence of European practices on national ones is best seen in the present clash between the EU and the UK government that is occurring in the area of financial investment and funding of property redevelopment. Since the early 1980s one approach favoured by the UK government has been to subsidise the works required to bring abandoned and derelict land and buildings back into economically beneficial use. This is seen by the EU to be providing a subsidy to the private sector (to specific developers), whereas the UK government sees the use of public funds as creating a climate where private sector funds can be levered in to redevelop a derelict site by bridging the 'gap' between cost and commercial profitability. This contravention of EU economic rules is being challenged. However, it is obvious that without state help in addition to EU funding the revitalisation of urban Europe will stall. There is an urgent need for a resolution of this dilemma.

In every urban regeneration case study the original aims of the programme were a mixture of economic, social and environmental ambitions. In some areas the primary aim was the return of vacant and derelict land and buildings to profitable uses. In other areas it was employment creation through inward investment or indigenous growth. In yet others social inclusion has been a major concern. The growing competition between cities and the importance of *image* has been a major driving force shaping many regeneration programmes. The work of the Merseyside Development Corporation and its restoration of the Albert Dock is one such example of a combination of physical reclamation with environmental enhancement and the creation of a marketable image of the city. An important aim of the Emscher Park IBA was to improve the image of the area for inward investment. Indeed, in most of the city centres studied economic development is the primary aim. However, in the inner urban areas such as Delfshaven and Vauxhall social aims tend to dominate.

In some areas these basic aims have become overlain by others as new agendas have emerged. Environmental improvements were and remain common features of many regeneration programmes, but over the last decade many have moved on to include more sophisticated aims for *sustainable development*, taking a broader view of the role of these areas and how their regeneration might minimise future environmental degradation and the loss of natural resources. The Emscher Park IBA gave particular prominence to such aims. Related to this has been the belief that, by regenerating inner-city areas, a greater proportion of development can be retained in in-town locations. It will thus be possible to ease the pressure on peripheral and agricultural land: that is, to limit urban sprawl. This has been a major objective in Britain and the Netherlands. Connections are being made between regeneration and health improvements. The UK government's effort in relation to *health action zones* is notable in this respect.

In many cities there has been a process of encouraging cultural developments. In Lille the social and cultural spin-offs of the Vieux Lille and Grand Palais projects have added a new dimension to the regeneration of the city, where the main aims had previously been confined to the economic revitalisation of the metropolitan area. In Belfast the development of the Waterfront Hall in the Laganside area has had a similar effect. The berthing of famous Tayside-built ships such as the *Discovery* in Dundee has given a focus to the waterfront area. The cultural developments in Liverpool (such as the Tate Gallery, Maritime Museum, and Ropewalks Partnership) have achieved a similar effect. Another aspect of this has been the use of annual events or special occasions to give character to a city, which can be used to promote tourism. Major sporting events, pop concerts and art festivals are all being used by cities to attract tourists, improve their image, and encourage investment and job creation. A European Champions' League football match in Dortmund, for example, will attract up to 60 000 spectators, many of whom stay overnight and spend money in local hotels, restaurants and other services. The immediate economic impact is significant, and the long-term impact is to create many thousands of 'ambassadors' for the city.

More recently it has been perceived that the need to create jobs and bring local populations back into the economic mainstream is often complicated by the fact that these populations are not homogeneous. The problems of local decay, economic and physical, often compound and are compounded by social, religious and ethnic differences between groups. The need to overcome these extra barriers is now recognised, and regeneration programmes are adding the task of tackling social exclusion to their range of targets. The New Deal for Communities programme in Kensington, Liverpool, is such an example. A similar social purpose can be found in the regeneration of Rotterdam.

In essence, the agenda for regeneration has evolved in line with the widening set of objectives for spatial planning and public policy as a whole. In so doing, the number of agencies with a stake in regeneration has increased, and it is no longer the prerogative of one department or set of experts but in every case now requires 'joined-up' policies and 'inter-corporate' working. Examination of the evolution of the mechanisms for running programmes suggests that there does not appear to be any single administrative structure that gives better results than any other. However, there is a common trend across much of Europe that is leading to the devolution of power to tackle these problems to authorities close to the local population.

In Germany the *Land* governments have always held considerable power. In Belgium constitutional changes have given the Wallonie region a great deal of autonomy in matters of planning, regeneration and social policy. In the French example of Lille and in Rotterdam large metropolitan authorities are the focus of the action, although they fit into clear national programmes. A similar process is occurring in Scotland and Northern Ireland. However, in England there still seems to be excessive central government control of the objectives and the financing of regeneration, but the situation is fluid, and new combinations of agencies are emerging. The new regional development agencies that will locally interpret government policy in collaboration with other local agencies may in time prove a more effective and locally responsive structure than that which has been in place to date.

It is clear that, in tackling the problems of structural change in Europe's cities, political stability, leadership and vision are important ingredients, and these need to be allied to a sound and stable professional staff with a long-term commitment to the process of reshaping our urban heritage. The continuity of the process in Lille contrasts sharply with the changing project teams and political uncertainty seen in Liverpool and other UK cities.

Key actors in urban regeneration outside government are landowners, investors, land users and local communities. The formulation of policies that have the desired effect on the behaviour of all, without provoking unanticipated side effects, and the seeking of synergies between each constitute a major task for the public sector in urban regeneration. There is a varied approach to this issue, ranging from the willing intervention of the public authorities in France to the tentative in the UK and the example in Belgium, where the region of Wallonie has only recently acquired the strong powers necessary to support its desire to intervene.

An interesting revelation from the case studies has been the extent to which regeneration has related to other planning policies and programmes. In Wallonie, regeneration is clearly part of the mainstream planning process. In the Netherlands, although the schemes are larger and have their own administrations, they appear to dovetail well with the local and national plans, and are integrated into their strategies. In Milan a primary objective has been to enable a previously rigid planning system to evolve to deal with regeneration areas and to develop the flexibility to adapt to such needs as they arise. Similarly in Lille both case studies are linked into the new Schéma Directeur and to the local plans of the constituent *communes*. In the UK the situation is more complex. In Northern Ireland there is an obvious desire to integrate the regeneration programme with other programmes for housing, transport and economic development through the Area Plan. However, in both Dundee and Liverpool the 'normal' planning process appears to be something apart from the regeneration process. The responsible agencies are clearly answerable to different clients, the financing is separate, and the professional teams engaged on the programmes are autonomous. There does not appear to be a clear set of objectives encompassing the total spatial planning process. The impression is one of a process of *shifting programmes* where, when one initiative has run out of steam, another appears in response to a newly perceived political need. Planning theory experts would recognise this as *disjointed incrementalism*.

In terms of delivered results, the most obviously 'successful' examples have been those where the land is in public hands or can be easily brought into the public sector. The cases of Euralille and Bovisa demonstrate this. The more difficult challenge is to achieve results when the regeneration process is something more than a public sector land development exercise. The case of Roubaix is therefore in many ways an interesting demonstration of the new direction of urban regeneration policy in France. Paradoxically, while it has been easy to point to structural flaws in the UK cases, the challenges posed to the agencies there have been of a different dimension from that faced by some continental cities. To begin with, land that was once was 'public' is now subject to the commercial objectives of its owners – railways, utility companies, even local authorities. The challenges in terms of social integration and economic rebirth are infinitely more complex in peripheral cities such as Dundee, Liverpool or Belfast than in the more centrally located and more affluent cities of Rotterdam, Lille or Milan, where a main strategy is to reintegrate regeneration areas with their more prosperous neighbours. The peripherality of the UK examples does raise the question of the extent to which urban regeneration programmes can reverse the decline that is in part caused by geographical location. Such desperation in changing programmes and projects is less evident in more centrally located UK cities such as Birmingham or Bristol, where economic growth seems more assured.

The issue of whether the funding of urban regeneration should be private or public, and what role each sector should play, is another issue running through the review. Although this is central to the *gap funding* debate, it obscures another aspect of financing that is equally important. This is the stability of both institutions and financial flows. The UK example of constantly evolving subsidy mechanisms, competitive bidding, an obsession with short-term achievements and a narrowly defined concept of *value for money* is inimical to the delivery of strong, long-term regeneration strategies. The French and Dutch models appear to accommodate evolving aims within relatively constant and stable administrative and financial frameworks, and seem to work better. The example of the Caisse des Dépôts as a stable, long-term 'mutual' source of financial support for urban regeneration in France requires further examination, but it appears to offer a funding mechanism free from the vagaries of national treasury policies that can give continuity to programme implementation. Similar, if not so spectacular, organisations exist in Germany and the Netherlands, and are emerging in Wallonie. Perhaps in its debates on gap funding the EU might give some consideration to the creation of a more stable *public* sector banking system as an adjunct to the European Central Bank to support urban regeneration, rather than continuing to rely on programme-based initiatives funded through its structural funds.

In summary, successful urban regeneration appears to be more likely in situations where appropriate powers have been devolved to secure, stable and adequately funded local governments working in partnership with local communities. A strong planning framework, incorporating modern concerns about sustainable development and social inclusion, is also essential to ensure regeneration that is economically efficient, socially useful and environmentally beneficial. The challenge is for the European Union and national governments to learn the lessons from the past and to be strong in their support for urban regeneration. With these mechanisms and policies in place we truly can look forward to an urban renaissance across Europe.

Bibliography

Chapter 1

Ball, M., Harloe, M. & Martens, M. (1988) *Housing and Social Change in Europe and the USA*. Routledge, London.

Berting, J., Geyer, F. & Jurkovich, R. (eds) (1979) *Problems of International Comparative Research in the Social Sciences*. Pergamon, Oxford.

Breakell, M.J. (ed.) (1975) *Problems of Comparative Planning*. Department of Town Planning, Oxford Polytechnic.

Commission for the European Communities (CEC) (1990) *Green Paper on the Urban Environment*. CEC, London.

Cooke, P. (ed.) (1989) *Localities: The Changing Face of Urban Britain*. Unwin Hyman, London.

Couch, C. (1990) *Urban Renewal: Theory and Practice*. Macmillan Education, London.

European Institute for Urban Affairs (EIUA) (1992) *Urbanization and the Functions of Cities in the European Community*. Regional Development Studies No. 4, Commission of the European Communities, Brussels.

George, V. & Lawson, R. (eds) (1980) *Poverty and Inequality in Common Market Countries*. Routledge, London.

Gibson, M. & Langstaff, M. (1982) *An Introduction to Urban Renewal*. Hutchinson, London.

Hall, P. & Hay, D. (1980) *Growth Centres in the European Urban System*. Heinemann, London.

Hass-Klau (1988) *New Life for City Centres*. Anglo-German Foundation for the Study of Industrial Society, London.

Masser, I. (1986) Some methodological considerations. In: *Learning from Other Countries* (eds I. Masser & R. Williams). Geo Books, Norwich.

Newman, P. & Thornley, A. (1996) *Urban Planning in Europe*. Routledge, London.

Nijkamp, P. & Perrels, A. (1994) *Sustainable Cities in Europe*. Earthscan, London.

Norton, A. & Novy, K. (1991) *Low Income Housing in Britain and Germany*. Anglo-German Foundation for the Study of Industrial Society, London.

Oxley, M. & Smith, J. (1996) *Housing Policy and Rented Housing in Europe*. E. & F.N. Spon, London.

Power, A. (1993) *Hovels to High Rise*. Routledge, London.

Thomas, D. *et al.* (1983) *Flexibility and Commitment in Planning: A Comparative Study of Local Planning and Development in the Netherlands and England*. Mariinus Nijhoff, The Hague.

White, P. (1978) *Towards an Improved Methodology for Cross-national Comparative Planning Research*. Centre for Urban & Regional Studies, University of Birmingham.

Wild, T. & Jones, P. (1991) *Deindustrialisation and New Industrialisation in Britain and Germany*. Anglo-German Foundation for the Study of Industrial Society, London.

Wilmott, P. & McDowel, L. (1977) *Poverty and Social Policy in Europe*.

Yin, R.K. (1982) Studying phenomenon and context across sites. *American Behavioural Scientist*, **26**, 84–100.

Chapter 2

Bastie, J. (1964) *La Croissance de la Banlieue Parisennne*. Presse Universitaire de France.

Cipolla, C.M. (ed.) (1973) The emergence of industrial societies. In: *Fontana Economic History of Europe*. Collins/Fontana.

Department of the Environment, Transport and the Regions (2000) *Our Towns and Cities: The Future*. The Stationery Office, London.

Department of the Environment, Transport and the Regions (2001) *Neighbourhood Renewal*. London.

Dezert, B., Metton, A. & Steinberg, J. (1991) *La Periurbanisation en France*. SEDES.

European Commission (2000) *Compendium of Spatial Planning Systems; Belgium, France, Germany, Netherlands, UK, Italy*. EU, Luxembourg.

European Commission (2000) *European Spatial Development Perspective*. Brussels.

Fraser, C., Le Ny, L. & Redding, B. (2001) *Living in Towns*, Interreg IIc Project Report. South Bank University, London.

Gibson, M. & Langstaff, M. (1982) *An Introduction to Urban Renewal*. Hutchinson, London.

Giddens, A. (1999) *Runaway World: How Globalisation is Reshaping our Lives*. Profile Books, London.

Held, D., McGrew, A., Goldblatt, D. & Perraton, J. (1999) *Global Transformations*. Polity Press, London.

Hall, P. (1992) *Urban and Regional Planning*. Routledge, London.

Hoskins, W.G. (1957) *The Making of the English Landscape*. Hodder & Stoughton, London.

Jackson, A.A. (1973) *Semi Detached London*. George Allen & Unwin, London.

Martikainen, T. (2001) *The Turku Cathedral: Religious Consumption Experience*. Weimar.

Miles, S. (2001) *Consuming Cities; Consuming Youth; Young People's Lifestyles and the Appropriation of Cultural Space*. Weimar.

Ministry of Housing, Spatial Planning and the Environment (VROM) (2000) *Fifth National Policy Document on Spatial Planning 2000–2020*. The Hague.

Sueur, J.-P. *Changer la Ville: Pour une Nouvelle Urbanité*. Editions Odile Jacob.

Urban Task Force (1999) *Towards an Urban Renaissance*. DETR, London.

Woods, N. (2000) *The Political Economy of Globalization*. Macmillan, London.

Chapter 3

Brauner, S. (2000) Regeneration without confrontation. *Regeneration and Renewal,* 20 October 2000.

Couch, C. (1990) *Urban Renewal: Theory and Practice.* Macmillan Education, London.

Couch, C. (2000) Urban renewal and grants. In: *Introduction to Planning Practice* (eds P. Allmendinger, A. Prior & J. Raemakers). Wiley, London.

Couch, C. (2003) *City of Change and Challenge.* Avebury, Aldershot (forthcoming).

Couch, C. & Dennemann, A. (2000) Urban regeneration and sustainable development in Britain: the example of the Liverpool Ropewalks Partnership. *Cities,* **17** (2), 137–147.

Cowan, R., Hannay, P. & Owens, R. (1988) The light on top of the tunnel: community-led regeneration by the Eldonians. *Architects Journal,* 23 March, 37–63.

De Groot, L. (1992) City Challenge: competing in the urban regeneration game. *Local Economy,* 7, 196–209.

Department of the Environment (1977) *Change or Decay: Final Report of the Liverpool Inner Area Study.* HMSO, London.

Department of the Environment (1996) *City Challenge, Interim National Evaluation.* The Stationery Office, London.

Gibson, M. & Langstaff, M. (1982) *An Introduction to Urban Renewal.* Hutchinson, London.

Giddens, A. (1999) *Runaway World: How Globalisation is Reshaping our Lives.* Profile Books, London.

Gillespie, C. (1998) *The single regeneration budget challenge fund: is it targeted?* MSc thesis, Liverpool John Moores University, Liverpool.

Liverpool City Challenge (1991) *City Challenge: Liverpool City Centre East, Preliminary Submission.* Liverpool City Council.

Liverpool City Council (1995) *Speke Garston SRB Bid.* Central Policy Unit, Liverpool City Council.

McIntyre, B. (1995) *The effectiveness of urban policy, a case study: the Liverpool inner city ward of Vauxhall.* MSc thesis, Liverpool John Moores University, Liverpool.

Meegan, R. (1993) Urban development corporations, urban entrepreneurialism and locality. In: *British Urban Policy and the Urban Development Corporations* (eds R. Imrie & H. Thomas). Paul Chapman Publishing, London.

Robson, B. & Parkinson, M. (2000) *Urban Regeneration Companies: A Process Evaluation.* Department of the Environment, Transport and the Regions, London.

Topping, P. & Smith, G. (1977) *Government Against Poverty? Liverpool Community Development Project 1970–75.* Social Evaluation Unit, University of Oxford.

Urban Task Force (UTF) (1999) *Towards an Urban Renaissance.* E. & F.N. Spon, London.

Chapter 4

Bazley, K. (1992) Urban Regeneration and Economic Development. In: *100 Years: Town Planning in Dundee*, pp. 40–47. Duncan of Jordanstone College of Art, Dundee.

Dewar, D. (1998) *Social Exclusion in Scotland*. Edinburgh: The Stationery Office.

Dobson Chapman, W. (1952) The City and Royal Burgh of Dundee: Survey and Plan 1952. Part Two: The City Plan. Dobson Chapman Partners, Macclesfield.

Doherty, J. (1992) Planning the harmonious whole. In: *100 Years: Town Planning in Dundee, Centenary Celebrations: Duncan of Jordanstone College of Art, 1892–1992*. University of Dundee, Dundee.

Keating, M. & Boyle, R. (1996) *Remaking Urban Scotland: Strategies for Local Economic Development*. Edinburgh: Edinburgh University Press.

Lyle, R. & Payne, G. (1950) The Tay Valley Plan. Burns & Harris Ltd, Dundee.

McCarthy, J. & Pollock, S.H.A. (1997) Urban regeneration in Glasgow and Dundee: a comparative evaluation. *Land Use Policy*, **14** (2), 137–149.

Pocock, D.C.D. (1968) Dundee and its region. In: *Dundee and District* (ed. S.J. Jones), pp. 174–190. British Association for the Advancement of Science, Dundee.

Ravetz, J. (2000) *City Region 2020: Integrated Planning for a Sustainable Environment*. Earthscan, London.

Wannop, U. (1995) *The Regional Imperative: Regional Planning and Governance in Britain, Europe and the United States*. Jessica Kingsley Publishers, London.

Ward, S.V. (1994) *Planning and Urban Change*. Paul Chapman Publishing, London.

Whatley, C.A. (1992) The making of 'Juteopolis, – and how it was. In: *The Remaking of Juteopolis, Proceedings of the Abertay Historical Society's Octocentenary Conference* (ed. C.A. Whatley). Abertay Historical Society, Dundee.

Chapter 5

Adair, A., Berry, J. & McGreal, S. (1996) Regeneration processes in Northern Ireland: the public sector and partnership structures. *European Planning Studies*, **4** (5), 527–543.

Bardon, J. (1982) *Belfast: An Illustrated History*. Blackstaff, Belfast.

BCC (1998) *Corporate Plan 1988–2002*. Belfast City Council, Belfast.

BCC (1999) *Sustainable Development In Belfast: A Framework for Action, 1999–2001*. Belfast City Council, Belfast.

BCCMSC (1999) *City Centre Management*. Belfast City Centre Management Steering Committee, Belfast.

BCP (1999) *Belfast City Vision: Our Vision*. Belfast City Partnership, Belfast.

Beckett, J.C. *et al.* (1983) *Belfast: The Making of the City*. Appletree Press, Belfast.

Bew, P. & Gillespie, G. (1993) *Northern Ireland: a Chronology of the Troubles, 1968–1993*. Gill & Macmillan, Dublin.

Bew, P. & Gillespie, G. (1996) *The Northern Ireland Peace Process, 1993–1996: A Chronology*. Serif, London.

Bew, P., Patterson, H. & Teague, P. (1997) *Between War and Peace: The Political Future of Northern Ireland*. Lawrence & Wishart, London.

Birrell, D. & Wilson, C. (1993) Making Belfast work: an evaluation of an urban strategy. *Administration*, **41** (1), 40–56.

Boal, F.W.C. (1995) *Shaping a City: Belfast in the Late Twentieth Century*. Institute of Irish Studies, QUB, Belfast.

Brett, C.E.B. (1986) *Housing in a Divided Community*. Institute of Public Administration, Dublin.

Buckland, P. (1981) *A History of Northern Ireland*. Gill & Macmillan, Dublin.

Connolly, M. & Knox, C. (1988) Recent political difficulties of local government in Northern Ireland. *Policy and Politics*, **16** (2), 89–97.

Deloitte & Touche (1997) *Making Belfast Work: Review*. MBW, Belfast.

Department of the Environment (NI) (1988) *Shaping Our Future: Draft Regional Strategic Framework for Northern Ireland*. The Stationery Office, Belfast.

Department of the Environment (NI) (1997) *Housing Statistics*. HMSO, Belfast.

Fitzsimons, D.S. (1995) Spearheading a new place vision: the Laganside Corporation. In: *Reimaging the Pariah City: Urban Development in Belfast and Detroit* (eds W.V.J. Neill, D.S. Fitzsimons & B. Murtagh), Chapter 3. Avebury, Aldershot.

Gorecki, P. (1995) *Economic implications of peace through peace to prosperity*. Northern Ireland Economic Council, Occasional Paper No. 3, NIEDO, Belfast.

House of Commons (1996) *Northern Ireland Affairs Committee*. HMSO, London.

Knox, C. (1998) Local government in Northern Ireland: emerging from the bearpit of sectarianism? *Local Government Studies*, **24** (3), 1–13.

KPMG *et al.* (1995) *The Economic Consequences of Peace: Report to the Forum of Peace and Reconciliation*.

Loughlin, J. (1998) *The Ulster Question since 1945*. Macmillan, Basingstoke.

Macrory Report (1970) *Report of the Review Body on Local Government Northern Ireland*. Review Body on Local Government in Northern Ireland, HMSO, Belfast.

Maguire, W.A. (1993) *Belfast*. Ryburn Publishing, Keele.

Matthew, R. (1963) *Belfast Regional Survey and Plan*. HMSO, Belfast.

Neill, W.V.J. (1995) Lipstick on the gorilla? Conflict management, urban development and image making in Belfast. In: *Reimaging the Pariah City: Urban Development in Belfast and Detroit* (eds W.V.J. Neill, D.S. Fitzsimons & B. Murtagh), Chapter 2. Avebury, Aldershot.

Neill, W.V.J. (1999) Whose city? Can a place vision for Belfast avoid the issue of identity? *European Planning Studies*, **7** (3), 269–281.

NIHE (1991) *Brick by Brick*. Northern Ireland Housing Executive, Belfast.

NIHE (1998) *Review of the Northern Ireland Housing Market 1998/99–2000/2001*. Northern Ireland Housing Executive, Belfast.

Northern Ireland Property Market Analysis Project, Quarterly Issues 1997 to 1999. School of the Built Environment, University of Ulster, Belfast.

RICS (1999) *Response to Review of the Northern Ireland Property Market*. Royal Institution of Chartered Surveyors, Belfast.

Chapter 6

Caisse des Dépôts et Consignations (2001a) *Urban Regeneration: Success through Innovative Financing.* Direction du Renouvellement Urbain, Paris.

Caisse des Dépôts et Consignations (2001b) *Le Renouvellement Urbain: Une Méthode pour l'Action.* Direction du Renouvellement Urbain, Paris.

Direction Interministerielle a la Ville (2000) *Les Grands Projets de Ville.* Les editions de la DIV, Paris.

L'Agence de développement et d'urbanisme de Lille Métropole (1998a) *Lille after Euralille: The Changing Metropolis.* Lille.

L'Agence de développement et d'urbanisme de Lille Métropole (1998b) *Lille Métropole en 2015.* Le Schéma directeur de Développement et d'Urbanisme de Lille Métropole, Lille.

Direction Générale de l'Urbanisme comme de l'Habitat et de Construction (2000) *Lille–Roubaix; l'Action Urbaine Levier Economique et Social Projet Urbain.* no. 20.

Paris, D. & Stevens, J.F. (2000) *Lille et sa Région Urbaine.* La Bifurcation Metropolitaine, l'Harmattan.

Simon, M. (1993) *Un Jour, Un Train: La Saga d'Euralille.* La Voix du Nord.

Chapter 7

Couch, C. (1990) *Urban Renewal: Theory and Practice.* Macmillan Education, London.

Dieleman, F.M., Dijst, M.J. & Spit, T. (1999) Planning the compact city: the Randstad Holland experience. *European Planning Studies,* **7** (5), 605–621.

Europa (1999) URBAN Community Initiative 1994–1999: Netherlands, Rotterdam. www.europa.eu.int/comm/regional_policy/urban2.

McCarthy, J. (1996) Waterfront regeneration in the Netherlands: the cases of Rotterdam and Maastricht. *European Planning Studies,* **4** (5), 545–560.

Pinder, D. & Rosing, K.E. (1988) Public policy and planning of the Rotterdam waterfront: a tale of two cities. In: *Revitalising the Waterfront* (eds B.S. Hoyle, D.A. Pinder & M.S. Husain). Belhaven Press, London.

Priemus, H. (2001) A new housing policy for the Netherlands (2000–2010): a mixed bag. *Journal of Housing and the Built Environment,* **3–4**, 319–332.

Rodenberg, P.J. (2001) Personal interview.

Teule, R. (1999) Urban renewal and housing rehabilitation in the Netherlands. In: *Housing Renewal in Europe* (eds H.S. Andersen & P. Leather). The Policy Press, Bristol.

Van den Berg, L., Van der Meer, J. & Olgaar, A.H.J. (1999) *The Attractive City.* EURICUR, Erasmus University, Rotterdam.

Chapter 8

Bruwier, M., Dhondt, J., Hansotte, G. & Lebrun, P. Essai sur la Revolution Industrielle en Belgique 1770–1847. *Histoire Qualitative et Développement de la Belgique au XIXe siecle*, Tome II, Vol 1.

Dachouffe, M. (2000) Les sites d'intérêt regional. Contribution a l'Esquise d'une nouvelle image de La Wallonie. *Les Echos de l'Aménagement et de l'Urbanisme.*

European Commission (1997) *The EU Compendium of Spatial Planning Systems and Policies.* EU, Belgium, Luxembourg.

Fraser, C., Le Ny, L. & Redding, B. (2001) *Living in Towns*, Interreg IIc Project Report. South Bank University, London.

Gouvernement Wallon (1998a) Code Wallon de l'aménagement du territoire, de l'urbanisme, et du patrimoine. *Les Echos de L'Aménagement et de L'Urbanisme*, Edition Special, no 19, Direction Générale, Aménagement du Territoire, Logement et Patrimoine.

Gouvernement Wallon (1998b) Information Notes: *Zones d'Initiative Priviligées, Revitalisation Urbaine, Rénovation Urbaine, Sites d'Activité Économique Desaffectés.*

Gouvernement Wallon (1999) *Schema de Développement de L'Espace Régional.* Namur.

Milward, A. & Saul, S.B. (1997) *The Development of the Economies of Continental Europe*, Chapter 3. Allen & Unwin, Belgium.

Vandendorpe, L. (2000) Les metamorphoses de l'économie Wallonne. *Les Cahiers de l'Urbanisme*, nos. 28–29.

Ville de Mons (1997) *Schéma de Structure.* Mons.

Voye, L (2000) 1958–2000: une période de turbulences, un temps d'affirmation identitaire. *Les Cahiers de l'Urbanisme*, nos. 28–29.

Chapter 9

Ambrosini, P. & Rossi, C. (2002) Un territorio che cambia pelle e sostanza. In: *Bovisa: Paradigma di Milano che si trasforma* (eds V. Erba & C. Morandi). Libreria Clup, Milano.

Bolocan Goldstein, M. & Pasqui, G. (eds) *Politiche di sviluppo territoriale epianificazione: riflessioni ed esperienze nella regione milanese e lombarda.* Archivio di Studi Urbani e Regionali, no. 64.

Comune di Milano (2001) *Ricostruire la grande Milano. Documento di inquadramento delle politiche urbanistiche comunali.* Il Sole 24 Ore, Milano.

Dalmasso, E. (1971) *Milano capitale economica d'Italia.* Franco Angeli, Milano.

Erba, V., Molon, M. & Morandi, C. (2000) *Bovisa: una riqualificazione possibile.* Unicopli, Milano.

Fossa, G. (1996) *Il Sempione. Grand axe del territorio Milanese.* Gangemi, Roma.

Minotti, L. (2001) *Progetti infrastrutturali e territorio nell'area milanese e lombarda.* Centro Studi Pim, Milano.

Morandi, C. (1992) L'adeguamento del sistema infrastrutturale di Milano tra l'Unità e la fine del secolo. In: *La Milano del Piano Beruto (1884-1889)* (ed. R. Rozzi), pp. 191–217. Guerini e associati, Milano.

Morandi, C. (1994) *I vantaggi competitivi delle città: un confronto in ambito Europeo.* Franco Angeli, Milano.

Morandi, C. (2001) Le trasformazioni delle aree industriali a Milano: una riflessione su alcuni recenti progetti. In: *Se i vuoti si riempiono, Aree industriali dismesse: temi e ricerche* (eds E. Dansero, C. Giamo & A. Spaziante). Alinea, Firenze.

Pasqui, G. (2002) *Confini milanesi. Processi territoriali e pratiche di governo.* Franco Angeli, Milano.

Provincia di Milano (1998) *Accompagnare lo sviluppo. Guida alle politiche di sviluppo locale nell'area milanese.* Milano.

Urbani, P. (2000) *Urbanistica consensuale. La disciplina degli usi del territorio tra liberalizzazione, programmazione negoziata e tutele differenziate.* Bollati Boringhieri, Torino.

Chapter 10

Almaas, I.H. (1999) Regenerating the Ruhr (IBA Emscher Park project for regeneration of Germany's Ruhr Region). *The Architectural Review*, **205** (February), 13–14.

Blotevogel, H.H. (1998) The Rhone–Ruhr metropolitan region: reality and discourse. *European Planning Studies*, **6** (4), 395–410.

Bömer, H. (2000) The changing economy and evolution of development policies in the Ruhr 1978–1998. In: *Economic Restructuring, Urban Change and Environmental Policy in the Ruhr and Merseyside 1978–1998* (eds C. Couch & H. Bömer). Dortmund University.

Bömer, H. (2001) *The Ruhr context.* Lecture, 2 April, Dortmund University.

Brandolini, S. (2000) Paradise Found (the transformation of Germany's Ruhr region). *Architecture*, **89** (November).

Couch, C. (1995) Guidelines for regional planning in Germany. *International Report*, October, 18–26.

Danielzyk, R. & Wood, G. (1993) Restructuring old industrial and inner urban areas. *European Planning Studies*, **1** (2), 123–147.

Fox, K. (2001) *Selling NRW: marketing and urban regeneration in Germany.* Unpublished paper, South Bank University, London.

Griffiths, R. (1998) Making sameness: place marketing and the new urban entrepreneurialism. In: *Cities, Economic Competition and Urban Policy* (ed. N. Oatley), Paul Chapman, London.

Healey, P. *et al.* (1992) Property-led urban regeneration: an assessment. In: *Rebuilding the City: Property-Led Urban Regeneration* (eds P. Healey, S. Davoudi, S. Tavsanoglu, M. O'Toole & D. Usher D). E. & F.N. Spon, London.

Hotchkiss, G. (2002) *An examination of the way in which the environment has played a central role in the redevelopment of the Ruhr.* Unpublished paper, South Bank University, London.

IBA (1999) *Internationale Bauausstellung Emscher Park: Short Information Including Large IBA Map.* IBA, Gelsenkirchen.

Knapp, W. (1998) The Rhine–Ruhr area in transformation: towards a European metropolitan region? *European Planning Studies*, **6** (4), 379–393.

Kommunalverband Ruhrgebiet (undated) *The Ruhrgebiet: Facts and Figures*. KVR, Essen.

Kurpick, S. & Weck, S. (1998) Policies against social exclusion at the neighbourhood level in Germany: the case study of North Rhine Westphalia. In: *Social Exclusion in European Cities: Processes, Experience and Responses* (eds A. Madanipour, G. Cars & J. Allen). Jessica Kingsley Publishers, London.

Kushner, J.A. (2000) Social sustainability: planning for growth in distressed places: the German experience in Berlin, Wittenberg and the Ruhr. *Journal of Law and Policy*, **3**, 849–874.

Madanipour, A., Cars, G. & Allen, J. (eds) (1998) *Social Exclusion in European Cities: Processes, Experience and Responses*. Jessica Kingsley Publishers, London.

NRW State Government (1998) *Ideas, Impetus, Initiative*. Düsseldorf.

Redgrove, N. (2002) *Planning for sustainable development in the Ruhr*. Unpublished paper, South Bank University, London.

Shaw, R. (2002) The International Building Exhibition (IBA) Emscher Park, Germany: a model for sustainable restructuring? *European Planning Studies*, **10** (1), 77–97.

Stohr, W.B. (1992) *Global Challenge and Local Responses: Initiatives for Economic Regeneration in Contemporary Europe*. The UN University, Tokyo.

Watson, A. (1994) *The Germans: Where Are They Now?* Mandarin, London.

Chapter 12

Bailey, N., Barker, A. & McDonald, K. (1995) *Partnership Agencies in British Urban Policy*. UCL Press, London.

Barlow, J. & Hill, S. (1995) Single regeneration budget: hope for those inner cities. *Housing Review*, April 1995.

Chapter 13

Brownhill, S. (1990) *Developing London's Docklands, Another Great Planning Disaster?* Paul Chapman, London.

Cars, G., Healey, P., Madanipour, A. & de Magalhaes, C. (eds) (2002) *Urban Governance, Institutional Capacity and Social Milieux*. Ashgate, Aldershot.

Cochrane, A. & Jonas, A. (1999) Reimagining Berlin: world city, national capital or ordinary place? *European Urban and Regional Studies*, **6** (2), 145–164.

Couch, C. & Fitzharris, T. (2002) *Merseyside Health Action Zone: Safe and Warm Housing Project – Interim Report*. Liverpool Health Authority, Liverpool.

Fernie, K. (2002) Changing patterns of social exclusion in Dundee. In: *Planning in the UK: Agendas for the New Millennium* (eds Y. Rydin & A. Thornley). Ashgate, Aldershot.

Fox, K. (2001) *Selling NRW: marketing and urban regeneration in Germany*. Unpublished paper, South Bank University, London.

Gibbs, D.C. (1999) Sustainable cities in Europe. *European Urban and Regional Studies*, **6** (3), 265–268.

Griffiths, R. (1995) Cultural strategies and new models of urban intervention. *Cities*, **12** (4), 253–265.

Hall, P. (2000) Creative cities and economic development. *Urban Studies*, **37** (4), 639–649.

Hambleton, R. (1990) Urban Government in the 1990s: lessons from the USA. SAUS Occasional Paper 35, University of Bristol, Bristol.

Knapp, W. (1998) The Rhine–Ruhr Area in transformation: towards a European metropolitan region? *European Planning Studies*, **6** (4), 379–393.

Loftman, P. & Nevin, B. (1995) Prestige projects and urban regeneration in the 1980s and 1990s: a review of benefits and limitations. *Planning Practice and Research*, **10** (3/4), 299–313.

Smyth, H. (1994) *Marketing the City*. E. & F.N. Spon, London.

Van den Berg, L., Braun, E. & van Winden, W. (2001) Growth clusters in European cities: an integral approach. *Urban Studies*, **38** (1), 185–205.

Ward, D. (2002) Forget Paris and London, Newcastle is a creative city to match Kabul and Tijuana. *The Guardian*, 2 September.

Ward, S. (1998) *Selling Places*. E. & F.N. Spon, London.

Index